Shenandoah Religion

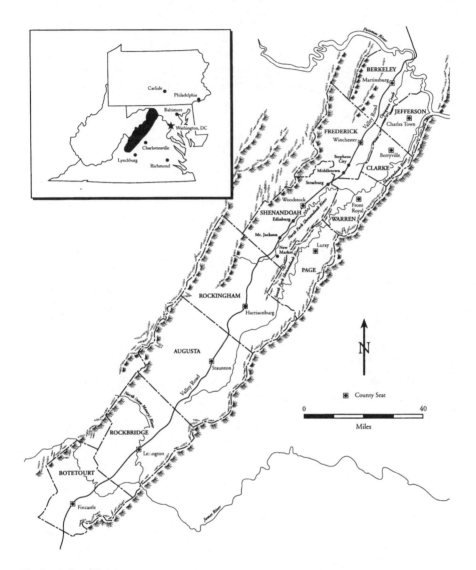

The Great Valley of Virginia.

Frontispiece: The Great Valley of Virginia, from *After the Backcountry: Rural Life in the Great Valley of Virginia, 1800–1900*, Kenneth E. Koons and Warren R. Hofstra, eds. (Knoxville: University of Tennessee Press, 2000). Map published courtesy of the University of Tennessee Press.

Shenandoah Religion:

Outsiders and the Mainstream, 1716–1865

Stephen L. Longenecker

Baylor University Press
Waco, Texas

Published by Baylor University Press
Waco, Texas 76798

Cataloging-in-Publication Data

Longenecker, Stephen L., 1951-
  Shenandoah religion : outsiders and the mainstream, 1716-1865 /
Stephen Longenecker.
      p. cm.
Includes bibliographical references and index.
  ISBN 0-918954-83-5 (pbk. : alk. paper)
  1. Shenandoah River Valley (Va. and W. Va.)--Church history--18th
century. 2. Religious minorities--Shenandoah River Valley (Va. and W.
Va.)--History--18th century. 3. Shenandoah River Valley (Va. and W.
Va.)--Church history--19th century. 4. Religious minorities--Shenandoah
River Valley (Va. and W. Va.)--History--19th century. I. Title.
  BR555.V8 L66 2002
  277.55'907--dc21
                              2002007993

Cover image: Rockfish Gap and the Mountain House, Plate 3,
Album of Virginia, 1858, by Edward Beyer, Courtesy The Library of Virginia

Printed in the United States of America on acid-free paper.

For Jean Longenecker,

my mother

Contents

Preface

"OUTSIDERNESS" HAS ALWAYS INTRIGUED ME. I grew up in Lancaster County, Pennsylvania, which styled itself the "heart of Amish country" in a tribute to some of society's most conspicuous outsiders (and also an attempt to stimulate tourist dollars). The "Heart of Amish Country" included numerous other small German traditions, one of which, the Church of the Brethren, had been spiritual home for the Longeneckers for several centuries. With such a heritage, by the time I left home for college, outsiderness was deeply imprinted into my persona. I was on campus during the Vietnam War, when nonconformity was a way of life, but I aspired to my own peculiar level of nonconformity. I kept my hair short while all my friends embargoed their barbers. I wore an olive green twill jacket, very military looking, and pinned a "Beat Army" button on it with a peace sign superimposed on the letters. When I walked into the gym, the coaches, not quite comprehending the blend of symbols, asked if I was a Navy fan.

Outsiderness was no less a companion on my journey as a scholar. As an undergraduate and master's student, I often wrote term papers on Anabaptism, fascinated both by my heritage and by the opportunity to pick a topic about which my professors knew very little. After receiving my master's degree and embarking on a teaching career in the public schools, I spent summers writing about a family of German Anabaptist printers in colonial Pennsylvania who were very conscious of their nonconformity. Then I studied a Church of the Brethren mediator in the Selma,

Alabama, civil rights struggle, who parlayed his outsiderness, i.e., his affiliation with an obscure, pacifist denomination, into a neutrality that facilitated his peacemaking mission. After eleven years in front of the chalk board, I returned to graduate school at Johns Hopkins and studied with Timothy Smith, who refined my understanding of nonconformity. Smith, himself devoted to a small denomination, the Church of the Nazarene, had a keen appreciation for the role of all outsiders, and he directed me towards a dissertation on Pennsylvania German Pietism.

After reincarnation as a "doctor of philosophy," I came to Bridgewater College in the Shenandoah Valley, Virginia, where issues of outsiderness remain prevalent. As in my Pennsylvania home, my neighbors in the Valley include numerous Anabaptists, some of whom have all-but-abandoned traditional nonconformity while others wage a determined effort to remain outsiders. On the way to church we routinely pass horse-and-buggy Mennonites enroute to their meeting. My own congregation, a Church of the Brethren fellowship, built atop a hill a grand, eye-catching facility that bears little resemblance to the simple meetinghouses of its tradition.

My new academic home at Bridgewater stimulated a more intentional study of outsiderness. Previously, my study of nonconformity had been coincidental in that all of the questions that interested me happened to involve outsiders; but at Bridgewater several faculty, including myself, began to think more specifically about this concept. The catalyst was the drastic nationwide decline in Church of the Brethren membership from 200,000 in 1960 to 140,000 in 1990. Bridgewater is a Brethren-related institution, and our interdisciplinary faculty group, the Forum for Religious Studies, brought this serious problem under academic scrutiny with much of the discussion focusing on the decline of nonconformity within the denomination. The ensuing conversations with my forum colleagues and forum-sponsored conferences, plus a major publication by one of the forum scholars[1] matured my understanding of outsiderness significantly. I learned that the histories of many traidtions, not just my own, included a puzzling drift into the mainstream. As with most successful academic quests, increased study led to more questions. I became especially curious about why some outsiders retain their nonconformity while others lose it. This led to the study that became this book.

Consistent with the topic of this book, *Shenandoah Religion* may represent the work of an academic gadfly caught between antiquarianism and current academic fads. On one hand, this volume is neither a textbook of Shenandoah Valley religion nor a comprehensive history of the early Shenandoah Valley. It lacks the detail necessary for these genres, and this type of local history is not my purpose. I have also attempted to avoid preoccupation with the race/gender/class triumvirate or other forms of thick analysis that so often encumber modern studies. To be sure, these approaches can be productive, and this study uses them when appropriate. But often these lenses, to borrow a phrase from "scholarese," overpower the story itself, adding layers of density that cloud rather than clarify understanding. My task is to explain the influence of daily nonconformity, or daily crosses, on outsiders and the mainstream in a border South valley during four revolutions, and I hope that what follows is a direct, straightforward account of this impact. Whether this story is simply-told or over-simplified is for others to judge. But I had fun doing it.

Steve Longenecker
Harrisonburg, Virginia

Acknowledgments

MANY ASSISTED ME IN THIS ODYSSEY, and I cheerfully but inadequately acknowledge my indebtedness to them with these few brief words of thanks. The papers written by my friends at the Southeastern Colloquium for American Religious Studies and the Shenandoah Valley Regional Studies Seminar advanced my scholarship, and the criticisms of these scholars improved my papers. This project also benefited from the comments of numerous scholars at conferences, and I especially appreciate their tactfulness. I will never forget one listener who, after I said something rather stupid during the session, quietly approached me and advised me not to "push that too hard." They were wise words spoken tactfully. Russell Richey and Donald Kraybill provided excellent guidance during the early phase of the project. Dan Bly, an office neighbor and departmental colleague at Bridgewater College, read the manuscript and patiently answered spur-of-the-moment questions about local history. Ronald Walters pointed me in the right direction at the beginning of the project and then read a draft of the manuscript. John Heatewole, Terry Barkley, and Ruth Doan also contributed their time as readers and offered very helpful suggestions. Jewel Spangler also expertly evaluated the manuscript, and she has been particularly supportive throughout the life of the project. Warren Hofstra and Robert Calhoon were the readers for Baylor University Press, and they made the manuscript much better with extremely useful criticism. My editors at Baylor Press, Janet Burton and David Holcomb, have been tolerant of my mistakes and pleasant to work with. Under their guidance the manuscript improved significantly.

I am also grateful for the assistance of my employer, Bridgewater College. Elizabeth Moore and Lisa Houff provided clerical help. My department head, Robert Andersen, has been wonderfully encouraging, and President Phillip Stone and Dean Arthur Hessler have been generous with research and conference travel, photocopying, and a semester-long sabbatical.

Many librarians were gracious with their time and facilities. I am indebted to the following: Bridgewater College, Eastern Mennonite University, the Harrisonburg-Rockingham County Historical Society, the Massanutten Regional Library, the Virginia Baptist Historical Society at the University of Richmond, the Rare Book Room at the Handley Public Library in Winchester, Virginia, Alderman Library at the University of Virginia, the Rare Book Room at Washington and Lee University, James Madison University, the Lutheran Theological Seminary in Gettysburg, Pennsylvania, Mary Baldwin University, and the United Methodist Historical Society—Lovely Lane Museum in Baltimore. Edwin Schell at Lovely Lane very kindly sent the Bridgewater College Library a copy of the Minutes of the Baltimore Conference

Finally, let me thank my family—Carol, Lew, and Ada—for their patience with me during this project. Without their understanding, this would have been impossible.

Shenandoah Religion

Introduction

ONE DAY IN THE EARLY NINETEENTH CENTURY George
Baxter, the president of Liberty Hall, a boarding school
in Lexington, Virginia, lectured to his students about
society's lack of respect for the Christian lifestyle. Baxter, an
ordained Presbyterian, conceded that the world admired some
traits of Christ's followers, such as integrity and "sober moral
deportment," and he told his young listeners that if these were the
only characteristics of a Christian life, the world would find
Christians "much more pleasing." But, according to this pious
educator, from the beginning of the faith Christian character had
been at odds with the world, and although almost everyone professed approval of piety, many non-believers found it "disturbing"
when they actually confronted it.[1]

Like most good teachers, Baxter oversimplified. While his portrayal of the timelessness of the tension between the faith and the
world was accurate, his description of a dualistic world consisting
only of Christians versus non-Christians made better theology
than history because it overlooked the complexity of outsiderness.
Baxter was correct that nearly all Christians intend to confront the
world—the majority professes to covet minority status—but he
failed to mention the tremendous variety of nonconformity. If
some believers are so different that the worldly consider them
bothersome, others resist the world so passively that non-believers
find them quite acceptable. Baxter also did not explain that the
faithful regularly disagree on how to oppose the world; except for
obviously detestable acts, such as public drunkenness or adultery,

they lack consensus on what constitutes worldliness. He could have added that many lose nonconformity without a deliberate decision. While intending to oppose the world, they unconsciously become part of it. Had Baxter more accurately described outsiders and the mainstream, he most certainly would have confused his students because though all believers desire outsiderness, their approach is multifaceted and fulfillment often elusive.

This study, aimed at a more sophisticated audience than Baxter's young charges, asks why so many outsiders struggle to stay on the margins when so many affirm the concept. Why do some find it easier to remain at odds with the world than others, i.e., why do some outsiders drift back into the mainstream while others retain their nonconformity? Why do some fellowships, generation after generation, remain on the fringes of society while others slowly sink into the majority?

Outsiderness has only recently found a place on the historiographical map. Most generations of American historians, including those as recent as the consensus school of the mid-twentieth century, favored stories of assimilation rather than tales about those who were different. They stressed similarities among Americans and often portrayed the loss of outsiderness as a beneficial and inevitable contribution to the process of Americanization. In the 1960s, however, when higher education became available to the children and grandchildren of America's most recent immigrants and when the civil rights movement inspired historians to value minorities of all types, bottom-up scholars discovered the value of outsiderness and developed curiosity about its characteristics.[2]

By the 1980s scholars had completely rethought outsiderness and now placed it at the heart of the American experience. Instead of writing about unity, conformity, and assimilation, they celebrated distinctiveness and diversity. As one survey of the literature describes the new viewpoint, historians exchanged the metaphor of "the melting pot for that of the salad bowl." Rather than a temporary obstacle in the path of progress, many now approved of outsiderness and dubbed it as typically American. Nathan Hatch's influential study of antebellum Christianity uncovered outsiders who practiced popular faith, who created a vibrant democratizing trend embraced by the fastest-growing denominations, and who "storm[ed] heaven by the back door." In Hatch's view such populists have become a recurring and distinctive component of American religion. Laurence Moore similarly explains outsiderness as the norm in American religion, finding evidence of it among a variety of traditions and periods, including Mormons, African Americans, Catholics, and fundamentalists. According to Moore, most American Christians think of themselves as nonconformists; his version of the mainstream has an outsider self-image.[3]

Anabaptist scholarship contributes another dimension to the literature on outsiderness. Although outsiderness has always enjoyed prominence in Anabaptist thought, the recent decline in membership among many Anabaptist denominations has added a new twist to their scholarship on this topic. Once unquestioned nonconformists, this is no longer a given among them, and since 1960 the Anabaptist denominations most closely associated with the mainstream have suffered the largest declines in membership, sometimes at alarming rates. These two trends—the decline in membership and the loss of nonconformity—have caused much soul-searching, and led some students of these traditions to argue their linkage, i.e., that the surrender of distinctive beliefs and practices yielded a damaging loss of identity. They claim that as Anabaptists became more like mainstream Protestants and less separate from the world, loyalty to these relatively small and obscure religious movements lapsed. In short, for some Anabaptist scholars, the relationship between loss of nonconformity and loss of members, whether coincidental or cause and effect, has been compelling.[4]

Scholars of Southern religious history have also been thinking about outsiderness, particularly its waning among antebellum evangelicals. Much of the effort has gone towards identifying the signposts of this trend. Many scholars agree that growing fondness for college-trained, professionalized clergy and large, dignified church buildings were unmistakable markers of conformity.

Mainstreamed evangelicals no longer provoked a harsh reaction from the public, and their worldview increasingly invoked values, such as manliness or gentility, consistent with those of the larger society. Gendered and racial behavior similarly pointed towards the center. White males increasingly turned evangelicalism into a patriarchy, and white women found correspondingly fewer opportunities for leadership; instead, the "Southern evangelical lady," governing the home and bounded by domesticity, appeared. African Americans, as well, lost stature, now segregated in the galleries of the grand meeting houses, and evangelical tolerance for slavery became nearly universal. Among Methodists, the denomination attracting the most scholarly attention, an aging clergy abandoned itineration for permanent placement. Evidence of conformity is abundant, and few scholars doubt that antebellum Southern evangelicals became mainstream.[5]

But few place the beliefs of the rank and file at the heart of this nonconformity. Although the path of Southern evangelicals from the margins to the mainstream is fairly well-marked, most of the markers located by scholars are behavioral and sociological rather than theological and intellectual. Rhys Isaac's influential description of eighteenth-century Virginia relies heavily on cultural anthropology and sociological details, such as court days or tavern life, to draw large conclusions about the conflict between evangelicals and the gentry. Hatch's landmark work, though not confined to the South, also includes a heavily sociological emphasis on "a social struggle with power and authority" that suggests class warfare. Hatch explains that the battle between evangelicalism and orthodoxy in the early Republic belonged to a larger contest between the right of elites to make decisions for others and authority based on popular appeal. Revivalists, says Hatch, were so successful that the orthodox copied them to keep pace, blurring the lines between rebels and old regime. Hatch also credits Charles G. Finney, a "crucial figure, a bridge between classes," for making revivalism respectable by polishing it for the middle class. Donald Mathews concludes that evangelicals responded to the "needs of an increasingly proud and numerous middle class." William Henry Williams, on Methodists, speculates that "perhaps revolutionary movements have a life cycle of their own" and that the "early, radical phase" of Methodism evolved into "a more conservative and accommodating phase." Or maybe, Williams says, powerful social, economic, and demographic forces finally overwhelmed the movement. John Wigger is convinced that "popular religious movements are limited by the boundaries of the broader culture in which they take shape." He writes that the lines between Methodism and the larger American society inevitably blurred because early Methodists co-opted so much from popular culture, but as this approach attracted large numbers of ordinary Americans to the movement, they in turn compromised their new denomination. The orientation towards social history causes observers to overlook the importance of faith to identity, and it encourages the portrayal of outsiderness in behavioral rather than theological terms.[6]

This study, then, emphasizes the theological or spiritual causes of outsiderness. I am not convinced of the inevitability of assimilation, and I aim to identify conditions within traditions that either enhanced or weakened their chances of remaining separate. To be sure, outside forces, such as wars, politics, and the economy, also provide opportunities for nonconformity, but these pressures change and are beyond the control of the faithful. Whatever the external conditions, however, fellowships with a strong theological sense of outsiderness and with reinforcing practices that emphasize separation from the mainstream in daily life stand a better chance of remaining on the margins.

The Shenandoah Valley between 1700 and 1865 is an ideal location to ask these big questions. This period has more than enough variation to reveal the impact on outsiderness of shifting conditions, represented in this study by four revolutions: the American, the Methodist, the market, and the Southern. The term "revolution" for the American independence movement is commonplace and, likewise, "market revolution" is a frequently used term, but the other "revolutions" may need explanation. "Methodist revolution" refers to the new wave of revivalism and emotional worship that swept Protestantism in the early nineteenth century. This movement, which I have named after its best-known adherents but which embraced other traditions, brought so much change in worship style that it polarized Protestantism, and the denominations associated with revivalism grew so fast that "revolution" appropriately describes this phenomenon. The "Southern revolution" pertains to the movement to protect slavery and withdraw from the Union. Although secession was a conservative cause defending the racial *status quo* and safeguarding planter dominance, Southerners portrayed their movement as their version of the American revolution, and their attempt to create a new nation seems enough change to justify the term "revolution."[7]

The Shenandoah Valley, a small place, is particularly well-suited for a regional study because of its pluralism, which included groups of varying size and theology and representatives of diverse ethnicity. English, Germans, and Scots Irish embodied Anabaptism, Calvinism, confessionalism, and evangelicalism and worshipped as Methodists, Presbyterians, Baptists, Lutherans, Reformed, Dunkers, Mennonites, Anglicans, Quakers, and others. Even sectional identity lacked consensus. In this border region some traditions were southern branches of fellowships with a Northern outlook while others were the northernmost extension of groups with a Southern orientation. African Americans, though institutionally barren, contributed still further complexity. Shenandoah society was a little quilt with a fascinating assortment of patches of all shapes and sizes.

During these changing times in this diverse valley, Protestants maintained in one chorus that the world, the darkness, held dangerous temptations. They almost uniformly characterized the world as proud, vain, wicked, profane, and frivolous. They depicted its wisdom as "foolish," its pleasures, although momentarily delightful, as "deceitful" and ultimately "empty." Worldly wealth was "at best but frail and transitory." Believers could not, as one Mennonite wrote, be like the world and still belong to God because what men "highly esteemed" was "abomination" to God. The world's values and God's were incompatible, like light and darkness, a favorite metaphor. "What fellowship hath righteousness with unrighteousness?" asked a Lutheran, "and what communion hath light with darkness?" A Dunker periodical added that "just as darkness and light, life and death, good and bad, right and wrong, truth and falsehood" were opposites, so were the world and the Bible.[8]

Consequently, preachers and writers warned the faithful not to conform to the darkness. They were to avoid "men of the world" and ignore what worldly persons thought of them. When interacting with the world, the "Christian spirit" of believers should be apparent. "Christ has purchased for himself a peculiar people," wrote a Lutheran periodical that circulated in the Valley, and a Presbyterian preacher encouraged his Winchester congregation to be "fools for Christ" (I Corinthians 6:8), that is, to be so different that the world would consider them foolish. A Dunker urged his brothers and sisters of the faith to "deny themselves and take up their cross daily."[9] Ideally the contrast between light and darkness, i.e., between the behavior of believers and non-believers, was obvious.

The consent that Valley Protestants shared about the world's sinfulness quickly broke down when they attempted to clarify where the light and darkness separated, and characterizations of outsiderness were as diverse as the variety of religion itself. With so many different interpretations of nonconformity, fellowships, in effect, shaped their own definitions of the world and then cast themselves as nonconformists because they avoided a mainstream of their own design. Presbyterians, for example, with generations of grievances against English royalty and Anglican bishops, easily pinpointed the English Anglican establishment as the darkness, but Anabaptists, who suffered at the hands of a variety of European governments and ecclesiastical authorities, developed a more generalized fear of the world, less dependent on opposition to political authority. All fellowships condemned broad inventories of vile behavior, such as lying and stealing, and all agreed that sexual misconduct, including fornication and adultery, were beyond the pale. But some found any use of alcohol unacceptable, others identified only drunkenness as darkness, and a few labeled the temperance movement itself as part of the sinful world. Similarly, worldly dress seemed evil but difficult to define. Some said little other than to quote the Scriptural admonition to avoid "braided hair, gold, pearls, or costly apparel"[10] without adding specificity. Others withheld condemnation of fashion as sin but still hoped that their members would avoid flamboyant clothing on the basis of thrift, efficiency, or common sense. Yet another viewpoint was that members of God's kingdom should dress noticeably different from those who were not. Regarding slavery, most Shenandoah Protestants believed that the South's institution did not contribute to the darkness, but the Valley was also home to a minority who stubbornly opposed bondage, which was unusual for a Southern community. Thus, if Protestants spoke in one chorus about resisting the world, they became polyphonal when they tried to identify what that meant.[11]

While each tradition sang about the mainstream in a slightly different key, did a real mainstream still exist? Yes. To the myriad definitions of the mainstream, I add one more (Baxter's students would not be amused!), an actual mainstream rather than the Presbyterian, Mennonite, or Baptist version of it. The Valley's mainstream consisted of those who formed majority opinion. Both religious and non-religious Shenandoans contributed to this prevailing current, and, therefore, within the mainstream differences between these two were not especially sharp. Although religious Shenandoans who inhabited the mainstream often termed themselves as outsiders, they nevertheless located the darkness so that its avoidance required little effort, and they moved easily in the secular world. While nonconformists deliberately separated from a world that was dominant and local, the mainstream defined the sinful world as distant, outlandish, or specific to a minority, such as women or youth. While nonconformists were a self-conscious minority that took positions that might bring risk or embarrassment, the religious mainstream's conception of worldliness allowed them to live much like their non-religious companions in the mainstream. Although separation from the world was popular in theory, fellowships that in reality appeared indistinguishable from secular attitudes were in and of the mainstream, not outside it.

Six chapters in this book describe the tensions between outsiders and the mainstream. Chapter 1, "The Valley," introduces the region's religious groups and demonstrates nonconformity through diversity. Chapter 2, "The American Revolution," reveals outsiderness through the creation of alternative faith communities to the larger society and through political opposition. Chapter 3, "The Methodist Revolution," describes resistance to popular religion. The next two chapters illustrate outsiderness through separation from popular culture: Chapter 4, "The Market Revolution," recounts conflict with material culture, especially fashion, much of it the result of a pervasive economic trend; and Chapter 5, "The South's Revolution, I: The Slavery Debate," discloses outsiderness through antagonism towards slavery, deeply imbedded in both the popular culture and the political economy. The final chapter, "The South's Revolution, II: The Civil War," returns to outsiderness through political opposition, but in this case the most conspicuous outsiders defied political authority rather than merely criticizing it.

As the four revolutions swept over the Shenandoah Valley, the ability of ideologically or theologically motivated individuals practicing daily nonconformity to create outsiderness became apparent. During this period, matters that affected every-day-persons altered; issues that once created passion became less vital or irrelevant while fresh questions arose to define identity for new generations. As environments shifted, groups that averted the daily cross but relied on other foils often slid closer to the mainstream, but sometimes determined walls against the world, like the Anabaptists' doctrine of nonviolence, functioned more noticeably in new circumstances, such as the Civil War. Additionally, those accustomed to erecting barriers against the world found it natural to renovate them or reconstruct new ones as times changed.

In 1850 Daniel Webster spoke in Boston about the sectional divisions that split Methodists into two denominations. He complained about religious extremists.

> In all such disputes, there will sometimes be found men with whom everything is absolute; absolutely wrong or absolutely right.

They see the right clearly; they think others ought to see it, and they are disposed to establish a broad line of distinction between what is right and wrong. . . . They are ready to mark and guard [that line] by placing along it a series of dogmas, as lines of boundary on the earth's surface are marked by posts and stones.[12]

The God-like Daniel, whose alcoholism and womanizing left little doubt about his personal worldliness, may have been correct about the impact of narrow-mindedness on the political system, but he was wrong about the danger of a "broad line of distinction" in religion. These "posts and stones," which he denounced, indicate for laity where the world lies and prevent separation from the world from being empty rhetoric. The more visible the stones and markers, the more likely that the group will resist the mainstream.

The Valley

T HE SHENANDOAH RIVER'S COURSE is short but dramatic. Rising in the mountains of western Virginia, the Shenandoah's several branches meander through a long, narrow valley, bounded by the Blue Ridge on the east and the Alleghenies to the west. For forty-five miles Massanutten Mountain, a steep ridge, rises from the Valley floor to separate the Shenandoah's North Fork and South Fork branches. Denied its own outlet to the sea, the river joins the Potomac in a breathtaking confluence at Harper's Ferry, made famous by John Brown's assault on slavery and Thomas Jefferson's pronouncement that this spectacle alone justified a trek across the Atlantic. From headwaters to Harper's Ferry the Shenandoah's path is generally southwest to northeast, but within the Valley the Shenandoah flows from south to north; the upper Valley is in the south, and the lower Valley in the north. Therefore, residents say that the river runs "down the Valley" though on a map its northward course looks like "up."

By the eve of the American Revolution the earmarks of religion in this picturesque valley had emerged. This remarkable region had become populated by a variety of settlers with a wide assortment of religious traditions. Nearly all embraced the concept of outsiderness but each used a slightly different grip.

In 1716 Virginia's governor, Alexander Spotswood, led an expedition of gentlemen-pathfinders into the Shenandoah wilderness. Spotswood's motivations mixed official and personal aims; he hoped that settlement of the west would simultaneously enhance his personal investments and also protect the empire. With Spotswood in his chaise and the gentlemen on horseback, the party descended the Blue Ridge and camped for two nights by the Shenandoah River, which they named the Euphrates. The explorers toasted the King with champagne, the Prince with burgundy, and the rest of the royal family with claret, firing a volley after each toast. The well-stocked expedition, unlikely to perish of thirst, also lugged Virginia red and white wine, brandy, shrub, two kinds of rum, cherry punch, cider, and other beverages across the Blue Ridge. These genteel explorers bore little resemblance to Frederick Jackson Turner's rugged egalitarian pioneers, whom he credited with the building of American democracy.[1]

Spotswood, his genteel companions, and the many Europeans who followed in the footsteps of these pathfinders, found a congenial climate that produces abundant vegetation. Average annual rainfall is 32 inches. The average high temperature in January is 42 degrees, the low 21, and the average high and low in July are 86 and 61. Lengthy autumns last well into November, prompting one nineteenth-century resident to inform Northern relatives that "winter does not really set in much before Christmas." Ice storms, however, caused by heavy, cold air trapped between the mountains, plague the Valley. Prior to European settlement deciduous hardwoods, including hickory, poplars, walnut, and a variety of oaks formed the Valley forest, while pines grew on steeper and higher locations and grass carpeted open areas along stream beds. American chestnut trees spread forage for animals across the forest floor. Early farmers preferred the limestone portions of the Valley, although a limestone-shale contact zone created edge habitats, abundant with game, and numerous springs. The principal native American route through the Valley, the "Warrior's Path," may have followed this. One traveler claimed that frogs were so plentiful that neighborhoods held "bull frog frolics" in which participants shot into ponds with large populations of croakers. When the dead frogs floated to the surface, specially trained dogs brought them out. Revelers discarded the head, body, and shoulders, but the legs made a tasty soup or fricassee.[2] The fertile, breathtaking landscape impressed visitors. "Some of the finest land I have seen," extolled one traveler. "Small hills and narrow vales," according to another, "abounding in copious springs and bold rivulets," bestowed the smallest tract with a beautiful spot for a house, "a fine southern slope for a garden, and a brook of water as pure as the dew of the heaven."[3]

The first whites to "discover" the Valley's small hills and brooks of heavenly dew found them uninhabited. Aside from an isolated village or scattered family units, Native Americans journeyed through the Valley rather than occupying it. Iroquois from northern New York, for example, traveled the Shenandoah on their way to tributary groups in Virginia's Piedmont and the southern Appalachians. But Native Americans nevertheless created a presence in the Shenandoah wilderness. Spotswood's explorers descending the Blue Ridge found it impassable until they located a trail marked by Indians. As new settlers constructed cabins and farms, contact increased with passing Native Americans. An early minister described the natives as generally traveling in groups of fifteen to twenty, requesting food at every house they called upon and taking it if not freely offered. He also recalled sporadic murders.[4]

Disputed claims over the small hills and brooks of heavenly dew, at least those in the northern Valley, virtually guaranteed that Shenandoah society would be diverse, even in its earliest stages of settlement. Disagreement developed because Thomas, Sixth Lord of Fairfax, had inherited a proprietary grant between the Potomac and Rappahannock rivers and the boundaries of this "Northern Neck" were unclear. Although by the late 1720s all acknowledged that the Rappahannock began on the Blue Ridge, Fairfax believed that the Potomac's headwaters were deep in the mountains and that a line drawn from it to the Rappahannock's origins put the northern Valley in his claim. But Virginia's governor, William Gooch, maintained that both rivers began at the Blue Ridge, meaning that the entire Valley was outside Fairfax's claim. Gooch acted first. He conferred large grants in the Valley, an action that asserted the colony's supremacy over the territory, and he stipulated that the grantees quickly settle their lands in small allotments, which he hoped would hastily create a buffer between eastern

Virginia and the growing alliance between the French and Native Americans in the west. Two of the early grantees were Pennsylvanians born in Europe: Jost Hite, a German, and Alexander Ross, a Quaker from Ireland. They naturally recruited their countrymen and women, attracting an ethnically mixed population of small farmers to settle portions of the northern Valley. Fairfax's agent, the wealthy planter Robert "King" Carter, responded to Gooch's initiative with a more aristocratic vision of the lower Valley by bestowing generous-sized patents without restrictions on eastern Virginia aristocrats, thus laying the foundation for large estates in the lower Shenandoah.[5]

In the upper Valley landholding patterns were similar. Here Governor Gooch held uncontested control, and as in the lower Shenandoah, he bestowed large grants but required rapid settlement on relatively small distributions. But, as in the low country, large landowners nevertheless predominated. In 1769, more than seventy-one percent of Augusta County freeholders owned less than four hundred acres, but their share of total acreage was only thirty-seven percent and a majority of Augusta County men remained landless. Still, the upper Valley avoided the large disparities of wealth that characterized eastern Virginia, and small holders drawn from middling Pennsylvanians, especially Scots Irish, seeking cheap land were conspicuous.[6]

Policy makers did not set out to create Shenandoah pluralism, but the Board of Trade, which managed the empire's colonies in London and whose policies Gooch implemented, did covet a well-ordered zone of white, Protestant small holders. This was pragmatic, not idealistic. The board considered yeoman ideal for militia duty and expected these future Protestant militiamen to protect the empire from the growing French Catholic and Native American threat. The Shenandoah's whiteness was intentional, too. The Board of Trade feared that an unpopulated backcountry might spark low country slave insurrection, as it did in Jamaica, or create a tempting haven for runaways, but planting small holders there would spawn a population that required few slaves and displayed hostility towards fugitives. The Shenandoah would become a slaveless belt between the mountainous west and the enslaved east. Low country leadership, therefore, must have been pleased to see in the backcountry a reasonable facsimile of its stratified society with large landholders atop the social ladder. Still, the mixture of Scots Irish and German small holders with scions of low country planters kept the Valley from being a carbon copy of eastern Virginia.[7]

Despite the designs of the Valley's planners, African Americans, though only four percent of the Valley's population in the 1750s, eventually added to the Valley's pluralism. Tidewater-style slave plantations were less prevalent in the Valley than in eastern Virginia, "King" Carter's efforts notwithstanding, but prominent members of the community, sometimes including preachers, were conspicuous slaveholders, just as they were across the Blue Ridge. Most African Americans were from eastern Virginia, although one of the earliest and most remarkable, Edward Tarr, a free black, moved to the Valley from Lancaster County, Pennsylvania, with his Scottish-born wife. In 1753, traveling Moravian missionaries identified Tarr as the only blacksmith in Augusta County and a reader of German-language sermons. In the next decade Tarr became a landholder, established a shop along the Great Wagon road between Staunton and Lexington, and joined the Timber Ridge Presbyterian congregation. But unspecified morals charges were brought against his wife, and in an obvious attempt at intimidation, the court ordered the display of an executed slave's head on the road that led to his shop. Tarr got the message; he sold his land at a loss and moved to Staunton. Tarr, a bilingual free black with a Scottish wife, embodied the Valley's diversity but also its tendency, from its first generation, to be Southern on race.[8]

In the middle of the eighteenth century this diverse population and its fertile Valley occupied the edge of mid-eighteenth-century British North American civilization, which placed it on the front lines between the competing geopolitical interests of three powers: the British Empire, the French Empire, and Native Americans. This tripartite conflict converged at the Forks of the Ohio, the site of modern Pittsburgh. The French had already established outposts along the Great Lakes and in the Illinois country, and they hoped that their control of the strategic confluence at the Forks would box in the British along the Atlantic seaboard. British policy makers schemed to disrupt the growing French sphere of influence in the North American backwoods and separate French Canada from French Louisiana by controlling the same area. Native Americans, increasingly exasperated by spreading English settlement, simply sought to hold on. With cheap land still available in the Valley, all this held little interest for Shenandoans, but low country Virginians became increasingly drawn into this remote but strategic area. Investors headed by Lord Fairfax considered the Forks of the Ohio profitable, and the colonial government, standing in for the Empire, desired to demonstrate authority over the region. In 1754 Governor Dinwiddie, perhaps thinking about his own purse as well as the Empire's stature, sent George Washington to warn the French out of the Ohio country, but they ignored the twenty-two-year-old aristocrat. Dinwiddie quickly sent Washington back to the Ohio, this time with muscle—Virginia militiamen—including recruits from the Valley. The inexperienced commander ambushed a small party of French, but in the process killed—murdered, claimed the French—an ambassador on a diplomatic mission. (One of Washington's Indian allies crushed the ambassador's skull with a tomahawk after he was captured.) A few weeks later Washington found himself surrounded by French and Indians in a meadow at Fort Necessity and surrendered under embarrassing circumstances that included an apology for the French emissary's death. The opening shots of the Seven Years' War had been fired deep in the North American wilderness.[9]

The following year the Empire assigned General Edward Braddock's Redcoat regulars, accompanied again by Valley units, to dislodge the French from the Ohio country, but after his now-famous defeat, the war suddenly came much closer to the Valley. Braddock's debacle left the Virginia frontier defenseless, and up and down the mountains Native Americans attacked with impunity. Panic set in. In the Valley rural residents flocked to towns, and those in towns headed east. Washington complained that the "Crowds of People who were flying, as if every moment were death," made it difficult to cross the Blue Ridge.[10]

The war did little to distinguish between soldiers and civilians. Both sides shot on sight, and those without protection faced high risk. John Rhodes, for example, a Mennonite preacher, was shot in his doorway, and his murderers then killed his wife and three sons. Rhodes's oldest daughter and his youngest child escaped through a hole in the barn, but the raiders marched off with four other children as prisoners. When a young son could not keep pace, they killed him, and two of his sisters who then refused to go any further lost their lives as well. The survivor of these four remained with the Indians for three years before returning home.[11]

To protect families from these depredations, Dinwiddie put Washington in charge of Virginia's perimeter defenses, which amounted to a string of forts and blockhouses along the frontier. Sometimes no more than cabins surrounded by a stockade and isolated from one another by ten or twenty miles, these diminutive citadels were targets as much as bastions. Still, they allowed families to huddle together rather than risk attack in isolated farmsteads, and they prevented the backcountry from becoming completely depopulated, which would have given Native Americans a strategic victory. Most of the forts were in the mountains to the west of the Valley, but several were near Woodstock, and Fort Loudon, a significant point in the defense system, protected Washington's headquarters in Winchester with twenty-four cannon and barracks for 450 men.[12]

Despite the proximity of the carnage, Shenandoans only half-heartedly supported the war. Many backcountry residents dismissed the conflict as a scheme to protect the fortunes of low country planters and a private company of investors. They viewed the militia's mission as a local one of self-defense rather than as serving the king and empire. The consequent lack of cooperation frustrated authorities. When Washington commandeered seventy-four wagons from the Winchester area, owners only surrendered ten of them. Winchester residents routinely violated Washington's orders not to sell alcohol to soldiers; in fact, satisfying thirsty soldiers was profitable, and the number of tavern licenses increased noticeably during the war. Further annoying Washington was the soldiers' practice of selling stolen military equipment to raise cash to pay for the grog. He ordered a random search of private homes to recover missing equipment, but local officials refused to participate. Washington complained that "in all things" he "met with the greatest opposition." One civilian, he recounted, had threatened to blow "his brains out." Imperiled by enemy raiders but with a localist mentality, Shenandoans viewed the Seven Years' War much differently than did Virginians in the eastern low country.[13]

In this frontier environment, religion also lived on the edge, even during peacetime. As backcountry religion evolved, its pluralism matched the Valley's social diversity, but its religious authority was even more dispersed than the Valley's moderately tiered social structure.

Not surprisingly, religion on the Shenandoah frontier was just as raw as the rest of the new society. Backcountry settlers and later generations agreed that "moral waste and desolation" best described the Shenandoah frontier. An early minister represented his new charge as "a wilderness in the proper sense" without any church order and with but "a few Christian settlers." According to antebellum era legend, when someone complained to "old Father [John] Craig," one of the Valley's first Presbyterian preachers, about the character of the officers in his congregation, he promptly replied in his Scots Irish brogue, "Faith, an when ye can't get hewn stone, ye must ain tak durnies" ("dornies," an English term for wooden doorways).[14]

Craig's "durnies" might have answered that their ministers were hardly hewn stone. Early preachers themselves often reflected the immature institutional life of the backcountry with ordinations that were unacceptable in Europe. William "One-eyed" Robinson, who intinerated through the Valley from eastern Virginia, was a graduate not of a Scottish seminary but of William Tennent's log college, a one-room schoolhouse that trained young ministers in Pennsylvania. (Robinson had lost an eye from smallpox, thereby gaining his nickname.) Alexander Miller had been deposed in Ireland, but he appeared so repentant before the synod of Philadelphia that they restored his ordination and he filled a pulpit in the Valley. Another backcountry pastor, Desolate Baker, adopted an alias, "James Loveall," to conceal a checkered past of promiscuity, bigamy, and syphilis. Baker's partners included black and Native-American women, which made his transgressions even worse for his congregation. In 1746 Mill Creek Baptists excommunicated him for immoral behavior. John Craig had been a divinity student in Glasgow but did not graduate. In Virginia he taught school for a year, then "read" or studied the scriptures for two years and received ordination.[15]

Like Pennsylvania, no tradition dominated, and the Church of England, the established denomination in England and Virginia, possessed only a tentative toehold in the Valley, sometimes a decade behind other denominations in organizing congregations. Despite benefiting from established status, institutional weaknesses plagued Anglicanism in America and in the Shenandoah. Only bishops could ordain, but North America had none, so candidates for ordination had to travel to London. Furthermore, colonial Anglicanism suffered from deficient educational facilities. Prior to the College of Philadelphia (1749) and King's College (1754), the only Anglican-affiliated institution of higher education in the colonies was William and Mary (1693) in Virginia. Not surprisingly then, Anglicans suffered from a shortage of priests. To make matters worse, scandal plagued the relatively small numbers of clergy. Between 1723 and 1743 the character of twenty Virginia ministers suffered challenge, though perhaps nine of the attacks were frivolous. Similarly, between 1743 and 1776 fourteen serious accusations surfaced.

Institutional frailties and ministerial deficiencies especially impaired Anglicanism because for Anglicans the church played a central role in salvation. Anglicans believed that humans were naturally weak, but the rational Anglican God understood this and was ready to forgive. Individuals, however, only received this necessary forgiveness, or grace, through faith, which they acquired in a lifelong journey as they followed the church's guidance through its liturgy, sacraments, and hierarchy. Hence, without ministers to lead worship, administer the sacraments, and provide spiritual authority for weak sinners, Anglicanism drifted.[16]

In the Valley Anglican membership was so low that occasionally vestries conducted business without quorums and filled out their ranks with non-Anglicans, especially Presbyterians. The Augusta County parish, created in 1738, waited until 1746 to organize its vestry, but eight of the first twelve vestrymen were Presbyterians. By the 1760s Presbyterians still held a majority on the Augusta vestry, so the Virginia Assembly dissolved it, but a new election in 1771 changed little. Perhaps because of this Presbyterian presence, several of the early Anglican clergy had Presbyterian backgrounds, though they possessed Anglican ordinations. The first priest in Augusta County, John Hindman, was born in Ulster. A horse-racing fan, his estate included twenty-three race horses, racing equipment, five wigs, and fifteen books of sermons. In 1773 Staunton Anglicans hired another former Presbyterian, Alexander Balmaine, who stayed only until the Revolutionary War broke out; after the war Balmaine settled in Winchester. So slowly did Anglicans organize that not until 1763 did Augusta Anglicans complete their first church building, a brick structure, and later that decade they secured a glebe to support their priest. After the Revolutionary War, several Anglican buildings in the Valley fell into disuse although Anglicanism enjoyed a resurgence among the wealthy planters in the eastern part of Frederick County. Staunton Anglicans, however, as late as 1818, only had eighteen communicants, and they waited several decades into the century for their reawakening.[17]

With Anglicanism so weak, Valley religion became a polyglot of ethnicity, theology, and varying size. Ethnic and denominational identity remained sharp, and ethnic groups clustered in neighborhoods. As late as the antebellum and Civil War periods Germans still attracted the attention of travelers, either for their crudeness or for their husbandry's contribution to the Valley's beauty, depending upon the observer's viewpoint. Ethnic enclaves, however, were small, and residential mixing created strong patterns of tolerance and cooperation, similar to the middle colonies. Shenandoans often had neighbors of a different ethnicity, and small business transactions frequently transcended nationality.[18]

Perhaps the most conspicuous minority group were the

Germans, many of whom were Lutheran and Reformed. Lutherans traced their birth to the moment that Martin Luther nailed his ninety-five complaints to the church door. Rejecting the notion that believers could earn their salvation through sacraments, obedience to ecclesiastical hierarchy, or, worse yet, relics, Luther concluded that redemption from sin came by faith alone, which was a divine gift from a warm and compassionate God. To emphasize the need for individuals to respond to God, Lutheran services encouraged congregational singing, preaching, and reading the Bible in the vernacular. On the other hand, early Lutheranism also had a conservative side. It preserved the belief in Jesus' literal presence in the communion elements and continued the Mass, albeit in altered form, for two centuries. By the seventeenth century, Lutheranism had fallen under the influence of the "scholastics," who urged the acceptance and verbatim memorization of precise doctrinal statements. A countermovement led by Pietists at the university in Halle sought re-invigoration through heart-felt faith and intimacy with Christ, and the organizer of American Lutheranism, Henry Melchior Muhlenberg, carried this to the colonies.[19]

The Reformed tradition descended from John Calvin in Reformation-era Geneva. More than Lutherans, who found gentleness in the divine, Calvinists stressed an absolutely powerful but distant God and the complete inability of humans to take steps towards their own salvation. Instead, God elected, or predestined, certain individuals for redemption. Believing that God was revealed primarily through the word in sermons and the scriptures, they stripped their churches of ornamentation, including statues, crosses, and candles, placing only the Ten Commandments on the walls. The austere surroundings removed distractions and reminded worshippers of God's power. They recognized only two sacraments, baptism and communion, rather than the Catholic seven. Although Calvin's followers firmly denied that works earned redemption, their constant doubts about personal salvation led to intense self-scrutiny and concern about morality and behavior. German Calvinists, or the Reformed, accepted a compromise with Lutheranism, the Heidelberg

Confession, which emphasized moral activity motivated by thankfulness, a Lutheran influence, and deemphasized predestination.[20]

Both Lutherans and Reformed suffered from organizational weaknesses in the Shenandoah, especially a shortage of ministers, not just in the backcountry era but throughout the period of this study. In 1747 early Lutheran and Reformed settlers joined to build a union church in Strasburg, and in 1753 they acquired a lot, but it took another eleven years to lay the cornerstone. Still without a minister, they called one from Baltimore to help with this ceremony. Clergy from across the Blue Ridge served early Lutheran congregations until the first resident pastor, Peter Muhlenberg, son of Henry Muhlenberg, arrived in 1772. The young Muhlenberg's invitation came from an Anglican parish that had insufficient numbers to attract a rector, and he made the long trip to London to secure ordination; then returned and held dual ordination until he took up arms in the Revolutionary War. After the war, Muhlenberg returned to Pennsylvania and embarked upon a political career, leaving Valley Lutherans once again without ordained leadership. (Muhlenberg was elected to the United States Senate from Pennsylvania.)[21]

After the Revolutionary War Lutherans found a minister in Paul Henkel, from the mountains of western Virginia, who after preaching to several congregations, took letters of recommendation from four of them to the Ministerium in Pennsylvania and received a license to preach for a year. After that he made another trip to Pennsylvania for ordination. In 1793 Henkel and three other Lutheran clergy in Virginia organized the Virginia Ministerium, and later that year the new organization held its first meeting in Winchester. Early in the next century Virginia Lutherans ordained several Shenandoans, but in 1809 they still had forty-eight congregations in Virginia served by only eight pastors, four of whom labored in the Valley.[22]

The Reformed were even more poorly organized. Throughout the eighteenth century their clergymen in the Valley begged the Coetus, the Reformed governing body, for help but not until 1825 did Reformed Virginians get their own classis when four ministers and five elders gathered in Woodstock to organize it. The shortage of clergy never abated, however, and by the 1840s, when membership still numbered only approximately one thousand, the Reformed blamed it for their struggles. One Valley pastor attributed a membership decline in his seven (!) congregations from 800 in 1830 to 373 in 1841 to the dearth of clergy. Other signs of declension were competing denominations worshipping in former Reformed buildings and congregations that failed to meet their full financial obligations to the classis. The Winchester congregation was so weak that it needed assistance to construct a building, and the classis requested donations from other congregations; customarily town congregations were among the strongest societies rather than those requiring subsidization. Despite the Valley's large German population, the Reformed never became a large part of its religious life.[23]

Smaller German-speaking fellowships—Mennonites and Dunkers—and the English-speaking Friends added to the Valley's salad bowl. Mennonites and Dunkers belonged to the Anabaptist wing of the Reformation, which held that Luther and Calvin had neglected reform by insufficiently imitating the New Testament church. "Anabaptist" means rebaptizer and refers to the belief in adult baptism, which in Reformation-era Europe meant a second baptism for those who had previously received the sacrament as infants in established churches. Mennonites acquired their name from a Dutch monk, Menno Simons, a sixteenth-century organizer of scattered and persecuted Dutch and North German Anabaptists. They taught firm adherence to what they considered simple Biblical truths, particularly those in the New Testament, such as adult baptism, obedience to the community of believers, avoidance of luxury, nonviolence, and nonswearing of oaths. William Penn's offer of tolerance appealed to them, and in the early eighteenth century they contributed to the wave of German immigration to Pennsylvania. In 1728 the first Mennonites arrived in the Shenandoah Valley, and soon permanent settlers established Massanutten, near present Luray, but an Indian raid during the Seven Years' War nearly destroyed these settlements. Most fled back to Pennsylvania, but when the danger subsided, others returned, establishing farms mostly in Augusta and

Rockingham Counties. By the time of the American Revolution Mennonites had a secure foundation in the Valley.[24]

The Dunkers came to Anabaptism several centuries after the Reformation. Their German founder, Alexander Mack, Sr., was initially drawn to Radical Pietism, which called for a personal relationship with Christ so intense and intimate that the organized church often became irrelevant. Mack concluded that this neglect of the spiritual community was an error, so in 1708 he and seven followers created a fellowship, often called simply the Brethren, that fused heart-felt faith with the Anabaptist emphasis on the community of believers. In many ways Dunkers resembled Mennonites, but they differed from their Anabaptist cousins because of their form of total immersion baptism ("trine immersion"—three times under) and because they included feetwashing in their celebration of the Lord's Supper. (Some Mennonites practiced feetwashing, but Dunkers made it a point of emphasis.) In the early eighteenth century they migrated to Pennsylvania and in the 1750s followed the Great Valley into Virginia.[25] In 1788 Valley Dunkers had grown enough that church leaders needed to draw a line at Market Street in Harrisonburg, dividing the fellowship into northern and southern districts for administrative purposes, and by the turn-of-the-century Dunkers had held three denominational Yearly Meetings in Virginia, two in the Valley.[26]

Friends were a small, innovative English-speaking community. Emerging from the period of the English Civil War, they concluded that God lay within each individual in the form of the Holy Spirit, or Inner Light, which placed them at the opposite end of the theological spectrum from Calvinists, who thought God remote and humans depraved. This piece of God entered every person at birth, and early Quakers acquired their nickname by shaking when this realization hit them. Yet this inner light was tender, easily overwhelmed by worldly influence. Especially determined to protect their children's delicate spirit from carnal influence, Quakers developed families that were exceptionally child-centered for that time. Rather than sending grown children away isolated or alone into the world, Quaker parents provided them with farms within the community, also unusual. This was costly,

and William Penn's offer of cheap land in the New World especially attracted Quakers from the less prosperous northwestern
England and northern Wales. When land prices in Penn's colony
eventually rose, most Pennsylvania Quakers moved into the trades
and protected their children's gift of grace with cash as well as
land. A few families, however, followed the great Wagon Road
south and west into the Valley. In 1732 the first Friends arrived in
the Shenandoah from New Jersey and Pennsylvania, and soon
they formed the Hopewell Monthly Meeting, under the supervision of the Chester Quarterly Meeting in Pennsylvania. Migration
from Pennsylvania to northern Virginia continued until the
American Revolution, and Quakers established a strong presence
in the lower Valley with seventeen meetings.[27]

Valley Friends and Anabaptists augmented the Valley's
Pennsylvania image. Quakers founded that colony, while Dunkers
and Mennonites were among the small, ethnic denominations
that made Penn's Woods so rich in variety. Demographically, these
small denominations were overwhelmingly Northern, and their
Valley branches retained strong kinship and organizational ties
with their Northern co-religionists. Although Quakers had pockets of settlement in other parts of the South, the Anabaptists had
few Southern members outside the Valley. The Shenandoah representatives of these groups, therefore, look like Southern minorities
in Northern denominations or like Northerners in a Southern
locale.

The Valley's other significant non-English ethnic group were
the Scots Irish, who were almost always Presbyterian.
Presbyterians were the Scottish and Ulster version of Calvinism
and, therefore, similar in theology to the German Reformed.
Large numbers, almost always in families, followed the Great
Valley south from Pennsylvania into the Shenandoah, and in some
places became so dominant that they infiltrated Anglican vestries,
as described earlier. Like everybody except the Anglicans, their
early organizational home was in Pennsylvania, but in 1786
Shenandoah Presbyterians created the Presbytery of Lexington
and in 1794 the Presbytery of Winchester, both of which belonged
to the Synod of Virginia. Although these dates come not much

earlier than the founding of other religious associations in the Valley, the populous Lexington and Winchester Presbyteries were stronger than the Lutherans' skeleton-like four-parson organization, and exclusively Virginian. During its early years the Synod of Virginia met often in Winchester, including every year but two in the 1790s, because its boundaries reached to the Monongahela River and Winchester was a central location.[28] Presbyterians complemented their early institutional maturity with educational facilities, establishing in 1749 Augusta Academy, which soon became Liberty Hall near Lexington and eventually Washington and Lee University.[29]

The third large ethnic group in the early Valley, the English, most frequently worshipped as Baptists and Methodists. Baptists came in two varieties—Regulars and Separates—both of whom baptized adults by immersion. Regular Baptists were Calvinists, more predestinarian than the German Reformed. Sometimes called Particular Baptists, for particular atonement (Christ died only for the elect, not for all), they flourished in Pennsylvania and New Jersey, where tolerance promoted stability and growth. The term "Regulars" suggests that they formed the heart of the American Baptist tradition. Separate Baptists, known in England as Generals, migrated to Virginia from New England, where they had acquired their nickname by separating from the anti-revivalist Congregationalist establishment. Separates were Arminian, i.e., Christ's atonement was universal and, therefore, all humans could achieve salvation by accepting or rejecting God's grace. (Calvinists taught that God's grace was irresistible; humans could not reject God once they had been elected.)[30]

Like almost everybody else in the Shenandoah, the first Baptists had a close connection with Northern co-religionists, but they quickly sustained themselves with local organization. In 1743 General Baptists from Maryland began a congregation in the northern Valley, and in the next decade another group organized the Linville Creek society in Rockingham County. Of the eleven who attended the first communion at Linville, six had belonged to Baptist congregations in southeastern Pennsylvania, and its first pastor, John Alderson, was from Germantown, Pennsylvania. For several decades Linville retained its ties with the Philadelphia Association. Eventually Virginia Baptists organized congregations into associations; in 1766 Linville and Opequon joined with two congregations east of the Blue Ridge to create the Ketoctin Association, named for its first meeting place. Valley Baptists never had their own association, instead holding membership in associations comprised mostly of congregations outside the Valley.[31]

Thus, rather than a vast geological melting pot, a basin of homogeneity stretching from ridge to ridge, the Valley was home to a society that more resembled the patchwork of its fields. Anglicans, Lutherans, and Reformed had been accustomed to established status and numerical preponderance in Europe, but in the Valley their organizational deficiencies, especially leadership deficits, left these traditions unlikely to overwhelm anybody and created space for those without a tradition of governmental support, especially Baptists, Dunkers, Friends, Mennonites, and Presbyterians. Long after the Shenandoah had lost its backcountry characteristics, it still resembled Pennsylvania because so many religious traditions remained distinct.

The Valley's vibrant pluralism gave each group the opportunity to claim outsiderness. Just as backcountry society with its independent-minded small holders evolved on a slightly different path than eastern Virginia, so Shenandoah religion contrasted from the low country with greater dispersion of authority and enhanced diversity. With numerous fellowships of varying size, ethnicity, and theology, pluralism was the norm in the Valley's religious landscape, a community of minorities. It would be a stretch to suggest that each fellowship possessed a unique definition of the mainstream, for the similarities between some groups—Dunkers and Mennonites, Lutheran and Reformed—were too great to allow each tradition to claim an original voice. But as waves of political, religious, economic revolution surged over the mountains, affecting successive generations, each fellowship defined the world just a bit differently.

The American Revolution

IN 1672 MICHAEL BRUCE PREACHED to a congregation in Carluke, Scotland, on the Valley of the Dry Bones. In this well-known Old Testament story, as the prophet Ezekiel spoke the bones came together, covered with sinews and flesh but lifeless until God's spirit breathed life into them. Bruce asked his listeners when the wind of God's spirit would breathe life into their dry bones? "O Carluke," he cried out, "What sense have ye of your own sad and doleful Condition?" Was there "any noise or shaking" among their lifeless skeletons? And, he questioned, were they aware "of the Sad Case and Condition" of the Church of Scotland and of the "sin that hath brought Sad judgments on both" the church and individual believers.[1]

Bruce's passionate words to Carluke typified the tendency of Scots and Scots Irish to join individual piety with the Scottish church. In practice, this meant commitment to the national church and its generations-long struggle with the English Anglican establishment, creating a distinct sense of outsiderness through opposition to political authority.

Prior to the American Revolution many communions in the Valley could claim outsider status through resistance to political authority. Anglicans, the established religion of Virginia, obviously could not, and Lutherans and Reformed, despite paying taxes like everybody else to support Virginia Anglicanism, had been established in Europe. Whatever their feelings about the Anglican establishment in the New World, their Old World heritage included political insiderness. But Baptists, Dunkers, Mennonites,

Presbyterians, and Quakers had strong histories of resistance to political and religious authority, and, therefore, the American Revolution had the greatest potential to alter their view of the center. But among these fellowships with dissenting traditions, only in Presbyterianism did political nonconformity occupy the bulk of the despised mainstream, and as a result the American Revolution affected their concept of outsiderness the most.

For Baptists, Dunkers, Mennonites, and Quakers political dissent was only one component of their outsidersness. All four had much in common. Dunkers and Mennonites, of course, shared Anabaptism, and Dunkers, Mennonites, and the English-speaking Baptists were so close that when eighteenth-century Baptists wrote a history of their communion in America, they included these German faiths. Each constructed a lifestyle and polity that gave them a self-identity apart from the mainstream and a counterculture in which resistance to political authority was merely one element.[2]

Each of the four emphasized the faith community as the primary source of spiritual authority, often in remarkably democratic ways, rather than a clerical or ecclesiastical hierarchy. Congregations were spiritual families with members bestowing the title of "brother" and "sister" on each other, except for Quakers, who recognized a special bond between members by calling each other "Friend." All prized unity within the community and expected members to be in harmony with one another. Baptists so cherished reconciliation between bickering members that they entered it into their church books. Members did not sue each other but relied on the fellowship to resolve financial disputes, especially those involving debt collection. Mennonites and Dunkers worked especially hard to achieve harmony prior to communion, typically employing elders on congregational visits or holding councils for the purpose of reconciliation.[3]

To strengthen the community, brothers, sisters, and Friends assisted each other in their spiritual walks and banished those who refused its guidance. Quaker monthly meetings, which had primary responsibility for exercising discipline, used overseers and visitation committees to monitor compliance and report deviance. Baptists disciplined at business meetings that usually met once a month on Saturday afternoons. Mennonites dropped a strict ban, or shun, urged by Menno Simons, that prohibited social intercourse or even eating with separated members, but they still excommunicated those whose sin threatened the purity of the faith community. Dunkers were more comfortable with this harsh form of discipline. Alexander Mack's first theological writing, *Rites and Ordinances*, condemned those who rejected the congregation's "discipline of love" as "lost," and he urged a ban on them "so that the entire body or church is not contaminated." The first generation of Dunkers applied the ban liberally on both sides of the Atlantic, and in one instance in Pennsylvania two congregations banned each other. Although Dunkers did not keep congregational records, evidence seems strong that they still used the ban during the era of the American Revolution; in the 1770s a Pennsylvania congregation shunned the founder's granddaughter for a sexual offense. For Quakers, Dunkers, Mennonites, and Baptists membership in the spiritual community required effort and conformity, and each group claimed the authority to expel deviant members.[4]

The body of believers also held ultimate power to select ministers. Dunkers, for example, allowed all members to vote for ministers. Among Quakers anyone inspired by the Spirit was free to speak, but silence was more frequent. Most members never commented, but those who did spoke regularly and were viewed as having a gift for it. Baptists allowed those who thought they had a preaching gift to demonstrate it before the fellowship, who then judged whether the candidate would continue to preach. For Mennonites, when the congregation nominated several candidates for the ministry, the final decision fell to the lot, which theoretically allowed heaven rather than humans to sway the decision. Each candidate received a book, but one of the volumes had a slip of paper inserted into it and the nominee whose book had the paper became the preacher. Both Anabaptist fellowships developed several tiers of ministers that consisted of elders, who were mature, experienced preachers, exhorters, who were less experienced and generally gave short responses to sermons, and deacons and deaconesses, who ministered to the needs of the poor and elderly. The differences between the three ranks were sharper among Dunkers, although they allowed all brothers to stand up and comment during worship, while Mennonites blurred the duties performed by elders and deacons. All were unpaid, self-supporting, "free" ministers who took time away from their vocation to serve. None of these groups required a university degree or even special training for ministers, inclining instead toward anti-intellectualism, and none empowered a bishop or an assembly of clergy rather than the fellowship to pick their preachers.[5]

Once selected, ministers remained under the authority of congregations. Quaker ministers often led quietly. It was not uncommon for Quaker preachers to call a special meeting and then sit through it in silence. Baptists warned ministers not to "Lord over the church" nor to act on the congregation's behalf without its approval. They noted that Christ appeared on earth "not in ministerial office" and that the New Testament church was congregational. John Alderson, Sr., minister of the Linville Creek Baptists, was so unconvincing in his rebuttal of accusations of misbehavior with a woman that his congregation suspended him until he repented three years later. Dunkers and Mennonite congregations enjoyed similar authority over their preachers. Mennonites controlled leadership by assigning teams of ministers to serve several meetinghouses rather than allowing a solo minister to possess a single congregation; this prevented individual preachers from staking out fiefdoms. While Anabaptist preachers enjoyed status and influence similar to their counterparts in other denominations, congregations and conferences could "bench" them if their beliefs or behavior no longer reflected community norms, and ministers, too, received warning visits if they strayed too far beyond the lines drawn by the fellowship. For Anabapists much of the authority of clergy derived from sensitivity to congregational mood rather than rank.[6]

Even in denominational polity Baptists, Dunkers, Mennonites, and Quakers reserved a large role for individual congregations, thereby preserving their status as communities set apart from the larger world. The most denominational were Dunkers, who called influential Yearly Meetings comprised of ministers who made decisions on polity and practice. Yet these leaders were adept at discerning attitudes within their congregations, and both Yearly Meeting and congregational councils, who usually had the responsibility of enforcing Yearly Meeting's decisions, relied on consensus for decision making. Friends likewise held annual gatherings, but Quakerism's core remained at the local level. Friends joined local meetings or congregations for worship, two or three of which typically formed a monthly meeting and conducted most of the business. Quarterly and yearly meetings created policy and heard appeals, which they seldom approved, but enforcement and interpretation occurred locally. Baptists, according to a seventeenth-century confession, considered "every [congregation] a compact and knit citie in itself," and denominationalism did not emerge among them until 1814 with the formation of the General Missionary Convention. To emphasize their independence from bishops and creeds, new congregations wrote their own covenants in which members agreed on faith statements, means of support for the congregation, and the role of members. Regional associations passed resolutions on vital matters of belief and practice, and they dismissed congregations for unsound doctrine or disorderly behavior. But congregations participated in associations on a voluntary basis and withdrew at will. Mennonites held no national meetings, although regional gatherings of ministers formed conferences and decided questions that vexed congregations. Until founding their own conference in 1835, Valley Mennonites relied on their more numerous and better-organized brethren in Pennsylvania for leadership, especially to settle disputes, and perhaps for supervision of ordination. Regardless of conference boundaries, in practice Mennnonite lines of authority were informal and tribal rather than bureaucratic. For example, prior to action against an individual, a representative of the conference might visit the accused for informal counseling. For all of these nonconformist denominations power flowed from the bottom up and empowered the local society, a stark contrast to the hierarchies embedded in the established faiths of Europe.[7]

Distinctive ceremonies further enhanced the identity of these fellowships. Baptists, Dunkers, and Mennonites all practiced adult baptism but each with a different mode: Mennonites sprinkled, Baptists immersed, and Dunkers immersed three times, one for each member of the Trinity and accordingly earning their nickname. Each rejected infant baptism and the catechising of children and instead insisted that baptismal candidates be adults. Other non-mainstream rituals included the kiss of charity or holy kiss (greeting members of the same gender with a kiss on the cheek), love feasts, anointing the sick with oil, and laying on of hands in ordination. Some but not all Mennonites and Baptists washed feet, and Dunkers practiced it universally. First-generation Brethren washed feet using the so-called single mode, in which a brother or sister washed and dried the feet of the next person; then this person did the same until all had participated. In the late eighteenth and early nineteenth centuries, some Dunkers developed a double mode, in which two moved down the line, one washing and the other drying, doing this to several, then allowing another pair to take over. Baptists, Dunkers, and Mennonites could point to any of a number of rituals and ceremonies that made them different.[8]

Friends, on the other hand, avoided all ceremony. Believing that outward forms, even speech and Bible reading during worship, flirted with pride and impeded holy conversation or the expression of the inner spirit, Quakers relied on silence. Though prayer and preaching might bring an inner experience, silence was more likely to allow the Holy Spirit to inspire, and Friends, especially in worship, measured words carefully and spoke only when necessary. Similarly, Quakers believed in baptisms of the Holy Spirit rather than water baptism. Although these "deep baptisms" often induced distress, they also washed away sin and the desire to commit future transgressions. Baptisms of the Holy Spirit usually came during a period of suffering or depression and could occur not just once in a lifetime but frequently. They also embodied the Quaker conviction that faith grew through the Inner Light, not outward ceremony. Mostly through subtraction rather than addition, Quakers developed a religious life as distinctive as any.[9]

Unique lifestyle added to the separation created by polity and ceremony. The records of eighteenth-century Valley Baptists are thin, but some evidence in eastern Virginia indicates that the austere and simple surroundings of Baptists, who tended to be poor and uneducated, contrasted with the prosperous display of the gentry pace-setters. Although the great differences in wealth prevalent in the low country were less pronounced in the Valley, Linville Creek Baptists carefully characterized "gentlemen and ladies" as part of larger society rather than their society, suggesting awareness of an elite class and the perception that Baptists did not belong to it. On the other hand, even eastern Virginia Baptists attracted men of distinction to their fellowship, and Baptists probably relied less on a contrast with the high-born than did other Valley dissenters.[10]

The outlines of the Dunkers' and Mennonites' emphasis on a nonconformist lifestyle built on simplicity and humility, especially in dress, are just a bit more clear. In Europe Mennonites gave little attention to these doctrines. Although Menno Simons had criticized lavish apparel and the pride of those who "parade" in silk, velvet, pins, buttons, and "such foolish finery," persecution rather than Menno's words on plainness cleansed the European fellowship of the lukewarm. But because Penn's colony was so tolerant and prosperous, the old emphasis on suffering and martyrdom was no longer realistic for Pennsylvania Mennonites. Consequently, they developed humility theology, stressing plainness, meakness, and lowliness, and they criticized fashionable dress with more intensity. Those exhorting Mennonites to greater faithfulness now complained that too many of the brothers and sisters imitated Joseph's coat of many colors or Solomon's splendor. Despite the conviction behind this jeremiad, non-Mennonite contemporaries did not report multi-hued or Solomon-splendored Mennonites. Instead, they noted that Mennonites avoided proud colors and metal buttons and that they expelled members for wearing buckles on their shoes or for having pocket holes in their coats. Beards on the men in a clean-shaven era added to their nonconformity. The Dunkers were probably even more plain. Observers described Brethren dress during the colonial period as "*bürgerlich*," or middle class, with "great plainness," and during the Revolutionary War their garb somehow identified them without being a sectarian uniform. In one instance a Loyalist passed through American lines by dressing as a Dunker. In all likelihood the dress of Dunkers and Mennonites was conspicuously simple and plain but not a separate style or cut.[11]

The lifestyle of Friends may have been the most marginal of all the outsiders. Quakers believed that "holy conversation" or interaction among the faithful communicated a meaning more revealing than any words could convey, and they more or less codified holy conversation into an intricate system of barriers, or "hedges," that effectively isolated them from the world. One of the most important hedges was distinctive speech, i.e., using "thee" and "thou" instead of "you." According to their understanding of the Bible, "thee" and "thou" were singular and "you" was plural; therefore, to call someone "you" proudly but falsely implied that they were two or more persons. Quakers also dressed plainly and refused to used titles, remove hats as a show of honor, swear oaths, or haggle over price. Swearing implied that without an oath the person might not tell the truth, and haggling was a form of lying because the declared price was not the desired price. Only partakers in holy conversation were fit marriage partners, and Friends disowned those who married persons engaged in carnal conversation, i.e., non-Quakers. Alternative behaviors in speech, dress, marriage, and commerce left little doubt about the relationship between Quakers and the larger society.[12]

The alternative worldview for three of these groups—Dunkers, Friends, and Mennonites—included misgivings about slavery and alternative attitudes about race. (Baptists were slaveholders.) Pennsylvania Quakers always had an antislavery element, and in 1776 this impulse received more emphasis when meetings disowned slaveholding Friends, described further below. Eighteenth-century Mennonites left a scant record of their opinion of bondage but little trace of their slaveholding exists, and individual Dunkers in Pennsylvania criticized the treatment of slaves and the inhumanity of the slave trade. They, too, leave little record of slaveholding. Although at this point only Friends disciplined slaveholders, Dunkers and Mennonites also took a minority position on race.[13]

These fellowships similarly held contrary standards on gender. Sometimes subtly and other times more openly, they gave women opportunities they lacked in the mainstreatm. Adult women who submitted to baptism made a choice about their faith that was independent of the men in their lives, and the Baptists' requirement to give a faith statement prior to baptism afforded women a rare opportunity to speak in public. In all four of the communions women participated in congregational councils and decision-making, including selection of ministers, and Friends empowered women with their own meetings. But Baptists, Dunkers, and Mennonites did not select women to leadership positions, other than deaconesses among the Anabaptists, and women's voices likely were unequal to men's in the various councils. Nevertheless, as tentative and vague as these measures on gender were, they represented another variance between these outsiders and the larger society.

Finally, for those who practiced free will conversion and adult baptism, prospective members knew that their decision to seek membership meant nonconformity. Their faith communities consisted not of children born into them but of rational adults who deliberately decided to join. Adult converts recognized that membership included a contrary lifestyle with bounds determined by the faith community. This applied less for Calvinist Baptists, who believed that grace was predestined and irresistible, and Quakers, who did not practice baptism, and these fellowships relied on discipline to maintain the community. But for Dunkers, Mennonites, and non-Calvinist Baptists the free will choice to accept God's grace accomplished both closeness to Christ and separation from society.

Thus, among Baptists, Dunkers, Mennonites, and Quakers their manner of relating to one another, their interaction with the larger society, and their approach to congregational affairs all pointed towards something different. When, according to the Linville Creek (Baptist) church book, adults like Mary Lincoln spoke to the congregation of her religious experience in "a short but very satisfactory" statement, she was baptized into a fellowship unusual according to the norms of the larger community. Sucky, "Brother Latham's molatto woman" (evidence of a Baptist slave-owner), gave "a very agreeable and satisfactory experience," had her words taken seriously by white men and women, and the council unanimously received her for baptism.[14] If bishops guided established churches and if rank and birth remained vital for eighteenth-century society, these nonconformist fellowships created an alternative community in which laity received uncommon influence, and fraternal relationships between peers—brothers, sisters, and friends—took precedence over top-down structures. Mary Lincoln, Sucky, and numerous Baptist, Dunker, Mennonite, and Quaker adult men and women chose to participate in communities with distinctive ceremonies and worship, democratic organizations, and nonconformist practices that reinforced their self-image as something different from the majority.

Being on the fringes created conflict with the center. In early modern Europe, where Dunkers, Mennonites, Baptists, and Quakers began, political, spiritual, and economic life were deeply intertwined, and those who tugged at one thread of civic fabric threatened the whole cloth and suffered the consequences. Both Baptists and Friends faced imprisonment or banishment for violating the English Parliament's Act of 1593, which punished those who practiced religion in an unauthorized gathering. Baptists encountered further conflict with the Church of England and political authority by insisting on congregational autonomy. The founding moment of the Baptist movement, when John Smyth baptized himself, came in Amsterdam because Smyth was in exile. In New England, Baptists suffered just as much intolerance as they had in the old country, and Puritans denied them the right to worship despite the common heritage of dissent. Authorities banished Roger Williams, an outspoken Baptist, to Rhode Island. As late as the American Revolution New England Baptists still felt discrimination from the Congregational establishment and withheld early support from the patriots' movement because they distrusted the colonial leadership who controlled it and because the majority culture had been so reluctant to recognize their rights.[15]

English Friends likewise endured jailings and frequent fines, often from actions influenced by their accent on individual conscience. Neither Royalists nor Puritans appreciated the Friends' emphasis on conscience, and both feared it threatened social harmony. Quaker indifference towards the aristocracy offended Royalists, who thought the gentry born to rule, and Quaker disregard for university-trained clerics provoked Puritans, who deemed clergy ordained to guide. Quaker attitudes about authority only confirmed to defenders of the *status quo* the dangers of unrestrained individualism. The small ways that Quakers repudiated authority, such as their refusal to use titles or remove hats in the presence of their social superiors, further convinced the mainstream of Quaker subversiveness.[16]

On the European continent Dunkers and Mennonites similarly suffered for their nonconformist beliefs. Sixteenth-century Anabaptists jeopardized German political and social cohesion by rejecting infant baptism, refusing to swear oaths, and declining to bear arms, whether to protect the town from military crisis, defend its herds from wild animals, or merely patrol walls. Authorities responded with anger predictable from those who felt their social foundation threatened, and early Mennonites endured so much imprisonment, banishment, beheading, burning, hanging, torture, and drowning that a compilation of their martyrdom by their eighteenth-century brethren produced a thick book, the *Martyr's Mirror*. After the Thirty Years' War Mennonites received greater tolerance because depopulated German principalities were desperate for settlers, even if they were peculiar. But jurisdictions that extended tolerance often denied Mennonites citizenship, and their property rights remained uncertain. Dunkers at their founding in the early eighteenth-century enjoyed a few small pockets of tolerance in minor principalities, but in most areas they faced persecution for unauthorized preaching, baptisms, love feasts, and feetwashing. They risked arrest, torture, and even enslavement on Italian galley ships. According to legend, recruiters for the King of Prussia seized one especially tall brother for the King's bodyguard, but he refused to serve because of his religious convictions. The rangy Dunker survived torture and when hauled before the King, repeated his inability to serve the crown because he already served Christ. This faith so impressed the monarch that he released his prisoner with a reward. Other incidents, however, did not end so happily.[17]

In Pennsylvania prosperity replaced persecution. Mennonites, in fact, flourished so much that they restructured their sense of outsiderness, replacing martyrdom with humility theology, as described earlier. Quakers also found it harder to sustain outsiderness in tolerant Pennsylvania; after all, they organized the colony and preserved political influence way beyond their numbers for decades. Some became wealthy, and Friends owned slaves in proportion to the rest of the population. But during the Seven Years' War Pennsylvania voters no longer indulged Quaker pacifism, and as voters pushed Friends onto the political margins, they rediscovered outsiderness, especially regarding slavery. A reform movement brought renewed pressure on slaveholders and others who drifted from traditional teachings. Whereas earlier in the century Quaker eccentrics, such as Benjamin Lay, a strict vegetarian who lived in a cave and abstained from tea and wool, were embarrassments and sometimes disowned, now nonconformists like John Woolman, who boycotted sugar because slave labor produced it, were tolerated or even embraced as role models. After several generations of being insiders, Quakers were again outsiders, but both Mennonites and Friends needed to make adjustments in Pennsylvania's persecution-free climate.[18]

As an extension of Pennsylvania the early Valley was similarly tolerant. Diverse faiths "lived in a common state of sociability," as James Ireland, a Baptist, affirmed. But, unlike Pennsylvania, complaints about intolerance occasionally surfaced. The Anglican establishment imposed religious taxes on everyone, popular with almost no one. Before the Revolution Dunkers grumbled that authorities "harassed" them over militia law and their refusal to swear oaths; Mennonites and Quakers probably had the same problems with militia musters although evidence of this surfaced only later during the American Revolution. Baptists noted that Christ's church was congregational rather than national, a rebuke of the Church of England (and Scotland, too!), and rivalry between Baptists and Anglicans ran strong. Two Baptist preachers, John Koontz and Martin Kaufman, each endured a beating for their faith. On one occasion bullies threatened Koontz as he approached Smith's Creek in Shenandoah County for a preaching appointment, but a local gentleman intervened and he was allowed to preach. But the next time Koontz came to Smith's Creek, his opponents hired a thug, who severely beat him with the butt end of large cane. Soon thereafter, Koontz went to a nearby location to preach, and his adversaries appeared once again. Koontz hid, but Martin Kaufman absorbed several blows before his assailants realized they had the wrong Baptist. Shenandoah Baptists who ventured outside the Valley experienced frequent presecution. When James Ireland and others preached in eastern Virginia without a license, which they commonly did, they risked arrest. (A contemporary suggested that Ireland's "fine commanding voice" and "easy delivery" may have given envious established clergy added incentive to suppress him.) Ireland spent time in Culpeper's jail, where he suffered a disagreeable keeper, but defiantly preached through the slats of his cell to listeners outside. On other trips to eastern Virginia persecutors tormented him with physical assault and verbal harassment. Nevertheless, despite occasional grievances brought by the dissenters, tolerance reigned in the Shenandoah.[19]

Nonconformists, then, appreciated the Valley's open-mindedness. All Shenandoans could point to the taxes they paid to support the Anglican establishment as an example of oppression, but only pacifists with militia fines and Baptists with their jailed itinerants and the Koontz/Kaufman incidents had additional complaints. Undoubtedly, intolerance suffered by previous generations contributed to denominational identity for all dissenters and enhanced outsiderness, but the tolerance of Pennsylvania and its spin-off society in the Valley muted this. Baptists, Dunkers, Mennonites, and Quakers still had their tightly knit faith communities and alternative practices, but religious tolerance in the Shenandoah backcountry made nonconformity different than in Europe.

In contrast to the Baptists, Dunkers, Mennonites, and Quakers, Presbyterians relied more heavily on political conflict to forge tension with the mainstream. To be sure, organization and ceremony contributed to Presbyterian identity as it did for other dissenters in the Valley, but the bitter rivalry with the Anglican establishment permanently scarred the Presbyterian soul and more easily transplanted itself into Shenandoah soil than did the oppressive systems faced by the other groups across the Atlantic.

Like the other nonconformist traditions, Presbyterianism boasted of distinctive practice and polity. Presbyterians, in fact, took their name from gatherings of ministers and elders—"presbyteries"—that devised policy and selected ministers. But in practice, especially in America, Presbyterians relied less on presbyteries and more heavily on sessions, i.e., congregational boards of lay elders, for enforcement and interpretation of policy. Sessions referred only difficult cases to the presbytery, and ministers were expected to win support from their congregations rather than presbyteries. Moreover, session members often were influential members of the community, and in America these boards appear more similar to Anglican vestries than to the spiritual families of Anabaptists, Quakers, or Baptists. While presbyteries offered identity and a denominational name, they must have encouraged outsiderness more in Scotland and Ireland than in the Shenandoah.

Communions also contributed to Presbyterian identity. Originating in Scotland as alternatives to Catholic pageants and holy days, communion celebrations became popular folk festivals lasting several days in the late summer and early fall. With preparation absorbing the week prior to communion and thanksgiving consuming the week after, seasons of communion occupied Presbyterian hearts for nearly two weeks. Often these holy fairs attracted large crowds who listened to several preachers. Communions generated spiritual revival, encouraged traveling and visiting, and provided young people with an opportunity to court. Additionally, communions became important moments in the life-cycle as parents had their children baptized at these gatherings and watched as an adolescent's first bread and cup marked the transition into adulthood.[20]

Communions, however, were more than a community revival or fall festival and served as a powerful articulator of nonconformity. Prior to the distribution of the elements, preachers traditonally described the characteristics required of a communicant, an elaborate warning about sin that included long lists of unacceptable behaviors based on the ten commandments. The unfit included swearers, gossips, scolds, liars, backbiters, and those who were divisive or who spoke of worldly things around the table. The climax of the service came when the ministers admitted communicants to long tables in front of the pulpit. As worshippers took their seats, they handed to deacons tokens of admission, small pieces of lead of varying shapes that only those worthy of the bread and cup had solemnly received the previous day. Tears of weeping were common. Then the preacher fenced off the area, sometimes literally, other times verbally, separating saved from unsaved and church from the world. For the American Revolutionary generation of Presbyterians community celebrations of the Eucharist were high points in the church year, brought lessons on outsiderness, and gave their denomination uniqueness.[21]

Thus, Presbyterian polity and ceremony complemented outsiderness, as it did for other nonconformists, but what differentiated Presbyterians from other Valley dissenters was their intense resistance to English political and religious authority. Conflict between England and Scotland had a lengthy history. English and Scots had waged fierce border wars against each other since the eleventh century, and, hence, it was natural that from the inception of Scottish Protestantism religion and politics overlapped. When John Knox, the founder of Scottish Presbyterianism, determined to purge the church of Catholic practices, his intent matched that of Scottish nobles who desired to end French political domination of Scotland. Similarly, Scottish and English political leaders at this time agreed to pursue religious independence from the Vatican. Parallel interests of Scottish religion and English politics ended with the ascension to the English throne of James I, who felt less dominated by Rome but preferred greater influence over Scotland. But politics and religion continued to mix. James understood that the presbyterian system of organization threatened royal and episcopal authority, and he hoped to consolidate the churches of his two kingdoms—Scotland and England—to contain Scottish Presbyterianism. To that end, James exiled and imprisoned leading Presbyterians, imposed an episcopal system on the Church of Scotland, decreed that communion would be received kneeling, and restored several holy days. For Presbyterians the beast now had two heads: Rome and London.[22]

The mandate to receive the elements kneeling especially aroused Presbyterian ire because it resembled Catholic practices, and when James interjected royal power into holy fairs by insisting on this, he struck a Scottish nerve. Rebellious clergy encouraged laity to withdraw from ministers who accepted the kneeling requirement and to seek the sacrament only from those who proferred it in the traditional way. Many heeded this advice. The rising popularity of unsanctioned communions alarmed Anglican authorities, who countered by requiring individuals to take communion in their own congregations, depriving Presbyterians of the right to seek communions awash with dissent in nearby parishes. Anglican authorities suppressed defiant preachers and big meetings in fields, but they failed to completely stamp out the movement.

Presbyterians found other forms of open defiance, including occasional armed resistance. Traveling preachers challenged the Episcopal system, ignored parish boundaries, and often attracted large crowds at communions. When in 1638 Charles I attempted to impose on Scotland a version of the English prayer book, Scots responded by circulating the National Covenant, which equated Presbyterianism with Scottish citizenship. In 1643 they added the Solemn League and Covenant, an affirmation of the presbyterian system, and this became another popular symbol of Scottish nationalism. Frequently worshippers signed these statements in public at the conclusion of Sunday worship. The Solemn League and Covenant was so important that after Charles I signed it, Scots were less confrontational, and his execution by Puritans repelled them, not just because Charles wore a crown but also because he had been a covenanting monarch.[23]

Theology reinforced these popular patterns of resistance. As Scots and Scots Irish searched for ways to purify their souls and their faith community, the most prominent contamination was English political and religious influence. When men and women repented and converted, they not only cast aside their former life of sin but also pledged to battle English influence in their national church. As exemplified by Bruce's *Dry Bones,* individual regeneration became nearly synonymous with salvation of the nation, and protection of Scotland's nationalism and religion grew inseparable, reinforcing one another.

After the Glorious Revolution, persecution declined, but the tradition of insurgency was so ingrained among Scots and Scots Irish laity that the language of resistance remained appealing. Presbyterians returned to power in Scotland, seizing control of parishes from Anglican priests—"rabbling" was the term for this—and with Presbyterian passions still running high, communion days became even more popular. In Ulster Presbyterian ministers were less aggressively nationalistic or disruptive, but Scottish itinerants blew through the region, drawing large crowds at emotional gatherings and encouraging the idea that silence was cowardice, then removing to Scotland, leaving the more cautious Ulster clergy to deal with the consequences of their fiery words. Especially along Scotland's southern border with England, which provided much of the immigration to colonial North America, Presbyterians continued to nurture a heritage of opposition, commemorating battles and marches against the English in community ceremonies and ballads. Generations of Scots and Scots Irish had resisted persecution and developed a pattern of resistance so strong that its momentum continued even when discrimination diminished.[24]

In the largely tolerant Shenandoah Valley, sporadic problems reminded Presbyterians of their antagonism towards the establishment. One early Presbyterian minister complained about the difficulty of implementing his denomination's system without giving "offence to the established church and government."[25] The sheriff in Winchester arrested a Presbyterian itinerant for preaching without a license although he soon released the preacher to continue his tour. Typically, however, Presbyterian preachers sought licenses and avoided arrest. They suffered no more and perhaps less intolerance than the nonviolent Anabaptists and Friends or itinerating Baptists. Nevertheless, the tradition of resistance remained powerful. In 1774 Virginia Presbyterians named their new college, located in Farmville, outside the Valley, after John Hampden and Algernon Sidney, martyrs of the seventeenth-century struggle against English tyranny. To be sure, Presbyterians still waited for the moment when they could drive a stake through the heart of the Anglican establishment.[26]

That moment came during the American Revolution, a far-reaching movement that shook the political and social landscape. As the embattled farmers gathered at Concord Bridge and other points to resist imperial authority, American nationalism was embryonic rather than developed, a child of independence rather than its parent. More than a simple colonial insurgency or expression of nationalism, the Revolution represented shifting attitudes about rank and deference, and in addition to national independence it endorsed egalitarian social relations. Moreover, in backcountry areas like the Shenandoah, the Revolution also stood for individual rights, local control, and resistance to distant authority. On all counts, the Anglican establishment was vulnerable.

The new attitude about personal relationships and social order spawned just as much change as the severance of ties with Britain. Eighteenth-century notions of deference, hierarchy, and birth fell out of favor, yielding to a new emphasis on talent and the independence of individual men (not women). Repudiating the old system of patronage, in which lesser men hitched their prospects to greater men, who rewarded this loyalty and deference with favor, Americans now regarded patrons as self-serving and insisted that common men could achieve success on their own. Ability rather than connections laid the path to office, and economic life would have equal and open competition. Paul Revere embodied the new order. A man of common origins, a silversmith who worked with his hands, Revere nevertheless enjoyed prosperity, considered himself a gentleman, and provided the patriots' movement in Boston with leadership. The new thought particularly detested hereditary aristocracy and emphasized hard work and social mobility. Ben Franklin, for example, bitterly observed that he was the youngest child of a youngest child for five generations. Primogenitor, rather than personal deficiencies, had caused the young impoverished Franklin to walk down a Philadelphia street and spend his last penny on a loaf of bread. Birth had placed Franklin in that low station.

Deference and rank, therefore, became conspicuous casualties of the movement. Early indications of the coming new order appeared in colonial religious life, especially in the eighteenth-century awakenings. Revivalists urged individuals to make choices about religion regardless of patriarchs, priests, or bishops, and political decisions independent of local political bigwigs were the next logical step. In colonial politics common people participated more directly in electoral politics, competing factions of gentlemen increasingly appealed to them for support, and contested elections for assembly seats became more frequent. Patriots expected these trends to flourish in a new American republic; the empire, they believed, protected the old ways of birth and privilege. In reality, pull remained important in the new regime, but the well-connected needed to exercise care not to flaunt their privileges. Connections were more fluid and more impersonal, and commitment to the Revolution or earned wealth, both exemplifying merit rather than birth, often created the new ties. Attitudes had changed, even if behavior lagged behind the ideal. Shenandoans, like most backcountry Americans, warmly embraced these concepts.[27]

The common cause resonated differently in the low country where Tidewater and Piedmont planters were less interested in eliminating privilege. Instead, they were attracted to freedom from indebtedness to English and Scottish merchants and creditors, whose financial hold over them threatened economic survival, and to independence from the King's ministers, whose intervention in Virginia politics jeopardized local control. Moreover, low country whites of all social rank, whether gentry or small planters, feared that King George III's policies, particularly his veto of Virginia's plan to limit slave importation, escalated the danger of slave rebellion to unacceptable heights. Whites surmised that more blacks would raise the population to a level hard to control. Debt, politics, and slaves turned low country planters into rebels.[28]

The Valley's viewpoint was different. During the critical 1774-75 period, as many Americans grew increasingly confrontational with London, Shenandoans looked westward. After recurring clashes with Native Americans along the frontier, Virginia's Governor, Lord Dunmore, sent two armies of militia, one from each end of the Valley, marching on a retaliatory expedition into the Ohio Valley. The southern column fought a battle at Point Pleasant, where the Kanawha River meets the Ohio, and both companies crossed the Ohio before returning to the Valley. While seaboard Americans wrestled with imperial taxes, sweeping search warrants, and customs officials, backcountry Virginians focused on the Alleghenies.

Shenandoans, like most inland communities, first became aroused when the British closed the port of Boston following the Tea Party, and they sent supplies to the beleaguered Bostonians, passed resolutions endorsing the resistance, and organized committees of correspondence. Support for the patriots' cause mounted, and the shots heard round the world reverberated in the Valley.[29]

No shots, however, were fired in the Valley, although many of its men saw action beyond its bounds. Early in the war Shenandoah units participated in the campaign that drove Dunmore out of Williamsburg and the state. Valley companies in the Continental Army fought at Brandywine, White Plains, and Germantown, and Valley militia were at Cowpens and Guilford Court House. Adam Stephen, a large landholder from Berkeley County, rose to the rank of major general, but after Germantown he was accused of drunkenness and relieved of duty. Prisoners of war from Saratoga and Yorktown were housed in Winchester. Alexander Balmaine, the Anglican curate in Staunton, served on the Committee of Safety and then left his pulpit to become a military chaplain, and Peter Muhlenberg's last sermon before departing for war is the stuff of legend. According to the story,

Muhlenberg, the Anglican in Woodstock, based his talk on Ecclesiastes 3: "For everything there is a season and a time for every matter under heaven . . . a time for war, and a time for peace." At the conclusion of his talk, he dramatically removed his vestments, revealing the uniform of a militia officer, and he proceeded to recruit.[30]

Daniel Morgan of Winchester exemplified the social mobility extolled by the Revolution by becoming a high-ranking general in the Continental Army. Morgan, who had been a humble teamster with Braddock's campaign during the Seven Years' War, raised a unit of riflemen from the Winchester area when the war broke out. So eager were recruits that he held shooting matches to determine who would be accepted, and Morgan marched off with ninety-six, twenty-eight more than requested. Morgan's militiamen, typically tall and in their early twenties, were armed with rifles, tomahawks, and scalping knives and clad in hunting shirts, leggings, and moccasins. Adam Stephen had recruited another company of hunting-shirt militia, and he and Morgan competed for the honor of being the first Virginia troops to join the Continental Army by racing their units overland to Boston, across the mid-Atlantic region under the summer sun. Morgan won; he departed on July 15 and arrived on August 6, while Stephen left two days later than his rival and entered the American camp on August 11. Morgan quickly rose through the ranks. He fought in the Battle of Quebec, where he showed uncommon bravery but was captured in the ill-fated expedition. After his release he commanded Americans at Cowpens, a major victory, and Guilford Court House. From teamster to war hero, Daniel Morgan represented American democracy.[31]

Localism and resistance to distant authority figured prominently in the Valley's wartime experience. Peter Muhlenberg's company, the first to be sent out of state, suffered heavy desertions as it marched south to defend Charleston, South Carolina. Later in the war, officials in several Valley counties sought escape for their constituents from taxes levied to pay for the war, and in Augusta and Rockbridge counties draft riots occurred in which armed men destroyed documents necessary for conscription.

Militiamen were particularly independent-minded. When a Rockbridge County militiaman murdered Cornstalk, a friendly Shawnee chief, authorities concluded that public opinion opposed conviction of white men for killing Native Americans, and they did not prosecute the case. After Morgan's hunting-shirt company arrived in Boston, it scored quick hits on unsuspecting British sentries, unaccustomed to the long range of the backcountry firearms, but soon wore out its welcome by shooting when ordered not to, by wasting ammunition in target contests primarily for entertainment, and by brawling. Early in 1776 an Augusta County rifle company was so unruly, burning a ferry house among other actions, that it earned a court martial trial.[32]

Militiamen particularly disliked leaving their homes to fight under low country leadership, and a popular anecdote about wartime heroism illustrates the Valley's arm's-length relationship with the east. According to local legend, during the British invasion of Virginia in 1781 the legislature fled from Charlottesville to Staunton, where it received word that Banastre Tarleton's Redcoats were in pursuit. The legislature bolted, but a Presbyterian minister, William Graham, just happened to be traveling to Staunton and encountered the fleeing politicians. While the politicians ran, an aroused Graham sent men off on roads south of Staunton to notify militia officers of the approaching enemy, and the next morning a sizable unit of Augusta and Rockbridge County militia assembled at Rockfish Gap, atop the Blue Ridge, to wait for the invaders. When the embattled Shenandoans learned that Tarleton was in retreat, some hurried to another gap where they suspected the British might appear, while others followed Tarleton east into the Piedmont. This group joined the Marquis de Lafayette's troops, but after surmising that the campaign would be lengthy, they returned to the Valley. The tale reveals the militia's aversion to venturing far from home and also illustrates western superiority over the east by comparing the retiring assemblymen, all eastern gentlemen, with the courageous hearts of the militia and Graham, who sounds suspiciously like Staunton's version of Paul Revere. For Shenandoans the Revolutionary movement meant local heroes, social mobility, an end to deference to birth and rank, and independence from distant authority, whether British, Virginian, or military.[33]

The impression this great upheaval left on religious outsiderness varied according to the manner in which traditions marked the mainstream. Those with minimal reliance on political boundary lines felt little impact, but Presbyterians, with their heavy emphasis on political nonconformity, experienced a drastically altered concept of the mainstream.

For Anabaptists and Quakers the Revolution sometimes reinforced traditional outsiderness by bringing intensified persecution. Nonviolence and other convictions brought tension with political authorities. In Pennsylvania patriots arrested Christopher Saur II, a leading Dunker, and confiscated his property because he maintained neutrality and refused to take an oath of allegiance to the American cause. (He cited the Dunkers' opposition to oaths.) Also in Pennsylvania, patriot authorities exiled influential Quakers to Winchester, where they languished in harsh conditions, an apparent lesson to local Friends about the ability of the common cause to suppress religious freedom. In May, 1776, Virginia ordered the enrollment of Mennonites and Quakers for militia service and stipulated fines for noncompliance, and the next year the state enacted heavier assessments for those who refused to drill or provide a substitute. Persons who refused oaths lost the ability to vote, hold office, or serve on juries until the Assembly restored these rights in 1783. Dunkers, Mennonites, and Quakers discovered that the new order could be just as oppressive as the old.[34]

On the other hand, the Revolution's emphasis on rebellion to distant authority made the Anglican establishment a natural target. Virginia, however, evolved rather than rushed towards its revolution in church-state relations, and during the Revolutionary period the religious establishment drifted in a legal twilight zone, neither enforced nor abolished. In 1776 Virginia's constitutional convention adopted a Declaration of Rights that exempted dissenters from Anglican taxes, a blend of toleration with establishment. But it suspended collection of all religious taxes until the next session and repeated this annually until 1779, when the levies ended altogether because it became too difficult to tell Anglicans from dissenters. (Anglicans dodged taxes by claiming to be something else.) The establishment nevertheless remained part of Virginia law.[35]

One path out of this legislative fog called for the establishment of all denominations. A proposal for this surfaced in 1777, and after the war the Assembly again considered permitting taxpayers to designate the denomination that received their religious tax. This version called for "incorporation" of all "teachers" of religion, meaning state support for preachers of all denominations through a property tax. Quakers and Mennonites were exempt because they had no formal clergy, a controversial part of the bill, and funds from non-believers or non-attenders would go to local schools. Furthermore, the bill would have made Anglicans independent of the state and given them control over their parish property. But the incorporation act also specified Anglican polity, including procedures for vestry meetings, elections, and voting, and it created a convention consisting of one clergy and one layperson from each vestry with authority to suspend or remove incompetent clergy. The scheme placed all denominations on an equal footing but left the state with a large role in religion.[36]

Supporters of general assessment consisted of primarily eastern Anglicans and several prominent politicians, including Patrick Henry, but in the Valley all of the denominations with dissenting traditions, led by Presbyterians, opposed general assessment.[37] The logic and depth of the Presbyterian case against the establishment testified to the feeling they held for this issue, fed by generations of resistance to English Anglicanism. Presbyterian statements dismissed past established religion as a "grievous burden" that had infringed on civil rights as well as conscience, and they opposed general establishment because it would continue to endanger the "unalienable right" to participate in religion according to their convictions. If the Assembly could levy a general assessment to support all denominations, then Presbyterians reasoned that it also had the authority to revive the old establishment or authorize a new one for another denomination. They further suspected that the power to establish or disestablish implied the power to regulate religion in general, including content or selection of preachers. Perhaps the fund-disbursing state, as "indulgent parent," might assume the power to punish religion as well as reward. Presbyterians also disliked the impact of establishment on the ministry. They observed that state-supported clergy were less accountable to their congregations, and too often past incorporation of clergy had resulted in "ignorance, immorality and neglect of their duties," a slap at colonial Anglicans. Instead, Presbyterians maintained that ministers' support should be based on their ability to care for congregations rather than favor they curried with the state. Presbyterian resistance to the establishment was passionate and well-reasoned.[38]

The energy, emotions, and numbers for disestablishment came from Presbyterians. A large Presbyterian convention in the Valley (Bethel, Augusta County) spearheaded opposition to general assessment, and petitions of protest, many but not all from Valley Presbyterians or Valley counties with heavy Presbyterian populations, poured into the capital at Williamsburg.[39]

With the groundswell overwhelmingly against general assessment, in 1786 the Assembly set it aside and instead passed Thomas Jefferson's act for "Establishing Religious Freedom." This ended the establishment, abolished religious requirements for office holding, and barred the state from requiring church attendance or supporting religious institutions, a landmark in American legal history.[40]

In the next century church-state issues remained on Virginia's legislative plate, but the dialogue now dealt with the ability of religious organizations to incorporate. Incorporation, which almost every other state in the Union permitted, gave congregations, schools, and other organizations greater control of their property and funds. Without it individual congregations required special action from the state legislature to buy or sell property, including land on which to build. Property was held in the name of trustees rather than the entire congregation or membership. Opponents of incorporation demanded an absolute interpretation of the Statute for Religious Freedom, but supporters requested what they said was a harmless and practical exception.

This arcane issue failed to excite the laity as had the debate over establishment in the previous century, and congregations only felt affected when they transacted business or if their treasurer died before church property could be transferred to another. It divided evangelicals, some of whom opposed incorporation because they feared it would benefit Catholics.[41] For generations of Presbyterians the mainstream had been the Anglican English establishment, and now it was gone. When Jefferson's constitutional wall between church and state went up, a boundary between Presbyterians and the larger society lowered.

The American Revolution and the resulting transformation in church-state relations affected Presbyterians most of all. Though Baptists, Dunkers, Mennonites, and Quakers matched the Presbyterian heritage of persecution, their tormentors comprised a variety of devils, not just English Anglicans. European Anabaptists suffered at the hand of German bishops and princes, who were very distant from the Shenandoah. The Baptist tradition of resistance included New England Puritans in addition to English and Virginian Anglicans and a few Valley ruffians, and while intolerance haunted Friends and Anabaptists in the late eighteenth century, their tormentors were American patriots rather than European priests or Anglican bishops. Only for Presbyterians was persecution limited to the establishment.

Presbyterians, therefore, relied more heavily on the establishment to define their mainstream. Presbyterians, like other dissenters, owned unique polity and practices, but these were less distinct than the democratic and alternative faith communities of the other dissenters and more infused with politics and nationalism. None of the other dissenters stressed political outsiderness as much as Presbyterians.

Thus, when religious establishment ended, Presbyterians more than any other group needed to redefine their center. Baptists, Dunkers, Friends, and Mennonites could still rely on distinctive practices, such as believer's baptism, feetwashing, silent worship, and nonconformist congregations. Furthermore, the lines of daily crosses yet to come had emerged. Dunkers and Mennonites had begun to use simplicity to create a distance between themselves and the world that would widen when pushed by the market revolution; and antislavery seeds sown by Anabaptists and Quakers would sprout in the next century and blossom as the sectional crisis expanded. Presbyterians, having lost their mainstream to disestablishment and without these boundaries against the world, entered into the Methodist and market revolutions without a clearly defined sense of what it meant to be on the fringe. What would breathe life into the dry bones of Presbyterianism in the next century?

The Methodist Revolution

I N THE MIDDLE OF A METHODIST SERVICE near the turn of the nineteenth century, a thunderstorm came up as the preacher gave out a hymn. During the prayer, the crashes became more intense. Then the preacher prayed for the thunder to come closer, and it did. He pushed his luck another time; "O Lord, send thy thunder still nigher!" A huge bolt of lightning lit up the meeting-house, and worshippers fell to the floor crying for mercy.

The next day one of the worshippers complained to the local magistrate that if the pastor had called out a third time, the entire congregation would have died, and the nervous Christian implored the authorities to prevent the preacher from further itinerating. But when the magistrate asked the worshipper if he thought the minister had influence with God, the complainant said "yes." The law officer replied that he had no authority over such a person.[1]

Even without thunder and lightning Methodists and other revivalists set off sparks. Heart-felt faith, including the awakenings led by George Whitefield and others during the colonial era, had always been controversial, but when a new round of enthusiasm arose with even more intense, more emotional behavior and with appeal more directly to popular thought, Protestants bitterly divided over it. This movement brought enough change and so successfully overwhelmed its competition and captured the soul of America that it constituted a revolution, broadly speaking. Its opponents were now the outsiders, and resistance to this new direction in popular religion became a strong marker of nonconformity.

This great upsurge of faith won advocates in nearly all denominations, split some, and gave birth to others, most notably the Disciples of Christ. The Disciples, however, only managed to plant a few congregations in one Valley county, and the Shenandoah groups most closely associated with the new enthusiasm were Methodists and the United Brethren.

Methodists, like many of the faiths that preceded them into the Valley, were born on the margins with a variety of characteristics that set them apart from both the world and other religious communities. English Methodists, from their inception in the 1730s among poorer students at Oxford University, were self-conscious nonconformists who sought a pious, moderate alternative to the undisciplined worldliness of wealthier Oxonians. John Wesley, their founder, compared the worldly to persons infected with disease and urged healthy Methodists to "keep their distance." They should not "play with fire, but escape before the flames" burned them. As the movement matured, it criticized the lifestyle of the mainstream, offered freedom of choice and intimacy with Christ as an alternative to Anglican ceremony and tradition, and appealed to those of lower status, generally ignored by the Anglican clergy. English Methodist preachers often found pulpits closed to them and held services outdoors. Itinerants, who usually led these unsanctioned gatherings, further represented challenge to the authority of Anglican parish clergy because they were interlopers competing for the allegiance of the laity. English Methodists, therefore, bequeathed to their Shenandoan brethren a strong tradition of resistance to the mainstream.[2]

In America distinctive organization and worship, especially classes, love feasts, and camp meetings, contributed to the image of Methodism as an alternative society similar to the spiritual families of Baptists, Dunkers, Mennonites, and Quakers discussed in Chapter 2. Testimonies, customary in all three of these Methodist gatherings, gave laity regardless of social rank, gender, or race an opportunity to speak. Like many of the other dissenter groups, Methodists called one another "brother" and "sister," although clergy tended to reserve the title of "brother" for themselves, exclusive of the laity. Classes, a division of the congregation into small groups for more intimate fellowship and growth, met once per week, were mandatory, and usually limited to members. Commonly arranged according to age, gender, and race, classes numbered between fifteen and thirty persons and featured lay leadership selected by the preacher. Described by one scholar as "subpastors" and "sergeants in the hierarchy of Methodist leadership," leaders were usually successful men in the community and male, even for women's classes. Meetings consisted of hymns, prayer, and examination of each member, and leaders encouraged participants to share their religious experience. Class meetings also introduced converts to Wesley's *General Rules*, which taught Methodists to avoid a variety of objectionable behaviors, such as profanity, brawling, drunkenness, quarreling, and tax evasion. Classes, unique to Methodism, provided individuals with critical denominational identity and sustained the alternative lifestyle of those in the new life with gratification for the faithful and discipline for the wavering.

Love feasts and camp meetings also contributed to Methodism's distinctiveness. Love feasts combined simple meals of bread and water with warm religion, such as emotional testimonies intended to evoke emotion. They usually coincided with quarterly conferences of preachers and, like class meetings, were closed to nonmembers, which enhanced the sense of Methodist exclusivity. As Methodism grew in the late eighteenth century, the press of business and growing numbers at the quarterly conferences began to overwhelm spirituality, sometimes literally forcing laity outdoors, so early in the 1800s Methodists employed camp meetings to feed the spiritually hungry without overloading local resources. These were carefully crafted events that lasted for several days. At the center of the camp were worshippers' benches, sometimes enough to accommodate thousands, and the preachers' stand, a roofed platform elevated approximately four feet off the ground. Tents and wagons ringed the worship area, and lamps and candles illuminated the camp ground after dark. Preaching, interrupted by singing and prayer, continued throughout the day. Camp meetings were neither a Methodist creation nor exclusively a frontier phenomenon despite their reputation; Presbyterians in

Scotland and Ulster staged communion seasons generations before camp meetings became a Methodist staple, and camp meetings were as frequent near urban areas, including Baltimore, as the frontier. Long after the Shenandoah ceased to be backcountry, Valley Methodists gathered in tents and under the trees. Neither were these events solely Methodist but instead attracted an inter-denominational congregation. Nevertheless, by 1811 American Methodists held between four and five hundred of these gatherings annually with perhaps one million participants, and camp meetings are more closely associated with Methodism than any other denomination.[3]

Whether in love feasts, camp meetings, or other spirit-filled occasions, Methodists became known for distinctive worship. Methodist preachers used plain language, simple but rousing music, and often spoke extemporaneously, a carefully constructed contrast to the elitism of Calvinist clergy. Their sermons included anecdotes drawn from common experience and humor, sometimes earthy, easily comprehensible by the popular mind. They attacked those they considered pre-occupied with high theology rather than common reasoning, and they appealed to experience, comprehensible to all, rather than a system of learning, comprehensible to few. The anxious bench, a pew or area designated for those desiring conversion and which enabled the preacher to speak directly to them, became so closely linked to revivalism that this hotly debated technique became the short-hand term for all of the new methods, including camp meetings. When critics denounced the anxious bench, they in fact challenged the entire system used by camp meeting enthusiasts.[4]

The release from sin and the intimacy of the Holy Spirit generated by these techniques unleashed a variety of emotions, another characteristic of revivalistic worship during the period. Weeping, shouting, jumping, fainting, spirited singing, loud preaching, and all-night services became common. Typical was a service in Harrisonburg in which the minister's "heavenly pathos, weeping eyes, and pungent truths," according to a participant, were strong enough to "melt down into tears the iceberg professors." The next night "shouting, weeping, and groaning" interrupted preaching until midnight. Sinners lay on the floor for approximately an hour, then arose shouting that they were converted. When the preacher declared that anyone who condemned shouting as the work of the devil actually did the devil's work, an African American in the gallery shouted his faith. Protracted meetings like these could last for several weeks until they ran out of momentum. Although unrestrained worship built on a precedent established in the eighteenth-century awakenings, revivalism in the Early Republic took enthusiasm to new heights. Common language, popular music, emotion, innovative methods, and noise (so their critics charged) marked Methodists with their own worship setting.[5]

Early Methodists lived a lifestyle that matched their alternative structure and worship for nonconformity. Although Wesley criticized Quaker-like apparel that distinguished church members, such as a broad-brimmed hat or a coat with only a few buttons, as "mere superstition," he conceded that the plainness of the Friends deserved imitation. He recommended inexpensive, grave, unfashionable clothing that was not "gay or showy," and the *Discipline* that Wesley's American followers adopted in 1784 urged local societies to hear their founder's "Thoughts upon Dress" annually.[6]

Wesley's followers did more than just listen to his thoughts. Ministers refused to wear ruffles or powder their hair, and they had authority to bar from love feasts women with "superfluous ornaments." Methodists in other parts of the country preached against powdered hair or required both genders to remove bows, ruffles, rings, and feathers. The Methodist meeting in Winchester expected one young convert to cut his fashionable hair because it did not have room for both "a man and a queue," and a Methodist school in Harrisonburg barred ruffles and powdered hair. Methodists also disciplined against drunkenness, adultery, and neglect of class meetings, and during the American Revolution Methodist leaders and laity outside the Valley suffered imprisonment, fines, beatings, and harassment for pacifism, opposition to slavery, or suspected Loyalism. Refusal to take oaths also brought suspicion upon Methodism, especially in the South, where a white man who refused to give his word had no honor.

Methodists relied heavily on ministers to enforce the discipline. As a circuit rider George Wells had expelled and suspended liberally for quarreling, dram drinking, and other offenses, but when he took a permanent position at Winchester, he discovered that his very popular predecessor had disciplined very little. Though standards were inexact, localized, and dependent upon individual ministers to define excess, Valley Methodists generally practiced what Wesley preached about resistance to the world.[7]

The United Brethren, with roots deep in German Pietism, resembled Methodists in theology and worship style but organized themselves more casually. The denomination evolved from informal gatherings of German Pietists in Pennsylvania and Maryland and dates its beginning from 1767 when its founders, Philip William Otterbein and Martin Boehm, encountered each other in a barn meeting in Lancaster County, Pennsylvania. Boehm was already a preacher among Pennsylvania Mennonites, but he experienced what he considered true conversion when he heard the voice of God while plowing his field. After visiting Mennonites and New Light Baptists in the Shenandoah Valley, he returned home and, probably in the early 1760s, led a series of nondenominational gatherings in barns and other atypical settings, similar to later camp meetings. Meanwhile in Maryland, Otterbein, a Reformed clergyman, organized colleagues attracted to faith of the heart. By 1789 the movement had become so strong that it organized a denomination, adopted the name United Brethren in Christ, and chose Boehm and Otterbein as superintendents, or bishops, but it only held its first denominational conference in 1815. The United Brethren had so much in common with Methodists that they frequently discussed merger, but United Brethren fondness for loose discipline, showing perhaps a Mennonite influence, blocked union. Unlike the Methodists, they admitted all believers to communion, and classes were optional for local congregations, who often favored instead informal prayer groups. Although the United Brethren encouraged baptism, feet-washing, and communion, they allowed members to determine the mode. They also differed from Methodists by electing delegates to general conferences and by electing bishops for four-year terms rather than for life. Francis Asbury, the organizer of American Methodism, particularly objected to the optional status of itineration for clergy and voluntary class membership for laity, and union waited until the twentieth century. (In 1946 the United Brethren joined with the Evangelical Association, another tradition rich in Pennsylvania German Pietism, to form the Evangelical United Brethren, which in 1968 merged with Methodists.) Despite their German origins and differences with Methodists over polity, the United Brethren nonetheless shared much with Wesley's followers and augmented the Valley's burst of revivalism.[8]

The United Brethren and Methodists enhanced several existing patterns in Shenandoah religion. The United Brethren were another small ethnic German, northern-based denomination, similar to Dunkers and Mennonites, and they made the Valley look diverse and Pennsylvanian. Methodists, far larger than the United Brethren and much more influential, made the Valley look more Southern. Early American Methodism blossomed first in Southern soil and had a Southern bent. Methodism's local dominance was also typically Southern, and the combined large population of Methodists, Presbyterians, and Baptists made Shenandoah religion resemble even more closely popular religion in the eastern part of the Old Dominion and other parts of the South.[9]

Growth rates in the Valley for the two revivalistic denominations were very different. The United Brethren began meeting in the Shenandoah at approximately the same time that the Methodists first gathered, but these German revivalists built congregations more slowly. They constructed their first meeting house in 1824 and had no full-time preachers until 1830, but as early as 1795 their circuit riders, exhorters, candlelight communions, and camp meetings added to the evangelical surge. In 1797, for example, Christian Newcomer, a circuit rider from Washington County, Maryland, toured the Valley preaching an emotional message of judgment ("I reprove and discipline those whom I love. Be earnest, therefore, and repent."—Revelation

3:19) and deliverance ("I am standing at the door, knocking; if you hear my voice and open the door, I will come in to you."— Revelation 3:20). Their worship, sometimes in both English and German and in schoolhouses, private homes, and borrowed church buildings, often evoked a fervor that matched that of the Methodists. In 1802 Newcomer recounted that during a meeting in a Rockingham County barn "a young woman fell down, crying for mercy." Then her sister, seated beside her, laid a child in her arms on the barn floor and similarly begged God for relief from sin. After this, the mother cried out "O Lord!—mercy, mercy for myself and [my] children." Meanwhile, the father took up the child to prevent its injury and stood beside his family with "tears streaming down his furrowed cheeks." Finally, Newcomer recalled, the entire congregation cried for mercy.[10]

Although the United Brethren remained a small fellowship serving primarily the Pennsylvania German diaspora, Methodism swept America like wildfire, increasing from 1000 members in 1770 to over 250,000 in 1820 and nearly 500,000 at the close of the next decade. By 1810 Methodism's rate of growth outpaced population growth rates in every state and major territory of the Union. In 1831 the Methodist national publication, the *Christian Advocate and Journal,* was the most widely circulating newspaper in America. With this amazing growth Methodists left their nearest competitors in the dust. By 1850 Methodists were thirty-four percent of total church membership in America, almost half again as large as any other Protestant group. They were ten times the size of Congregationalists, who in 1776 had been the most popular denomination, and they worshipped in 13,280 buildings, almost 4,000 more than the second-place Baptists. In 1860 nearly thirty-eight percent of all church buildings were Methodist. In 1860 Methodists had almost as many preachers (23,143) as the United States Army had active-duty military personnel (27,958). The rise of American Methodism was spectacular.[11]

Growth in the Valley was no less impressive. In 1788 Methodists organized the Rockingham circuit of the Baltimore Conference, and a few years later lower Valley Methodists created a Winchester circuit. Francis Asbury and other itinerants included the Valley on their preaching tours. Sometimes their seed fell upon the rocks; Asbury declared Shepherdstown "a poor place for religion," and on one trip he discovered that "Satan has been sowing discord" in Harrisonburg. But usually Methodist labor bore fruit. In 1790 Asbury preached in Rockingham County, where he found "the beginning of good work," and he observed that Methodists there "have a church built on a hill, that cannot be hid," a reference to its physical standing in addition to its spiritual condition. During several preaching trips through the Valley in the early 1790s he reported promising congregations at Stephens City (Newtown), Winchester, and Charles Town with "spacious" or "excellent" meetinghouses and capable local preachers guiding the societies between visits from itinerants. Methodists even managed to plant a small fellowship in stubborn Shepherstown after thirty years of intermittent preaching there.[12]

Statistical evidence confirms Asbury's sense of accomplishment. In 1819, the first year for which numbers are available but after the initial burst of growth had already occurred, Methodists counted 3092 members in the Valley (2426 whites; 666 blacks). This increased to 3600 (2917 whites; 683 blacks) in 1828 and 4786 in 1841 (3889 whites; 897 blacks). Most remarkably, Methodists achieved these successes as Valley population remained stagnant. In 1820 the total population was 100,190; in 1830 it increased to 113,576, but the 1840 census showed a small decline to 104,613, chiefly due to western migration.[13] By 1860, the most accurate church census in the Valley, Shenandoah Methodists had constructed 112 buildings, far outdistancing Presbyterians (42), Lutherans (36), and Baptists (32), their nearest competitors.[14]

Several factors contributed to this growth. Methodist itinerants traveled far and wide, and they provided inspiring leadership to localities, especially on the frontier, that suffered from a shortage of clergy. Between visits, local societies relied on home-grown shepherds, including class leaders and local preachers, while members of many other denominations had to wait for the arrival of seminary-trained clerics.

African Americans added to the groundswell of revivalism, discovering the Methodist Revolution to be much more attractive than other forms of Christianity for many reasons. Early

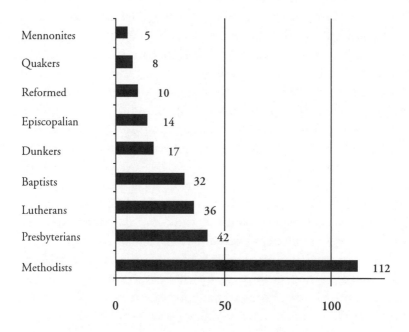

Church Buildings by Denomination, 1860

Methodist circuit riders were open about their distaste for slavery and correspondingly showed genuine interest in ministering to blacks. African Americans embraced the emotional side of revivalism; often blacks in the galleries took the first steps toward transforming a service from orderly to exuberant. Religious meetings became a gathering place for African Americans, and the unison shouting and singing of enthusiastic worship reminded this oppressed class of its collective identity. Much in evangelism resembled African customs. The tendency of evangelicals to eliminate boundaries between sacred and secular (the immanence of the Holy Spirit), the importance of singing, the antiphonal preaching style of evangelicals as the preacher proclaimed good news and the worshippers noisily answered back, and the Holy Spirit's power to physically overwhelm converts all had African counterparts. Finally, evangelicalism offered hope for the weak and the downtrodden. If whites abided by Christian ethics, justice would come quickly, but if not, evangelicalism ensured in the end rewards for the just and damnation for the unjust.[15]

But Methodism was much more than a frontier phenomenon or an appeal to a large, downtrodden minority. Critical to its attraction for all Americans, not just those in the backcountry or in chains, was the compatibility of Methodism, particularly its doctrine of free will conversion, with the emphasis on egalitarianism and rebuke of elitism so prevalent during the American Revolution and in the early Republic. Though Wesley agreed with Calvinists about human depravity, he departed from them by concluding that divine grace gave each individual the opportunity to choose or reject salvation. He argued that Christ died for all, not for the elect, that nobody was predestined for an eternal life in either heaven or hell, and that grace was resistible. Individuals, therefore, had a role in their own salvation. This was a remarkably democratic theology, especially compared to the elitism of Calvinism, in which salvation was available only for the select, and the hierarchy of Catholicism and Anglicanism, in which clergy and the church acted as intermediaries for individuals. In contrast, free will conversion required no mediators and granted individuals, even blacks, women, or the low born, direct access to God. Nothing could be more egalitarian.

Methodists were hardly the first to teach free will conversion, but their democratic worship style and the commonality of religious experience combined with their theology to make Methodism highly compatible with early Republican egalitarianism. Worship style and experience were related. In practice, the connection of a sin-sick soul to its Divine Savior often came suddenly and was an intense, emotional relationship. Personal conversion accounts often include noisy meetings, dreams, swooning, and shouting, and the continued presence of the Holy Spirit in believers following conversion meant that they would continue to exhibit these behaviors in future blessed moments, often among others in the faith community. This outward evidence of inner conversion showed that God could work in the heart of every man and woman, regardless of social rank.[16]

Once saved, or born again, believers of all ranks continued on a spiritual journey, a lifetime process requiring perpetual maintenance. The new life could be lost through back-sliding and continual re-examination was vital, but further growth following the new birth was also possible. According to Wesley, some could achieve a second rebirth that sanctified believers or placed them in a sin-free state of holiness. Or, as Wesley's brother Charles put it in his great hymn, "Finish, then, thy new creation; pure and spotless let us be." Sanctification freed individuals from sins of commission, i.e., deliberate rejections of God's will, but they still committed sins of omission that stemmed from human frailty. Sanctification made perfection available to the humblest-born, but although it held an important part of Wesley's theology, early nineteenth-century American Methodists de-emphasized it.[17]

Choice for all, experience, common worship, and sanctification promoted egalitarianism and appealed to non-elites, placing the Methodist Revolution in lock step with the American Revolution. Combined with organizational efficiency and popularity among African Americans, small wonder that John Wesley's American followers grew so rapidly and that the movement they led became the centerpiece of American popular religion.[18]

If the Methodist Revolution captured popular thought, consensus was something else, and with Methodist success came rancor as traditionalists held on. Most opponents of revivalism fell out of step with popular religion primarily because they disagreed with its salvation process and because they disliked its unrestrained excitement. But ironically they shared emotionalism with evangelicals, a legacy of the Pietism and the great eighteenth-century awakenings that infused almost all traditions with religion of the heart. In Lexington, for example, Old School Presbyterians organized a mission society that sent preachers into western Virginia, where their congregations were awakened, "melted into tears," and then sobbed aloud. As Daniel Baker, from Harrisonburg, surveyed one gathering, he expected that "the day would not pass over without some reviving mercy-drops," and he was not disappointed. (Baker was New School, which indicates that schism did not eliminate cooperation between the two.) On another of these mission trips into western Virginia George Baxter witnessed the "spirit overshadow" the proceedings when the preacher's heart was touched by a "live coal," then "melted; [and] the flame was communicated to the whole crowd, and all wept and sobbed in a very unusual manner." Old School preachers, such as Baxter, also led emotional services in their own congregations. At one of Baxter's services he was so overcome with emotion that he had trouble reading the text, and his sermons occasionally evoked tears among the listeners. At another Old School congregation the revival became so intense that converts later recanted with a "painful sense of duty," concluding that "under conditions of great excitement" they had made a mistake. If conservative Calvinists denied that humans contributed to their own salvation, mission work could still help the elect recognize what God had done for them, a realization that gave birth to warmth within the meetinghouse.[19]

Mennonites, generally outside the Methodist Revolution, and Dunkers, determinedly anti-revivalist, also enjoyed emotional moments. Their eighteenth-century predecessors had been heavily influenced by Pietism, and the first generation of Dunkers in the early eighteenth century underwent an exuberant phase of loud prayer and song, as if, a critic charged, God was hard of hearing. By mid-century the most common form of emotion among both Anabaptist groups was weeping, a practice that continued into the next century. John Kline, the Dunker preacher, found "much spiritual joy" during a service of hymn-singing, and he approved of tearful testimonies. Mennonites shed tears as they ordained new preachers, and a popular songbook, the *Harmonia Sacra*, written by a Valley Mennonite, was primarily a revivalistic work with expressions of torment and joy. Individual Anabaptists, especially Mennonites, participated in revivalistic meetings with members of other denominations. A Methodist preacher in Winchester noted that a "good old Dunkard" preached to his congregation—it was the third of four services that day—and contributed to a rewarding experience for the parishioners. (The pastor commented that the entire day was "a seeking time and the

largest company I have had yet.") Henry Boehm, Martin's
Methodist son, remarked that a Mennonite offered "a powerful
exhortation" when in 1800 he toured the Shenandoah Valley, and
an Augusta County Mennonite decided that a United Brethren
bishop was a "real Christian" after riding home with him from
Staunton. Frederick Rhodes, a controversial Mennonite, perhaps
led United Brethren revivals in prayer, and, according to critics,
preached loudly, like the United Brethren ministers, to his
Mennonite congregation. Valley Anabaptists and Old School
Presbyterians were no strangers to emotion.[20]

None of the Old School and Anabaptist revivalists, however,
mentioned shouting, fainting, or the anxious bench, and despite
sharing a fondness for emotion, observers noted a contrast in style
between Old School and New School. If Old School services
evoked piety, they also practiced "decorum." Though Old School
services sometimes encouraged emotion, other times they worried
that emotions misled, and they distrusted preaching that appealed
to the feelings but failed to "inform the mind." They took care to
avoid "improper" methods that would "terrify or alarm any one,"
and Old School conservatives disapproved of "ostentatious physical expressions." After listening to a service in which representatives of both viewpoints preached, an Old School Presbyterian
layperson conceded that the New School preacher was "striking,"
but he still found the prayer very offensive. Among anti-revivalist
exuberance had limits.[21]

Consequently, the revolution in popular religion divided some
fellowships. For approximately five years Harrisonburg-area
Mennonites bickered over the behavior of Frederick Rhodes, who
consorted with revivalists, until mediators from Pennsylvania
declared his behavior acceptable, noting that Mennonite and
United Brethren ministers in Maryland and Pennsylvania commonly traveled and worshipped together. Although Mennonites
generally fell into the anti-revivalist camp—a popular confession
proclaimed that "my experience can help you nothing; nor can
your experience help me anything,"—their polity had enough
flexibility to tolerate those more inclined toward the new measures.[22]

Resistance among the German Reformed also was stiff. Stung by recent defections of revivalists in the North, especially John Winebrenner's Church of God, Philip Schaff and John Nevin leveled a blistering counterattack against the innovators. In what came to be called the "Mercersburg Theology," Schaff and Nevin, professors at the Reformed Seminary in Mercersburg, Pennsylvania, denounced revivalism for replacing tradition and order with disruptive worship and a false sense of conversion. They also resented the respect the movement gave to unlearned men and upstart theologians. But revivalism also had friends among the Reformed, especially in the Valley, whose few clergy endorsed the new methods although noting the opposition of "formalists."[23]

Presbyterian and Lutheran opponents of revivalism defied it so strenuously that these denominations suffered schism. When in 1837 the Presbyterian General Assembly expelled its New School synods, Presbyterians in the Valley became predominately Old School, but it was a split decision. Southerners usually leaned toward the Old School, but in the Winchester Presbytery the vote for orthodoxy was close (fifteen to twelve), perhaps reflecting the influence of William Hill, a New School minister who had recently left a lengthy pastorate at Winchester. Five ministers and eight congregations left to join the New School while ten ministers and twenty-four churches remained Old School. The Winchester congregation divided with about one-third moving to a New School congregation on Loudoun Street. Old School sentiments were stronger in the Lexington Presbytery where New School defenders mustered only two votes, and the Presbytery's delegates to the General Assembly were firmly Old School. Only three Lexington congregations joined the New School—Union, Port Republic, and most of Cook's Creek—and another, Harrisonburg, divided.[24]

The rupture among Lutherans was deeper and longer lasting. New School Lutherans cast themselves as modern laborers in the mold of the heroic Henry M. Muhlenberg, whom they portrayed as their denomination's equivalent of Jonathan Edwards, John Wesley, and George Whitefield. The new methods, they argued, were consistent with those of Muhlenberg and the other "patriarchs of American Lutheranism," Pietists who had encouraged emotion, held prayer meetings, preached in barns and outdoors, and showed flexibility with the liturgy. New School adherents further pointed out that early Lutheran pastors had treated catechical sessions as opportunities to encourage religion of the heart in catechumens, a Lutheran version, they suggested, of Methodist class meetings. Muhlenberg even addressed catechumens during public meetings, which New School Lutherans likened to the anxious bench, and they surmised that had he witnessed this innovation in operation, the great organizer of American Lutheranism might have adopted it.[25]

Anti-revivalist Lutherans disagreed because they favored confessionalism, the traditional Lutheran step-by-step progress toward salvation, and they believed that the new methods subverted this. Confessionalists taught that Christians grew as they followed ecclesiastical and clerical direction and as they learned doctrine through the catechism and the sacraments. Tradition further contributed order for the community and direction for individuals. Revivalism undermined this gradual, supervised process by allowing individuals to achieve salvation in a moment, sowing confusion and, according to confessionalists, prompting "general ruin" to Lutheran doctrine. (The Mercersburg Theology of the Reformed was also confessionalist.)[26]

Accordingly, two synods competed for the loyalty of Valley Lutherans. Conservatives met with the Evangelical German Tennessee Synod, founded in 1820, while revivalists associated with the Synod of Maryland and Virginia. Conservative clergy arriving in the nineteenth-century wave of German immigration gave anti-revivalists momentum, but most of the Valley's conservative leadership was native born, especially the Henkels, a family of preachers with a publishing house at New Market. The Henkels and their fellow Old School sympathizers in the Valley added a layer of local, special conferences to coordinate resistance to revivalism, and they agreed on common measures, such as closing pulpits to itinerants.[27]

Cooperation between the Lutheran bodies was non-existent. The New School synod of Maryland and Virginia resolved not to recognize the ordination of members of the "so-called Tennessee Conference," and in New Market a congregation locked out its former pastor, an Old School proponent. Name-calling came from high places. A well-known New School clergyman, Samuel Simon Schmucker, denounced a prominent Old School rival as "a weak and illiterate man" and lambasted his publications as "crude, visionary, and inflammatory." Revivalists dismissed the Old School belief in the bodily presence in the communion elements as a "remnant of Romanism," harsh language loaded with meaning in a nativist era. By the 1850s relations began to defrost when the Virginia Synod rescinded non-recognition of Tennessee-synod ordination and elected a fraternal or observing delegate to their rival's conference, but reunion between the two schools waited until 1925.[28]

Two denominations—Dunkers and Primitive Baptists—objected so much to the new measures that their opposition became a boundary that separated them from the world. Despite sharing free will conversion and heart-felt faith with enthusiasts, Dunkers made it clear that their members should avoid the new measures, and they assailed revivalism for both theology and specific practices. The Dunker Yearly Meeting discouraged attendance at protracted meetings and decided against "innovations" like the anxious bench. The Brethren's annual gathering also censured benedictions with "uplifted hands," another practice of the enthusiasts, as unbiblical, and it urged that worship be "held in the order of the house of God," a thinly veiled attack on camp meetings and their alleged disorder. Peter Nead, a conservative and articulate Rockingham County preacher, was especially hard on revivalists. He mocked them for having "no established principles" except "to become numerous," and instructed his Brethren not to "make a public song" of their conversion, a slap at revivalists' alleged lack of humility. He condemned the prominence of singing among revivalists because the Bible did not mention it as a means to convert sinners. He also faulted revivalists for assuming too quickly that conversion had taken place, especially before baptism. "These people," Nead warned, "shout too soon," and he maintained that the Bible has no examples of persons rejoicing prior to baptism. True conversion, according to Nead, happened not when individuals claimed victory but when they obeyed Christ's teachings, as interpreted by the faith community. Nead and the Dunkers wanted conversion to include a deliberate decision to accept a Christian lifestyle, so they established nonparticipation in revivalism as a boundary that separated them from the world.[29]

For Primitive Baptists, even more than for Dunkers, condemnation of enthusiasm became a core belief that stood central to their identity. Primitives, who were traditional Calvinists, assumed that humans naturally rejected God. As one humble Valley Baptist put it, borrowing words from a popular hymn: "Prone to wander Lord, I feel it/Prone to leave the God I love." Conversion stories emphasized that God, not humans, brought salvation. Typical was the testimony of Emily Painter, who testified that if not for God's "working in my heart," she would not have become "sick of sin." Julia Sprinkel labored under the "heavy burden" of her sins but "felt that God was so far" that her prayers went unheard. After trying "every plan I could think of" with no results, she finally prayed to open her Bible to a passage "that might decide my fate." It worked, miraculously, and Sprinkel experienced "a joy unspeakable." She shouted and fell on her knees and face—even Primitive Baptists felt emotion—now receiving God's election after her own schemes failed. Specifically missing from Primitive Baptist testimonies were preachers, camp meetings, and other human intermediaries because, as one of their poets proclaimed, "Hearts are opened by the Lord."[30]

Consequently Primitive Baptists turned resistance to revivalism into a major crusade. They assailed free will conversion as false doctrine and complained that evangelical Baptists had reduced the faith to little but immersion baptism of adults, i.e., a narrow focus on ritual, and thereby had succumbed to the world. A newspaper, *Zion's Advocate*, located in Front Royal, Virginia, and published by John Clark, rallied Valley Baptists to the Primitive cause. Clark printed the conversion stories of Painter, Sprinkel, and others, mentioned above. He accused evangelical anti-Catholic nativists, another popular antebellum cause, of teaching Catholic-like doctrine because both groups recognized human action in salvation, evangelicals through free will decision and Catholics through the sacraments. This was similarity enough to earn Clark's condemnation. When a round of revivals swept the nation in 1858, Clark dismissed its converts as merely converting from one error to another. Primitive Baptists lamented that so many of the faithful had been "bewitched and carried away," i.e., they had defected to evangelical Baptists or Methodists, and Primitives fought what they considered a lonely battle, enduring as a faithful remnant.[31]

More than any of the new measures, Primitive Baptists despised mission societies. They charged that these humans agencies left "salvation to accident or chance" because their success depended on fund-raising abilities or on revivalistic technique, such as the ability to speak, sing, and pray or to manipulate the setting. All these banked on human ability rather than God's power. Primitive Baptists denounced mission societies as attempts to replace God's election with human effort, empty efforts that appealed mostly to pride. When Primitive Baptists prayed "not to be conformed to the world," they had mission societies in mind.[32]

Revivalism, then, gave enthusiasm and inspiration to its practitioners, outsiderness to its opponents, and identity to all. It grew so swiftly that it quickly embodied the center of American religion, stamping popular faith with an egalitarian theology and worship that fit the democratic spirit of early America. It divided some denominations—Presbyterians and Lutherans—and forced its foes—Primitive Baptists, Old School Presbyterians, Henkelite Lutherans, and Dunkers—into bucking a fashionable trend. Whether confessionalists and Anabaptists, who preferred a more gradual salvation process that involved clergy or the faith community, or Primitive Baptists, whose version of the mainstream engulfed mission societies, anti-revivalists built their opposition on a foundation of theology, but the noise, chaos, and disorder of the new measures was almost as unpalatable. Although revivalism involved worship life rather than daily interaction with the larger society, this practice was such a vital topic that vigorous defense of dogma clarified boundaries for anti-revivalists, and unbending public resistance to popular religion left them feeling marginal. The Methodist revolution placed the numerous revivalists, once on the fringes, in the mainstream, and swimming against this popular tide turned their fierce opponents into outsiders.

The Market Revolution

I N 1838 ON A PREACHING TRIP to the western Virginia mountains John Kline learned that a group of Native Americans had recently stayed with his host. While there, they had killed a wild turkey and then prepared the bird for the kettle in traditional style with two women stretching the bird between them, each holding a wing tip, and cleaning it. Then, the women cooked it in the same water they had just used to wash it.

Kline found it incredible that the Native American women had boiled the meat in dirty water. He compared this to Christians who cleansed themselves in church, then went into the world and mixed with it, making themselves unclean again.[1]

Many in the Valley agreed with Kline that Christians should remain uncontaminated by the world's dirty water. But they differed on the composition of unclean water, i.e., on what behaviors belonged to the sinful world. Some found unclean water everywhere, in all parts of life, requiring much effort from believers to remain unstained, while others defined the dirty world as more abstract and, hence, easier for laity to avoid. If all conceded that Christian behavior should be distinctive, varying traditions described those characteristics much differently.

Following the American Revolution in politics and generally coinciding with the revolution brought by Methodism in religion, an economic transformation, which historians call the market revolution, offered fresh opportunities to locate unclean water but made identifying it more troublesome. The market revolution reconstructed the economy, transforming a localized, subsistence, handicraft process into a market-oriented, cash and debt, industrialized system. Large quantities of inexpensive consumer goods enabled the middle class to attain new levels of fashion with surprising ease. Those who considered fashion, including clothing and other popular consumer items, as part of the sinful world had a harder time resisting it, but nonconformists with successful lines against popular culture, especially consumption, became even more separate. The market revolution made resistance to popular culture more challenging but also more meaningful.

The genealogy of the market revolution extends into early modern England. In the seventeenth and eighteenth centuries even small English yeoman produced for the market and calculated for profit, while at the other end of the social ladder nobility sent younger sons into commercial professions without embarrassment. Consumers eagerly acquired the trinkets of commercialization, including looking glasses, expensive fabric, silver, clothing, furniture, tea equipage, lace, ribbons, or ear rings. Eighteenth-century America likewise experienced developing forms of a market economy. Keeping pace with fashion became increasingly important, not just for the well-to-do but for all with social aspirations. Consumption ran strongest in towns and seaboard areas where the wealthy set the pace, but the middling sort, rural consumers, and backcountry spenders "aped" their superiors as best they could. Farmers routinely sold their surplus, often bartering it for consumer goods or raising cash to pay taxes. The outlines of the nineteenth-century market revolution had already emerged in the eighteenth century.[2]

Yet enough economic change came early in the next century to justify the term "market revolution." Economic relations became less local and personal and more regional, national, or international and increasingly impersonal. Misfortune in distant urban commercial centers caused far-reaching ripples, and cash shortages for international merchants could trickle down to the local level, depriving neighborhood entrepreneurs of the ability to purchase farm goods. International markets now linked subsistence farmers and handicraft artisans in rural hinterlands to sudden and frequent financial panics. Ruin came unexpectedly and mysteriously from unknown quarters. As markets expanded and competition increased, masters with access to capital cut costs by "putting out" sub-divided work tasks to families doing unskilled piece work in their homes or by organizing cheap, unskilled labor in large, centralized workshops, where supervision was easier. Traditional home manufacturing declined, and mechanization mushroomed; the spinning wheel, for example, commonplace in pre-market households, disappeared, replaced by water-driven looms in spinning mills, and Cyrus McCormick gave his reaper its first test-run on an Augusta County wheat field.

This economic revolution came with a large social impact. Among the losers were journeymen: with skills displaced by machines, it became increasingly difficult for them to amass the large amounts of capital required to establish themselves as independent artisans. They often slid into the ranks of unskilled labor and became permanent wage earners. Journeymen and apprentices no longer lived under the same roof as the master or considered themselves part of their employer's household. As labor relations became less paternal and more exploitative and impersonal, employers attempted to instill greater discipline in the workplace. In 1830 at the armory in Harpers Ferry, Virginia, a zealous superintendent banned loitering by non-employees, gambling and drinking on the job, and unexcused absences, and he issued a "Yellow Book" with stringent instructions for inspectors. An angry worker murdered the unfortunate disciplinarian. In 1842 another supervisor at Harper's Ferry installed a clock in the workplace, among other changes, and decreed a ten-hour work day. Armorers did not object to the length of day, which was reasonable by contemporary standards, but to its rigidity; the clock removed their ability to control the rhythm of the workday and, therefore, attacked their self-respect. So they went out on strike. From international panics to clock strikes, the market revolution possessed remarkable power to touch individual lives.[3]

As the Valley absorbed market economics, it remained agricultural, and manufacturing came slowly. A cement factory in Rockingham County was the Shenandoah's largest single employer with 150 laborers. Iron furnaces also contributed to the economy. The mountains that bounded the Valley contained rich iron ore deposits, their forests supplied charcoal, and quarries on the Valley's floor yielded limestone, another necessary ingredient in iron production. By 1860, however, Rockingham County's 220 manufacturing establishments, the most for any Valley county, employed only 638 persons. Rockingham's largest manufacturing sector, milling, produced fifty-two percent of the county's manufacturing output, but it employed only sixty-six workers. Sawmilling ranked second and employed fifty-one. The new economy left the Shenandoah's agrarian landscape generally intact.[4]

Manufacturing, however, was only one leg of the market revolution, and Shenandoah farmers experienced the full force of the new economy in other ways. Of course, much of what Valley farmers produced stayed home to maintain the farmstead rather than proceeding into the market. Corn was the most important secondary crop, but oats, rye, timothy, and clover also furnished food for humans and fodder and pasturage for animals. Swine were universal, and butchering them during the winter months was an annual ritual. But except for the first stages of frontier settlement, the market was always part of the Valley economy. Even in the eighteenth century and the very early stages of commercialization, many farmers fattened cattle raised in the mountains just west of the Valley for market. They bought herds in the fall, fed them on corn shucks and wheat straw over the winter, then pastured them in the summer before driving the fattened stock and their own surplus head to markets east of the Blue Ridge. By the 1830s cattle fattening had become big business, and small operators complained that a shortage of bank capital denied them credit necessary for this lucrative trade.[5]

The strongest link between Valley agrarians and the market revolution was wheat. A wheat boom emerged in the eighteenth century when Europe lost the ability to feed itself, and as wheat prices rose, farmers became increasingly commercialized. Between 1772 and 1819 the profitable wagonning distance for wheat doubled to one hundred miles. Although distillers converted grain into alcohol and shipped whiskey to cities east of the Blue Ridge, more frequently local millers ground wheat into flour and shipped barrels by wagon, railroad, or canal boat to Baltimore, Georgetown, Alexandria, Fredericksburg, and Richmond. Wagons returned with coffee, sugar, salt, plaster, and guano. By the late eighteenth and early nineteenth centuries Baltimore and Alexandria prices appeared in local newspapers, a sure sign of market influence, and in the 1820s this information, including prices from markets in Alexandria, Baltimore, New York, Fredericksburg, and Petersburg, was commonplace. By the 1840s Shenandoah wheat reached markets around the world, and local newspapers understood that international events, such as the Peninsular war, bad weather, currency conditions, and crop shortages in England and France, could set prices. In the decade prior to the Civil War ninety percent or more of Shenandoah farmers cultivated wheat with a large majority of crop destined for sale, signifying that the market revolution had reached virtually every farm.[6]

Critical to this increasingly complex version of capitalism were transportation improvements, first canals and then railroads, both of which greatly altered the physical scope of the market by shortening distances between rural producers and urban markets. Beginning in late 1824 long, low riverboats, or gundalows, floated down the South Fork of the Shenandoah River and to the Potomac at Harpers Ferry, where rivermen sold their boats for lumber and walked home. But the Shenandoah, a modest, not a mighty river, accommodated boats only at high water levels, which tended to be seasonal and often long after harvest season. The Valley turnpike, completed in the early 1840s, eased transportation north and south, and where east-west routes intersected it, the Shenandoah's two largest towns, Staunton and Winchester, grew. Wagon transportation, however, remained expensive, and, therefore, the first significant transportation improvement was the Chesapeake and Ohio Canal, which in 1833 reached Harpers Ferry from Georgetown and dropped the cost of shipping flour between these two points from approximately $1.25 to $.25–.40 per barrel. In the 1850s upper Valley farmers benefited from a canal that linked Lexington to the James River, and they began sending flour to Lynchburg and on to Richmond. The year after the canal came to Harpers Ferry, railroad transportation arrived there, shipping flour to Baltimore for $.33 per barrel. The first railroad inside the Valley, completed in 1836, connected Winchester with the Baltimore and Ohio railroad at Harpers Ferry; in its first four months of operation the Winchester and Potomac transported almost sixteen thousand barrels of flour to Baltimore, plus five thousand passengers to Harpers Ferry, and over thirteen hundred tons of merchandise back to Winchester. Soon, however, the westward extension of the Baltimore and Ohio and a new line between Alexandria and Front Royal afforded other transportation options, and freight along this once lucrative route quickly declined. Other railroads, however, laid tracks in the Valley before the Civil War. In 1854 the Manassas Gap Railroad connected Front Royal with points east of the Blue Ridge; in 1856 it reached Woodstock, and three years later locomotives lumbered into Mount Jackson. In 1854 railroads connected Staunton with Richmond, but not until after the Civil War did railroads link the lower and upper portions of the Valley with each other. Slowly but surely canals and railroads connected the Shenandoah with the national and international economy.[7]

Improved transportation that brought distant marketplaces and their economic power closer benefited typical Shenandoans in several ways. It increased income for farmers, generated more printed material, and broadened horizons. It provided consumers with new ways to add to their material life, which they eagerly embraced. Advertisements boasted of merchandise in the latest style and fashion, "selected in the Philadelphia and Baltimore markets, at the lowest cash prices," and presented readers with long, detailed lists of available items, especially store-bought clothing. Mrs. Thomas, her advertisement boasted to Winchester readers, "respectfully announces" the latest bonnets from Baltimore. Clark and Gordon informed customers of the arrival of their spring goods, which included "every article of French, English, German, and American manufactured dry goods in common use, together with a general assortment of hardware, queensware, and groceries."[8] Greater choices allowed consumers to demonstrate taste and develop middle-class politeness. Cast iron stoves freed women from the spark and smoke of fireplaces and placed oven-roasted meat and fancy pastries on Valley tables. Wall paper, this too "of the latest patterns and most fashionable style used in Philadelphia," graced homes. Another gift from the market revolution was new leisure time opportunities. Valentine's Day, for example, emerged from obscurity to become a major holiday. A Rockingham County newspaper noted that "Valentines comic, sentimental, romantic, breathing love, full of spleen and hatred, large, and small" had swamped Post Offices for days prior to February 14, and all of these Valentines—comic and sentimental—were store-bought fallout of the market revolution.[9]

The clothing, shoes, cheap furniture, carpets, draperies, carpet traveling bags, chisels, garden seed, umbrellas, parasols, valentines, nails, wall paper, and other boons of industrialization available to those with cash demanded that nonconformists make decisions about lifestyle and fashion where none previously had been required. As the market revolution gained momentum, making popular culture more materialistic, some Christians responded with potent barriers against its dirty water while others drank of it freely.[10]

In addition to economic complexity, the market revolution slightly increased the diversity of the Shenandoah's religious spectrum as Catholics arrived in the Valley more or less concurrently with the economic changes. Except for a few families here and there Catholics had been absent from the Valley until the appearance in the 1840s of Irish immigrants, mostly in towns and at a construction site for a railroad tunnel through the Blue Ridge. In 1841 the first priest in the Valley, Daniel Downey, an Irish immigrant, gathered less than a dozen worshippers for Mass in the home of a prominent storekeeper and slaveholder. A few years later the bishop in Richmond designated Staunton as a pastorate with missions in Charlottesville, Harrisonburg, Lexington, and Mountain Top, the tunnel site. Staunton's little congregation presumably met in homes until 1851, when it moved into a new brick building with a classical interior motif.

Yet, by the Civil War Catholics remained sparse in the Valley.

The Harrisonburg mission, for example, served only sixteen families, eight in the town and eight in the county. As recent immigrants, non-Protestants, and members of a despised fellowship, Valley Catholics must have felt very much like outsiders, but their small numbers made them a negligible part of religious life in the Shenandoah.[11]

As the market revolution added newcomers, leisure time, better transportation, distant markets, consumer choice, and popular taste to the Valley, it also provided fresh paths for the assimilation of nonconformists. On the other hand, now that consumption was such an important part of popular culture, resistance to fashion became a much more useful tool for nonconformists.

In the past, vague understandings of fashion had adequately described nonconformity, but with the rising availability of manufactured goods, separation from the fashionable world needed more precision. The lengthy lists of sins developed in the pre-market era condemned worldliness with a vast but vague brush; now they illustrated the difficulty of specifying the world in the market economy. Presbyterians, for example, inherited from communion celebrations a tendency towards broad cataloguing; one list, for instance, named "pride, self conceit accompanied with ignorance, passions, lusts, appetites, rebellious wills, evil company, and a whole army of natural corruptions" as among the "vices, follies, and vanity" of the world. A Lutheran inventory named "swearers, liars, defrauders, misers, fornicators, adulterers, [and] drunkards" and dispositions that were "covetous, wrathful, revengeful, spiteful, [and] uncharitable to the poor." The Baptist Ketocton Association defined works of the flesh as a roster of outrageous acts—adultery, fornication, idolatry, witchcraft, murder, and drunkenness—mixed with vague offenses, such as uncleanness, lasciviousness, hatred, variance, "emulations," wrath, strife, seditiousness, heresies, and "envyings."[12] Lists that mixed heinous acts such as adultery and murder, which nonbelievers also considered unthinkable, with ambiguous attitudinal flaws like wrath and covetousness did little to clarify the difference between a life in the church and a life in the world.

Other illustrations of the mainstream included more precise concepts but still relatively rare events in Valley society. Theatergoing and dueling, for example, were evident sins, according to their critics, and Valley Protestants read attacks on them in denominational periodicals published in Richmond or Baltimore. Theater provided a way to fill leisure time generated by the economic changes, but religious journals, another product of the market revolution, snubbed it as appealing to lower classes and "lower passions." Worse, actors cross-dressed, and both genders wore "every vice in fashion." Several journals reminded readers that in 1778 the Continental Congress urged the states to suppress the theater because liberty depended on "true religion and good morals." Valley preachers and their congregations, however, said little about the stage, perhaps because it was more common in urban settings. Although commercialization changed the Valley's economy, it remained largely agrarian and rural, making theatergoing a smaller temptation for believers in Harrisonburg or Timber Ridge than for the urban faithful in Richmond or Baltimore.[13]

Dueling likewise drew occasional condemnation but seemed distant from Valley society. George Baxter, at Washington College, warned the young would-be aristocrats under his care that the code of honor, an ethos that accompanied dueling, undermined republican institutions and destroyed public order. (Apparently Baxter could only think of secular arguments.) Others maintained that these contests created a taste for violence, established false standards of honor, and violated God's authority. Affairs of honor, however, were largely confined to the planter class, who used this extralegal and complicated system of ethics to define their elitism. In planter-dominated regions, criticism of dueling challenged the moral authority of those who controlled society, but the Valley lacked a large class of elite planters. This example of worldliness, therefore, was another far-away issue for Shenandoans, less meaningful than for other Southern Christians, and most of the criticism came from sources outside the Valley, as did the censure of theater. Assaults on dueling and the theater plainly labeled sin, but residents of the Valley, whether churched or unchurched, were unlikely to succumb to these largely symbolic temptations.[14]

The Sabbath, however, could be broken in rural as well as urban areas, and opposition to Sabbath-breaking became the most direct assault by many Protestants on the market revolution. A national movement to preserve the Sabbath emerged in the late 1820s in reaction to federal legislation, passed in 1810, requiring mail delivery on Sunday. The law attracted opposition almost immediately when a Presbyterian postmaster in Washington, Pennsylvania, was caught between his church, which called upon him to observe the Sabbath, and the state, which wanted the mail to move. The argument was about the movement of mail overland rather than door-to-door delivery, which was yet to come. Resistance gathered new energy when well-known evangelists Charles Finney and Lyman Beecher, backed by philanthropists Lewis and Arthur Tappan, climbed aboard the Sabbatarian band-wagon. By curtailing business activity, including mail delivery, on the Sabbath, the movement emerged as symbolic resistance to the alleged corrupting and materialist values of the expanding econo-my. With its petitions and local organizing, Sabbatarianism became an early grassroots political movement, but in 1830 the cause faded when Congress voted to continue Sunday mail. Nevertheless, the larger vision of protecting the Sabbath remained popular among reformers.[15]

Valley protectors of God's day focused on a variety of Sabbath-breaking activities. In the 1830s during the national movement's heyday the Lexington Presbytery condemned driving teams to market, running boats, driving cattle, pleasure driving, and travel-ing on the Sabbath. A Richmond-based periodical for border-state Presbyterians warned that visiting after church, common in rural areas, too often became a chat about farming, fashion, weddings, stocks, bonds, and markets (more evidence of the market revolu-tion). Sabbatarians feared that Sunday visits to the sick did not remain appropriate to the day but instead became an "idle hour" filled with "gossip or secular conversation." Misuse of Scripture to condone desecration of the Sabbath was another problem, as when Sabbath-breakers justified Sunday dinner parties by explain-ing that the disciples of Jesus picked ears of corn on the Sabbath to feed the poor. Sabbatarians expected children, as well, to honor the holy day. Joseph Travis, a Methodist preacher, remembered the piercing guilt he felt when as a youth near Harrisonburg he went birdnest hunting with friends on the Sabbath. Travis related this anecdote in his autobiography, but even if he embellished it, the tale nonetheless demonstrates the importance of the Sabbath to Travis as an adult. During the Civil War Thomas J. "Stonewall" Jackson, a native of Lexington, kept the flame of opposition to Sunday mail alive by tapping acquaintances to lobby the Confederate government against it. He argued that the Confederate government should reflect the faith of its citizens by repealing Sunday mail laws. "The Old United States," he judged, was too extreme on separation of church and state. For many, including Travis and Jackson, the Sabbath deserved special esteem.[16]

On the other hand, little emphasis on keeping the Sabbath emerges from congregational records, except for one or two cases of discipline for hunting and shooting on the Lord's day, and a wayward Presbyterian who tried to sell "various articles" on the Sabbath at a Methodist campmeeting.[17] Although individuals like Jackson and Travis enlisted in the Sabbath movement, congregations disciplined Sabbath-breakers infrequently. Moreover, Jackson was not a typical Presbyterian. He gave up theater, dancing, cards, smoking, and drinking when he joined the church, and won the respect of his contemporaries, who elected him to a deaconship, but they also considered him unusually disciplined and eccentric. Presbyterians seldom disciplined for Sabbath-breaking, perhaps because most faithfully kept this day or perhaps because this cause was a high priority for individuals but not fellowships. Regardless, those who kept the Sabbath were separate from the world and its marketplace, at least one day in seven.[18]

Other commonly drawn lines against worldly behavior—dancing, intemperance, and sexual misconduct—avoided rather than addressed the market revolution. These definitions of the mainstream focused on actions that were timeless and applied equally to pre-market and commercialized Valley society. All belonged to the list of vague sins so often cited by Protestants.

Opposition to dancing, like Sabbatarianism, urged a strict ban that left almost no form of modern-era dance acceptable and, therefore, offered tangible separation from the world. Critics acknowledged that it appeared in the Bible, but only, they asserted, for worship, and they claimed that biblical dancing was more similar to the Shakers' services than to social dancing. More tellingly, Salome's dance, though solo and confined to her mother's house, still led to evil—Herod beheaded the Baptist—and modern dances, such as the polka, allowed the lechery of Paris and Vienna to penetrate drawing rooms in Saratoga, Cape May, and Newport. "Bewhiskered villains" lurked on these dance floors. The Valley's spiritual shepherds considered dancing especially tempting for youth, but they fretted that their flocks, regardless of age, disregarded cautions.[19]

Indeed, laity often ignored these alarms, sometimes defiantly. Lutheran Charles Porterfield Krauth's sermon on "obscene concerts" and dance, for example, managed only to ruffle feathers in Winchester. Early in Krauth's message an attractive young woman walked out of the combined Lutheran-Episcopalian congregation in protest, with her brothers following. Krauth, perhaps exaggerating just a bit, contended that the entire town discussed his talk, and the next Sunday he stubbornly returned to the topic. He later published the sermon.[20] When John Skinner, pastor of the Lexington congregation, attacked the superintendent of the Virginia Military Institute for sponsoring a ball, members of the Washington College faculty resisted. Among those spurning Skinner's call to avoid dance were Henry Ruffner, the college president and a member of Skinner's session. Presbyterian preacher William Hill, in Winchester, similarly found conflict when he preached against dance. Hill fell into a long-running feud with his elders when three members of his congregation enrolled students in a dancing class while he was away at a meeting of the Presbyterian General Assembly. Dancing lessons were among the forms of instruction, including music, art, and language lessons, newly available to the middle class, courtesy of the market revolution. When Hill returned, he assailed these "frivolous exercises" and promised discipline for the dancers, including elders whom he claimed often opposed his exhortations for nonconformity. In rural Augusta County another Presbyterian preacher, Francis McFarland, likewise struggled against dancing with mixed success. McFarland's sons received an invitation to a Christmas eve party at the home of parishioners, but he feared that they might be confronted with dancing and drinking. The invitation, however, could not be declined, and McFarland's fears were confirmed when his sons and the sixty or seventy other guests found wine on the table and egg-nog handed round. After supper, dancing broke out in the basement, although McFarland's sons went to another room, or so they told their father.[21] Several days after the party the hostess expressed to him "her deep mortification" over events, and her husband claimed that the dancing began without his permission. McFarland, then, received a post-event apology, but Skinner, Hill, and Krauth faced open opposition to their injunction against dance.[22]

Clergy could only lament the inroads that dancing had made among the faithful. They resolved to do what they could to stop it but noted its popularity with many of their lay men and women.[23] In one unusual case a session took the rare step of disciplining one of its own for dancing and cards, but not before the affair divided the congregation. In most cases, however, Presbyterian sessions, controlled by laity, did not discipline for dancing, with the exception of members who owned taverns or organized dancing parties.[24] Although this cause campaigned against specific behavior, it lacked the necessary commitment from the laity to become a sharp boundary against the world.

The battle against strong drink held similar potential for a visible marker. Surfacing in the late eighteenth century among Quakers and Methodists, the temperance movement reacted to both an increase in alcohol consumption and concerns for social order. Consumption of hard beverages noticeably rose between 1800 and 1820 when western farmers increasingly converted corn to whiskey because they could transport it more easily to distant markets, yet another influence of the market revolution. The price of whiskey dropped considerably lower than coffee and tea, and Americans began to drink more frequently. Alcohol became an integral part of life, from bedtime snacks to elections. Many Americans believed that a glass of whiskey prior to breakfast promoted health and that alcohol was healthier than water. But the high level of consumption also produced a reaction, with reformers charging that strong drink led to widespread disorder, including crime, poverty, and economic waste. During the great revivals of the 1820s and 1830s temperance became a mass movement thoroughly committed to abstinence from all alcoholic beverages, not just "spirituous" or distilled drink.[25]

In the Valley soldiers in the holy war against demon rum included recruits from many denominations, both Old School and New School. After Maine enacted prohibition legislation, known as the Maine Law (1851), temperance men and women in Virginia hoped for a similar "Virginia Liquor Law." The *Lutheran Observer* (New School), published in Baltimore and read in the Valley, noted the order and quiet that came to that city's streets after the passage of its Sunday Liquor Law. The Lexington Presbytery allowed the local mayor to exhort it on temperance, and when in 1843 James McDowell, a Presbyterian who lived in Lexington, became governor of Virginia, his daughter remarked that "Old School Presbyterianism and total abstinence" enjoyed ascendancy in the Governor's House for one term at least. On Christmas Day, 1860, the Sons of Temperance and the Mt. Crawford Cavalry marched in Bridgewater, Virginia, and listened to an address by a local Methodist preacher. To be sure, many Valley Protestants endorsed this crusade.[26]

Only Dunkers and Mennonites objected to temperance societies. Although both groups reaffirmed temperance principles and urged members to avoid strong drink, Mennonites quietly stayed away from the organized movement, and Dunkers actively denounced it. According to Dunkers, if temperance organizations did good work—and they recognized that even the Masonic movement had "its good qualities"—believers nonetheless needed to "come out and separate" from all secular organizations because they lacked inspiration from Christ. If congregations suspected that candidates for baptism belonged to the Sons of Temperance, they had Yearly Meeting's authorization to ask about it. The Sons were doubly crossed for they were a secret organization and Dunkers disapproved of those, too.[27]

Other fellowships found harmony on temperance more difficult. Lutheran and Reformed temperance supporters mourned that many in their denomination opposed their cause, sometimes "with all their might," as a Reformed cold-water advocate lamented. The Baltimore Conference timidly charged its Methodist preachers to enforce the Discipline on spirituous liquors "mildly, but rigidly." Despite its popularity, temperance often failed to receive endorsement at the denominational level, and congregations in the Valley did not discipline for the use of alcohol.[28]

Instead, congregations expelled for misuse, i.e., for drunkenness. Buck Marsh Baptists, for example, disciplined Richard Alexander for being intoxicated and fighting during harvest time celebrations, and the Presbyterians in Shepherdstown suspended James Crawford for intemperance, refusing to lift the suspension when he wanted one of his children baptized. A congregation in Winchester fired its sexton for being under the influence while in the church building. In one of the most interesting cases, the Mossy Creek session investigated Abraham Hanna four times over a thirty-year period for intemperance. In 1829 the session accepted his apology for drinking too freely and also for selling spirits on the Sabbath, but in 1837 the elders suspended him for occasional intoxication. In 1855 Hanna confessed that again he had been drinking too much and called it his worst sin. Appearing before the session, Hanna promised that with God's help he would abstain from all intoxicating drink, and the elders took the unusual step of praying with him that God might provide the strength to carry out this rare cold-water pledge. A few years later the rumor mill again indicted Hanna, but this time he explained that his use of alcohol was only medicinal, and the session accepted this. Cases like these dot the records of Presbyterians and were among the most frequent causes of discipline.[29]

In condemning intemperance, Protestants fell in line with the secular mainstream. Although America may have been a republic of alcoholics, as one scholar has suggested, it consumed its rivers of alcohol sip by sip through the day rather than gulping spirits down in a binge, and this nation of problem drinkers frowned upon public drunkenness. Virginians made it a violation of the law. As Valley congregations removed drunks from their midst, they demonstrated the similarity between Protestant opinion and public opinion. Although abstinence helped individual participants find guidelines against worldly behavior, congregations and denominations did not endorse it. Instead, they concentrated on public drunkenness. Only the Anabaptists managed to make a wall out of the temperance movement, which they did by rejecting it.[30]

Intolerance of sexual misbehavior was no more successful in separating Protestants from the world than sabbatarianism or temperance. But there was no lack of effort on this front, and congregations willingly disciplined those judged at fault, often for fornication. Dunkers considered this transgression so severe that they would not even retain guilty members who expressed regret. Lutherans, who practiced infant baptism, sometimes recorded the baptism of illegitimate children on a separate page in the church book. Linville Creek Baptists excommunicated Elener Gum, whom, they said, was "basely begotten with child," and although she did not appear before the council when summoned, which added to her guilt, she had confessed her misdeed to a member. Linville Creek Baptists also excluded Hannah Price, another unmarried and pregnant woman, who admitted her condition to the two sisters appointed to visit her. Presbyterians showed comparable impatience with fornicators. Shepherdstown's Presbyterian elders suspended a member for marrying a woman whose husband had left her and for committing fornication with her prior to marriage. In 1842 Winchester Presbyterians disciplined a woman with a child born out of wedlock, but in 1900, after her death, the elders returned to the session minutes with their erasers to expunge her name. Apparently this anonymous woman had returned to close fellowship with her congregation following her discipline, and the elders recognized her faithfulness by removing her disgrace from the records. The Lexington Presbytery advised an elder to resign for marrying a young woman with an illegitimate child, which they suspected was his. Another suspected fornicator, however, escaped discipline because his case was "not ripe for decision in its present form." Perhaps birth had not yet occurred, and the Presbytery could not determine whether fornication occurred prior to marriage.[31]

Presbyterians extended the definition of sexual misbehavior to include marriage to close relations. Harry Stuart, for example, married the half sister of his dead wife and suffered excommunication. The elders at Bethel deliberated at length the case of a widow, whose new husband was also her uncle, admitting her to membership only after determining that her repentance covered all former transgressions, including this one. In Winchester William Hill once refused a communion token to the wife of the ruling elder at Timber Ridge because the elder was also her brother-in-law; she married him after her sister, the elder's first wife, died.[32]

Judging from the numbers of cases that came before Presbyterian sessions, fornication was more common than, say, dueling, and sanctions against it applied to actual behavior rather than conduct that rarely appeared in the Valley. On the other hand, the nature of the crime focused judgment on the unmarried, on women, and on the young, all limited populations within the fellowship rather than touching all members, especially white males. Furthermore, condemnation of sexual misbehavior was not unique to Protestants because, like drunkenness, both adultery and fornication violated civil law in Virginia. Rules against these behaviors, therefore, had limited potential to clarify boundary lines between the church and the world and said nothing about the market revolution.[33]

Fashion, unlike fornication, was something that married persons could do and offered boundaries for all, not just youth or the unmarried. Fashion, whether in church architecture or clothing, was commonly encountered, and exhortations against it confronted the market revolution. Criticism of fashion appeared in nearly all traditions, although attention sometimes focused on clergy. Presbyterians, for example, expected ministers to avoid the world in "dress, manners, and conversation" and to reflect the "plainness, simplicity, self denial, and holiness of life" so abundant in the early church. But whether for clergy or laity, the new economy offered fresh opportunities to resist fashion and to enhance plainness.[34]

The war against fashion, however, was a difficult fight, as illustrated by creeping shifts in meetinghouse architecture. Once church buildings had embodied simplicity and were devoid of fashion. Many eighteenth-century churches had been crude structures, little more than small rectangles of rough-hewn logs with earthen floors. Benches were backless; those nearest the pulpit rented for the most, with the price decreasing with distance from the pulpit, except for those against the wall (because they had a back). The only heat was in a separate small building, called the "retiring house," where mothers could take babies or footstones could be reheated during lunch break between sermons. Some scholars have noticed these plain buildings as evidence of a non-conformist mindset among evangelicals; the austere surroundings, so the argument goes, delivered an unmistakable message that the values of the faithful differed from those of the world.[35]

But even in the eighteenth century many congregations built more grandly when they could. As early as 1738 a Presbyterian fellowship north of Staunton had erected a stone building, naming itself the "Augusta Stone Church," and soon several other early Presbyterian churches also employed stone materials (New Providence, 1754; Timber Ridge, 1756; New Monmouth, 1789; Tinkling Spring, 1792; and Harrisonburg, 1793). In 1764 Winchester's Lutherans began work on a new gray limestone church to replace their log building; in 1790 it acquired two bells, cast in Bremen, Germany, and in 1795 an organ added to the sounds of worship. In 1805 Harrisonburg Methodists built a white frame structure with a steeple, bell, and high pulpit.[36]

At the other end of the spectrum, log structures enjoyed use into the nineteenth century until congregations rebuilt them, usually with brick. Bethel Presbyterian, for example, worshipped in a log building for nearly eighty years, replacing it with brick in 1821, and Mossy Creek, founded in 1767, had a dirt floor until raising a brick structure in the 1810s. St. Paul's in Page County, which served both Reformed and Lutherans, used its log church, built in the late eighteenth century, until acquiring one of brick in

1868 (construction began in 1860). St. Paul's in Strasburg used its 1769 log structure, which included an organ, until building brick in 1844. Occasionally nineteenth-century congregations used logs for new structures. St. James', near the head of Cedar Creek on the edge of the Alleghenies, built a log building in 1822, constructed another facility in 1840 that was still log, and used it until 1884; Bethel (Frederick County) used hewed logs in 1848 to build a new structure. Most of these buildings were in rural locations, near forests and an ample supply of inexpensive timber.[37]

By the 1830s some meetinghouses in towns adopted Greek architecture, participating in a national trend that influenced public building and private residences as well as religious structures. The Andrew Chapel, erected by proslavery Methodists in Harrisonburg, was a magnificent Greek Revival structure with a wooden belfry and a cornerstone laid by a Masonic Grand Master and seventy-five visiting Masons. Presbyterians in Lexington built a facility for their Sunday School and public lecture room with four fashionable columns surrounded by a pediment, and in the 1840s they added a new church, also in Greek style, described by a contemporary as the town's "chief architectural ornament." In 1841 Old School Presbyterians in Harrisonburg constructed a new building of Greek style with a portico and four large pillars and a cupola with a bell, and in 1853 the first manse at New Monmouth, a small frame house with gabled roof, included Greek revival interior with tall pilasters framing the windows and doors, classical mantels adorning the two west rooms, and pediments gracing the hallway entrances. The Reformed Church in Martinsburg (1846, Jefferson County), was a brick structure built in Romanesque style that included a cupola and cross, an impressive facade, pediment, and rounded arches. Trinity Reformed in Mt. Crawford (1848, Rockingham County) featured large doric columns, a portico, and galleries on three sides. This Roman and Greek influence was neither distinctly Lutheran, Presbyterian, or Methodist, nor even Christian, and the surroundings of these worship buildings exuded fashion rather than dissent.[38]

The Lexington Presbyterian Church, the town's architectural jewel.
Source: Robert F. Hunter, *Lexington Presbyterian Church, 1789–1989* (Lexington Presbyterian Church, 1991), 42. Published courtesy of the Lexington Presbyterian Church.

Indeed, the pattern of church construction of many of these congregations differed little from the Episcopalians, who have never been associated with simplicity. In 1747 Old Chapel Anglicans near Berryville built a log structure, but in 1790 replaced it with stone. In 1763 Staunton Anglicans erected a brick building, but by the early nineteenth century it had become obsolete, "an ancient church," an observer noted, "with a gray, moss-covered tower, clothed from base to summit with the Virginia Creeper." (Virginia Creeper is a vine-like plant that swarms over ground and trees alike without the aesthetic appeal of ivy.) So the Episcopalians tore down their decrepit building and replaced it with another brick construction ornamented with a cupola, front and back porches, a gallery, a raised pulpit, and a white fence. Front Royal's first Episcopalian church, built in 1854, was a wooden frame building. Anglicans, too, employed wood, brick, and stone.[39]

The piecemeal abandonment of plainness and the haphazard range of facilities that existed in the early nineteenth century— from humble logs to the noble Greeks—indicates that many Protestants never underwent a seismic shift in attitudes about church architecture. Instead, meetinghouse architecture suggests the importance of resources. Prior to the American Revolution most private homes were log, and as prosperity increased, construction materials improved. Many Protestants in the Shenandoah backcountry worshiped in structures similar to those in which they lived. When Francis Asbury rejoiced that Shepherdstown Methodists had acquired a structure "with two chimneys" (Asbury's emphasis), he anticipated being warm in addition to worshiping in a building that others might notice. Many congregations abandoned simple meetinghouses when they could afford it, and it seems unlikely that Protestants drew inspiration of nonconformity from plain architecture. More likely, as they sat in their log churches, they dreamed of the day when they could build more grandly. They built when funds were available, and the changes say more about economics than theology and indicate little commitment to simplicity as a religious principle. Many Protestants never possessed an understanding of church architecture that encouraged resistance to plainness; one editor advised that plain churches might be appropriate for poor congregations, but wealthier ones should build something better than logs and strive for beauty in church architecture. Thus, by the time of the market revolution church architecture provided little encouragement for nonconformity and scant shelter from the concept of fashion.[40]

If the surroundings of church buildings failed to reinforce proscriptions against fashion, neither did the words that flowed from their high pulpits. Most Protestants in the Valley endorsed general criticism of fashion, especially regarding apparel, but held little interest in resistance that required noticeable nonconformity.

Some thought that when Christians were the dominant culture, fashion and faith met rather than clashed, and resistance to the world became moot. According to this line of thought, Christians were always gentlemen and followed the "manners and customs of the world" as long as they were not unchristian. This viewpoint disapproved of oddity for its own sake or uncouthness merely to be contrary and assumed that unless the fashion was not obviously objectionable, nonconformists faced the burden of proof. In short, resistance to the world depended on circumstances. This wall against the world had a hole big enough to accommodate a hoop skirt.[41]

Others offered a *cassus belli* in the warfare against fashion that was secular rather than sacred, stressing what simplicity could do for the state rather than the church. Echoing growing American democracy, this reasoning championed republican simplicity. "Pride, luxury, and extravagance" and the tendency of the "rich to ape the manners of lords and ladies" violated the spirit of republicanism, and idleness was ungentlemanly and dishonorable. Americans should be satisfied with inexpensive pleasures, such as books and intelligent conversation, rather than balls, plays, and gratification of "Epicurean appetites." Furthermore, Biblical industriousness, consistent with true republicanism, could strengthen the economy, and simplicity in dress preserved life's necessities and respectability during a depressed economy. A "rusty" coat, for example, could be "turned" and appear decent again, which, one commentator reported, happened frequently during America's first two wars. He estimated that if a million men turned their coats, with each garment averaging thirty dollars in cost, the country would save thirty million dollars. Wearing old hats would additionally net between five and eight million dollars. Plainness was pragmatic and patriotic.[42]

Methodists especially fell into the tendency to dilute the war against fashion by invoking secular logic. While "costly apparel" and wearing gold remained a violation of the Methodist Discipline, the new interpretation of simplicity expected less of the laity, and distinctive clothing, such as a preacher's coat in the style of the "old preachers" with no "ornamentation," now belonged in the past. To accommodate clergy seeking respect, Methodists changed the Discipline, replacing a warning for preachers not to "affect the gentleman" with advice to "avoid all affectation," suggesting that gentlemanliness was now acceptable. The term "Methodistical" dress continued to have meaning, at least on occasion, but those who practiced simple dress became a minority, responding to the standards of a previous era.[43]

Critical to the Methodists' drift from plainness were new, less strenuous definitions for unacceptable worldly dress; they now denounced outlandish or unhealthy styles rather than encouraging distinctively plain garb. Instead of shunning jewelry, women were to cast aside only spare adornments. "Needle-working veils, caps, and collars" wasted years of Methodists' time, and the time and money dissipated on preoccupation with dress set a bad example for the lower classes. One wag humorously tolerated bonnets so large that they blocked the view of worshippers; perhaps, he quipped, churches should be built amphitheater style to allow worshippers a peak over the tall hats.[44]

Women who tightly laced their corsets received much criticism, and apparently Methodist women tugged hard at their laces. In fact, according to the national Methodist publication, the *Christian Advocate and Journal*, tight lacing, though a "barbarous custom," was nonetheless "universal" among Methodist women. Numerous rationalizations, noted by critics, further testified to the practice's popularity. Authorities urged women not to explain that "I do not lace so tight as other girls" or that "if it does require some strength to hook my frock, it feels perfectly easy when it is on!" Critics, however, emphasized the risks this fashion brought to health rather than its sinfulness. A "Doctor" cautioned that tight lacing caused heart disease by restriction of "the free passage of the blood from the lower extremities to the heart" and irritation induced by the "unnatural fixing of the chest." Many a "sickly, useless mother" paid a heavy price for her small waist. To be sure, a dress so tight that it interfered with motion destroyed Methodist women, but the punishment was now physical rather than spiritual.[45]

Some Methodist preachers still preferred greater distance from the mainstream, and they became increasingly frustrated. They counted many defects among contemporary Methodists, including the tendency of clergy to read well-reasoned sermons instead of preaching extemporaneously in ways that moved hearts, the descent of camp meetings into social events accompanied by fine food and dress, and the decline of classes and love feasts. But more than specifics, they detected that the zeal of the founders had been lost and that Methodists had accommodated themselves to fashion, wealth, and status. These men became known as "croakers," a widely used term for those who regretted the increased refinement of Methodism.[46]

Jacob Gruber, who served the Valley and western Maryland, was perhaps the best-known croaker, and he heaped sarcasm on fashionable Methodists. Once an unusually tall woman entered one of Gruber's services, and he stopped preaching to ridicule her bonnet. "Make room" for her, he commanded, adding that she appeared tall enough to achieve notice "without the plumage of the bird in her bonnet." A few days later the bonneted worshipper confronted Gruber about his rudeness, but he fired again. "O sister, was that you?" he inquired with mock innocence. "Well, I did not know it was you; I though you had more sense." Other times he directed rebukes to preachers, perhaps with gloves or canes, whom he thought too fashionable or those whom he thought "did not even appear like Methodists." Gruber reprimanded some of his colleagues for failing to preach against fashions or when they did, for allowing their exhortations for simplicity to disappear in the "trimming, rigging, muff, drums, bustles, and other fashionable gear of their wives or daughters." Once when he met a clergyman's family, including a grown son and daughter whom he considered too worldly, he introduced them to each other. Turning first to the preacher, he said, "This is your son; this fine, gay, fashionable young man, with his ruffles and nonsense about him, is the son of a plain Methodist preacher." He asked what the preacher's congregation would think of him when they saw his son. Then Gruber insulted the daughter: "Who that looks at you," he inquired, would guess that she was related to her mother, a "plain, old-fashioned woman?" Then, to the mother, he said,

This is your daughter, this fine-looking young lady, with her ruffles, rings, curls, locket, and silly needless ornaments. Some will think that, though you are plain yourself, you love to see your child gay and fashionable; but they will wonder who buys those costly toys and trinkets, father or mother? Some will fear that, with her beau-catchers, she will catch a fool and go to destruction.

Gruber professed surprise that his frankness went unappreciated, but his angry verbal barrages reveal the besieged mentality of those who supported the traditional position of plainness.[47]

Croakers remained a minority. Although most Methodists still pictured themselves as outsiders regarding dress, in reality they had reconstructed the wall that separated them from worldly fashion. They now encouraged the laity to consider frugality and health in clothing rather than separation from their neighbors, and they said almost nothing about the dress of men. John Kline, the Dunker preacher, observed the changes and wondered if contemporary Methodists would accept Wesley with his "plain dress and old fashioned ways." Instead of declaring themselves odd or avoiding the darkness, Methodists now defined simplicity in ways that allowed Methodist men and women to look more like non-Methodists.[48]

Presbyterians, because their bias leaned towards fashion rather than away from it, showed less movement than Methodists. Although communions had fenced off the world from the unworldly, they never identified fashion as one of the worldly sins.

To the contrary, preachers on both sides of the Atlantic had taught that dirty clothes signified sinfulness and urged communicants to wear their best apparel; laity might even buy or make new clothes for communions. In Scotland, where barefoot was common, dressing the feet showed special effort, and in western Pennsylvania Presbyterians carried their shoes and stockings, wrapped in a kerchief, to church; then put them on before entering. As one preacher remarked, "A church going people are a dress loving people," and clergy themselves dressed fashionably, including powdered wigs. Little in the Presbyterian tradition encouraged resistance to fashion, and they remained largely silent on this.[49]

Adding to the Presbyterian ambiguity about the mainstream in the new economy was the decline of communion seasons. Previously celebrations of the Eucharist, despite their encouragement of fashion, had in other ways delivered powerful messages about the sinfulness of the world.[50] But by the 1820s sacramental seasons fell out of favor, and communions became orderly and conformed more closely to middle-class respectability. In Harrisonburg, for example, elders still handed out clay tokens and the worthy sat at special tables, but the ceremony was no longer a season. Instead, the congregation held communion twice per year. The customary offer of alcoholic refreshment to those who had traveled some distance offended temperance advocates, and the courting that accompanied these large gatherings embarrassed reformers. Perhaps the several days of worship plus travel took too much time from work in an emerging capitalist economy. Eventually reformers did away with fencing and long communion tables, requesting communicants instead to remain in their pews, and they scheduled regular, more frequent communions, perhaps once a quarter, which made them more routine and less festive. At a time when the market revolution brought the "vices, follies, and vanities" of the world closer to the Valley, Presbyterians gradually lost one of their most dramatic lessons in nonconformity.[51]

Most Valley Protestants, then, did little to resist fashion. Whether Methodists, who yielded ground in the battle against fashion, or Presbyterians, who never had a strong commitment to simplicity, the majority did not define fashion so that laity had to avoid it.

Standing apart from these compromises with mainstream fashion were Primitive Baptists, Mennonites, and Dunkers. (American Quakers also continued to dress plainly, but by this time the population in the Valley had dwindled.) Believing, as one Dunker wrote, that "If I look like the world, talk like the world, do like the world, and go with the world in its vanities, I belong to the world,"[52] they endeavored to keep themselves different. Not only did these outsiders attack fashion with harsher words than other Protestants, but some of them adopted garb that specifically identified them as outsiders.

Primitive Baptists in the Valley, given voice in John Clark's *Zion's Advocate*, denounced extravagance as inconsistent with both common sense and Biblical instruction. Clark contrasted women who sat at the communion table, wearing "twenty dollar bonnets, fifty dollar dresses and five dollar handkerchiefs," with Jesus, "who had not where to lay his head," and he lampooned fashionable women who refused to teach Sunday school because they needed all morning to ready themselves for an entrance at church. While these admonitions might be extreme-case scenarios, Clark's criticism of jewelry offered commonsense guidance that all laity could observe. Jewelry he condemned as an invention of savages, but he also observed that it was simply bad taste to "burden the fingers with rings, the neck with necklace, and the ear with pendants." The *Zion's Advocate* wondered why wearers of jewelry wanted to attract special attention to their ears, neck, or fingers when Paul had told the faithful not to wear rings.[53]

Mennonites were similarly committed to plainness. Nineteenth-century Virginia Mennonites, however, left little record regarding dress, and those in nearby regions provide a trail only slightly better marked. Mennonites in Cumberland County, Pennsylvania, part of that state's great valley region, appeared noticeably different, "quite foreign," according to one traveler, and those in eastern Pennsylvania generally followed fashion but favored black without the ruffles and puffs. Statements by

Mennonite annual meetings or conferences on anything were relatively rare, but in 1865 a district meeting in the Valley, after discussing dress "at length," resolved to "guard against pride" and to keep the "fashions in their various forms out of the Church as much as possible."[54]

Instead, Mennonites, as befitting their reputation for gentleness, held fashion out of the gathered community primarily through persuasion and role models. In private correspondence they reminded themselves, almost ritually, that the hereafter was more valuable than the earthly life. They warned each other not to "spend time in the perishable things of the world" or that "a man's life consisteth not in the abundance of the things which he possesseth." Contemporaries described a Mennonite bishop as "scrupulously exact in his mode of dress," which "never varied in the color or cut." Male leadership set the example. Sometimes those who left the faith still looked different, as did a Mennonite-turned-Methodist whom Francis Asbury described as "plain in dress and manners."[55]

Mennonites also expected women to be plain. A widely used confession, published in Winchester, advised women to dress modestly "with shame-facedness and sobriety" and unfavorably compared hypocritical women, "who pretend to be converted" and yet obey the "fleeting fashions" of the world, particularly in hairstyles and hats, with the woman who wiped Jesus' feet with her hair. Unlike twentieth-century Mennonites, who adopted uniform clothing with standardized cut and color, the early nineteenth-century Mennonites defined plainness more informally and less rigidly but still distinctly enough to separate them from the mainstream. Moreover, if the evidence of Mennonite plain dress is thin, signs of resistance to plainness are even more scarce. Critics in Pennsylvania charged backsliding, but that movement, perhaps the Mennonite version of croakers, had not yet penetrated the Valley. Internal critics who might provide evidence of creeping fashion did not exist. No one accused Mennonite women of lacing themselves to death. Mennonites wanted to look different as they moved among their neighbors, and in the words of a Rockingham County leader, their garb should be so different that they would be "laughed or pointed at by a vain world." Without creating a list of rules, Mennonites developed a sense of simplicity, exemplified by their mentors.[56]

The Dunkers' campaign against fashion was unmistakably more formal and rigid. In the nineteenth century they became outspoken foes of fashion and freely criticized other denominations for their lack of nonconformity. "So-called Christians," they charged, claim to follow "the meek and lowly Jesus, [but] do not walk that narrow way" revealed by the Scriptures. Dunkers maintained that Christians must be "distinct, separate from the world," and that "their conduct, walk, and conversation" daily contrast with the world's standards. "True self-denial," John Kline asserted, "forbids conformity to the vain and useless style" of constantly changing fashionable society. Although Dunkers were not known for their sense of humor, John Kline told an anecdote that pointed to the folly of keeping pace with fashion. In Kline's story a father bought hats for his several grown daughters still living at home. On the way home, a friend stopped the gift-bearing father to converse, but he rushed off, apologizing that he had to get the hats home before they went out of style. For Dunkers faithfulness meant more than avoidance of worldly dress but verged on hostility to fashion.[57]

Numerous decisions by the Dunkers' Yearly Meeting, often responding to the market revolution's changing fashions, guided laity in self-denial. In 1849 the annual gathering banned fur or cloth caps and fashionable bonnets, and it objected to hoop skirts when they became popular. If fashionable men favored a casual, natural look with short curls close to the head that captured both the classical and romantic spirit, *à la Titus* or *Brutus*, as the styles were called, Dunkers parted their hair on top of the head and combed it straight down or back. Dunker beards were usually untrimmed, without a mustache, because "God made man with a beard," because Mosaic law as described in the Old Testament required it, and because Christ and his disciples wore untrimmed beards. When facial hair became fashionable, Dunkers reasserted outsiderness by criticizing those who trimmed beards "in conformity to the fashion of the world," and when mustaches became popular, Yearly Meeting banned them, too, unless with a beard. If admonishment or denial of communion failed to inspire conformity, whether in hoops, caps, or "high clothing" in general, the annual gathering authorized excommunication.[58]

Dunkers were determined to be separate. Peter Nead observed that a "living fish swims upstream, but a dead fish floats with the stream," i.e., true Christians went "against the current." Yearly Meeting banned a variety of behaviors, including sleigh bells, voting, and property insurance, and cautions against carpets and worldly furniture attacked direct results of the market economy. But limits on apparel were an especially significant contribution to the preservation of Dunker peculiarity because of the visibility of dress. When a visiting preacher of another denomination called the Dunkers "odd people," John Kline responded that he hoped that his fellow brethren would "always be odd."[59]

"When I survey the wondrous cross," sang Valley Protestants, "on which the Prince of Glory died, my richest gain I count but loss, and pour contempt on all my pride." The popularity of Isaac Watts' great hymn attested to the acceptance of anti-worldliness during the market revolution. But when most Valley Protestants tried to clarify "all the vain things that charm me most,"[60] another line from Watts's hymn, real life examples often eluded them.

Protestants interpreted vain things in a variety of ways. Sometimes they delineated the dangerous world so that the burden of separation fell on groups other than the male leadership who created the lines. Restrictions on dancing centered on youth, while dress and sexual morality often pressed women more than men. Only the Dunkers, who regulated the hairstyle of men, and Mennonites, whose male leadership wore distinctive clothing, drew strong lines on male fashion. Other lines, which involved the entire membership, never quite made would-be outsiders different on a daily basis or visibly segregated them from the secular. Eagerly sustained boundaries against fornication and drunkenness may have distinguished saints from sinners—they were the easiest ways to get kicked out of church—but because of the broad appeal of these restraints beyond the faith community, they failed to isolate the church from the world. Individuals, not fellowships, employed temperance to determine outsiderness, except for Dunkers who opposed temperance societies. Sabbath-keeping was genuinely nonconformist, but sabbath-keepers only needed to make decisions one day in the week, which limited this boundary's effectiveness. Plainness asked Christians to make judgments about being different every time they opened their purses or every time they dressed themselves, but most fellowships defined fashion so that their members escaped these difficult choices.

Yet amidst the market revolution clear lines were increasingly crucial. In the new economy goods were cheaper, more plentiful, more fashionable, and harder to resist, and those striving for non-conformity needed higher, more specific walls. Three denominations—Presbyterians, Methodists, and Dunkers—best illustrate the importance of clear definitions of the world for outsiders.

As the market revolution gained steam, Presbyterians lost their most visible boundary against fashion. Holy seasons, while only symbol and ritual, nevertheless had contained vigorous exhortations of vague concepts of outsiderness, but during the market revolution they passed into history. This is not to argue that individual Presbyterians did not live pious lives; Stonewall Jackson gave up just about everything (except war and slavery; see chapters 5 and 6), and religion made a difference in the lives of those who mended quarrelsome ways or who gave up a chance to see a circus. But as a faith community unaccustomed to stark nonconformity in daily life, issues of fashion never became especially important for Presbyterians, and so during the market revolution they struggled to define outsiderness in ways that significantly distanced them from the secular majority, except for Sabbatarrianism.

Methodists could boast, as did one Valley preacher, that "numerically, influentially and affluently" they compared favorably with any other denomination,[61] and, in fact, Methodists migrated farther from the fringes to the mainstream than any other group in this study. Several impulses pushed them along on this journey. As Methodists became more genteel, more polished, more middle class, the disclosure and self-examination of class meetings clashed with standards of polite society, and these weekly gatherings fell into disfavor and lost their ability to discipline. The overwhelming growth of Methodism also made outsiderness much more difficult. A popular movement by definition faces limits on its countercultural potential; the majority has difficulty behaving like a minority, and unity in a mass movement is a challenge. Finally, Methodism's core message and its conversion process made nonconformity difficult to sustain. The theme of forgiveness, freedom from sin, and salvation, plus conversion's suddenness, whether through solitary encounters with the Divine or amidst the fervor of a camp meeting, left little room for anxious sinners to contemplate the changed lifestyle that accompanied the new birth. Converts gained eternal life and freed themselves from the burden of sin, but thoughts about hairstyle or tightly laced corsets were less prominent. New Methodists probably did not encounter the detail of Wesley's *General Rules* until they attended class meetings. It would be a stretch to say that lifestyle was an afterthought, for Methodist preachers often denounced worldliness, but when individuals accepted Christ's call and joined the Methodists, their decision had more to do with the hereafter than the here and now. Sin and salvation, not a counterculture lifestyle, was not the most prominent feature of Methodist conversion. With large numbers of increasingly polite men and women embracing Methodist theology but not necessarily outsiderness, Methodists drifted towards vague definitions of the sinful world and modest-sized barriers overrun by the tidal wave of market-era economics.[62]

In contrast, Dunker conversion was less spontaneous. In the eighteenth-century Methodists and Anabaptists had shared much, including heart-felt faith, a history of persecution, plainness, and the new birth. But they always disagreed on the suddenness of conversion, and in the nineteenth century these distinctions became more pronounced as Dunkers rejected Methodist methods, especially camp meetings and other services that produced quick results and discouraged deliberation. Although Dunker brothers and sisters did not vote on new members, they nonetheless influenced conversion decisions more than Methodist societies, who more or less had to accept anybody who proclaimed for the Lord. Those who contemplated joining the Dunkers' gathered community—and conversion involved contemplation—knew what belonging to this fellowship of outsiders entailed, and they weighed this along with their anxiety about sin. Even the first step into the faith community, trine immersion baptism, signified acceptance of the special ways of the Brethren church in addition to a new life with Christ. Dunker converts understood that with their spiritual rebirth came a new lifestyle that would make them "odd" in the eyes of their neighbors.[63]

With a salvation process that encouraged the commitment of converts to an alternative lifestyle, a past that practiced nonconformity, and small numbers that facilitated consensus, market revolution-era Dunkers altered walls against the world first built in the previous century. For Dunkers the words of leadership and unequivocal decisions by the Yearly Meetings left little doubt about opposition to successive waves of fashion and created boundaries higher than the informal understandings of earlier generations. Dunkers were the only group to specify consumer goods other than clothing or jewelry as unacceptable. Accustomed to being different in daily life, during the market revolution they adjusted to preserve their outsiderness, and in a new era of expanded consumption this adamant opposition against popular consumption took on added significance.

Although condemnation of worldliness was universal, separation from the mainstream during the market revolution was easier said than done. Undoubtedly this economic upheaval brought popular culture closer than ever to Valley consumers, and the new economy made the world a more powerful foe than it ever was in the backcountry. On the other hand, the availability of fashion created new and effective opportunities to resist the mainstream, but only a few picked up that daily cross.

The South's Revolution, I:

The Slavery Debate

O N A LATE OCTOBER DAY IN 1806 Henry Martin challenged John to a wrestling match. John, a slave owned by
a miller in Port Republic, Virginia, refused the invitation,
as he had the previous evening, because he had no money with
him. A bystander, however, lent John fifty cents and held the
stakes while the black man and the white wrestled. (Apparently all
present assumed that wrestling involved wagering.)

John threw Martin. They bet another half dollar, and the slave
won again.

Martin wanted yet another chance, but John declined.
According to a witness, "when Martin pressed upon [John] to
wrestle he positively refused, pushed Martin away and said he was
a slave and did not want to wrestle." But Martin "wanted to have
another fall with him" and enlisted onlookers to urge the slave to
continue. Out of money, Martin pulled out a pair of silver sleeve
buttons and offered to stake them at fifty cents. (First modest
sums of cash, then barter; the market revolution had just begun to
penetrate the rural Valley.)

A spectator advised John, in a voice audible to Martin, that he
had just won a dollar and ought to give a man a chance to recover it. But while speaking he also shook his head no, advising John
to retire.

John claimed that he strained his knee and could no longer
continue.

At this point Martin "caught hold" of John, surprising and
throwing him, then claimed that he had just won a quarter dollar.

They exchanged angry words, and when John called the white man a "damned liar" for boasting of frequent victories over him, Martin had to be restrained from hitting John with a chair. For a moment, then, Martin appeared reconciled, but suddenly he stabbed John with a pocket knife. Martin admitted his responsibility for the deed on the spot, exclaiming "damn his soul if he did not kill" the slave. John had a one-inch wound on his left side and died several days later.[1]

According to a popular myth, slavery was milder in the Shenandoah Valley than elsewhere. In this version of history, the Valley's egalitarian-minded Germans withdrew from bondage altogether, and slaveholding Anglos became best friends with their African-American servants as they toiled together on the modest-sized Valley farms. According to this theory, laboring side-by-side beneath the Blue Ridge produced intimacy, not exploitation, a relationship unavailable on larger plantations further east and south. But the tragic conclusion to the wrestling match at Port Republic undermines this myth, as does the weight of other evidence.[2]

As the unfortunate John knew all too well, the Valley's ruling race behaved more or less like other Southern whites. On one hand, Shenandoah slavery gave blacks small openings to seek self-respect. John had the opportunity to compete physically with a white man, and he had small amounts of money (or credit). But John was aware of his subordinate position as slave, and when he "pushed Martin away," he likely withdrew from a clinch or an attempted wrestling move rather aggressively shoving John in open ground. He was winning and could have gone another round to further humiliate the white man, but he knew that this would come with a heavy price. So did the white spectators, who tried to end the contest. The slave's angry defense of his honor (he refuted Martin's boast of defeating him often) came at the expense of Martin's reputation and escalated the confrontation. It was a mistake; John went too far. First John was bullied, then killed. Undoubtedly, the Valley's mainstream on bondage flowed south.

Nationally, however, the mainstream divided over slavery, flowing in opposite directions. Prior to severing the Union, slavery destroyed the Whigs and divided Democrats, Presbyterians, and Methodists, the latter the largest non-governmental organization in the nation and the publisher of its most highly circulated journal. Bondage became so all-consuming that the six Lincoln-Douglas debates ignored the Homestead Act, tariffs, nativism, and the Trans-Continental railroad to concentrate exclusively on slavery politics. As sectionalism deepened on the national level, moderation receded on the local level, and majority opinion in the Valley defended its labor system with mounting vigor. Although the Shenandoah contained a wide spectrum of opinion that included determined objection to slavery, unusual for the South, most Shenandoans supported bondage. With slavery's increasing position in the spotlight, eventually leading to a Southern revolution, its ability to determine outsiderness through opposition to the political economy and popular culture correspondingly expanded, leaving the Valley's antislavery minority more conspicuously on the fringes.

Although slavery did not dominate the Shenandoah economy, it was commonplace. Overall, one Shenandoan in five was an African-American slave. Throughout the nineteenth century this percentage remained constant, slipping only a fraction of a percent over several decades, so slight that contemporaries seem not to have noticed. This happened while slavery declined almost ten percent statewide between 1810 and 1860. The Valley's rate of enslavement was lower than in the Piedmont and Tidewater, where slave populations were approximately fifty percent of the total population, but significantly higheer than in mountain counties to the west with slave populations of ten percent or less. Within the Valley differences in slave populations were considerable. Page, Rockingham, and Shenandoah counties in the central Valley were closer to ten percent, while Clarke County in the north was nearly half slave, and Rockbridge, on the Valley's southern end, approached one-third slave. All free residents must have known slaves, and interactions with them were commonplace and uneventful, John's tragic fate notwithstanding.

Slaves as a Percentage of Population:
Shenandoah Valley, 1790–1860

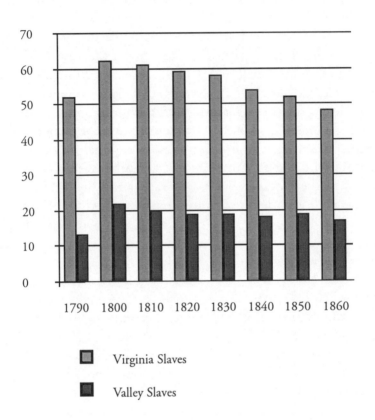

Source: United States Census, 1790–1860.

Although only a minority of the white males owned slaves, slaveholders typically were the wealthy few atop the social pyramid, replicating another Southern pattern. Forges, such as William Weaver's in Rockbridge County, used slave labor, which enabled them to meet competition from Northern operations. Even in the lightly enslaved central Valley, in 1850 five of Page County's six manufacturers used slaves, including an ironmaster with seventy-seven, a tanner with twenty, and a miller with four-teen. Samuel Gibbons, an entrepreneur who built a toll road across Massanutten Mountain and the Blue Ridge and who also served as magistrate of Page County and sheriff in Rockingham, owned sixteen persons. Another toll road builder owned one thou-sand acres and nine slaves.[3]

Hiring out slaves further extended the institution's influence, creating two masters, owner and renter, for each bondsperson. Labor-poor entrepreneurs annually traveled across the Blue Ridge in search of workers in the slave-rich piedmont counties, but some Valley masters also hired out slaves, usually locally. Owners pro-tected their investment by insuring their human property at three-fourths of their value. Transactions took place at the end of the year and stipulated owners' and renters' obligations in detail. Even older children were hired out; one advertisement offered a twelve-year-old boy with knowledge of housework and another offered two boys, aged fourteen and sixteen, for farm work. Francis McFarland, for example, the Presbyterian preacher, struck a deal, incidentally during a severe cold snap, calling him to furnish bed-ding but not a blanket. Masters typically consulted servants before dealing them out for the year, providing slaves with modest oppor-tunities to negotiate although whites almost always held the upper hand. During the Civil War, for example, Stonewall Jackson wrote home with instructions to hire out several of his slaves, including the suggestion that "Albert" should be hired "to any one with whom he desires to live." Critics denounced hiring as the "worst kind of slavery" because it pulled servants from their homes and left them with little stability from year to year. William Hill cut short a ministry in Prince Edward County and returned to Winchester because the congregation raised money for his salary by renting slaves to the highest bidder.[4]

Most Shenandoah slaves, whether hired or owned outright, labored on wheat farms. Whites could reminisce fondly about "waves of fireflies [that] rose and fell" over the fields at sunset just before harvest, but wheat farms involved hard work. Slaves sowed the seeds and harvested, stacked, and threshed the mature crop, sometimes singing hymns to accompany the rhythm of their labor. Between planting and harvest, wheat requires little effort, but masters kept their servants busy while the green shoots turned into golden brown stalks and during the non-growing season. Slaves cleared and removed stones from fields, cut wood and hauled it to town, railroad depots, or sawmills. They removed manure from barnyards and spread it on fields, built and maintained fencing, tended cattle, hauled coal, toiled in gardens, shucked corn, made butter and cheese, mended harnesses, and repaired roads. After farmers cut their wheat, they often grew clover over the stubble to replenish the soil with nitrogen; clover required mowing, raking, and stacking as hay. The wheat farms of the Shenandoah lacked the notoriety of the disease-ridden rice swamps of Georgia and South Carolina or the year-round intensity of Virginia's low country tobacco fields, but a wheat farmer's work was never done.[5]

Keeping slaves on the farm depended on physical force, just as it did in other parts of the South. A Staunton newspaper, the *Spectator*, advocated whipping "as a last resort" to prevent runaways or to force slaves to work. William Weaver, the forge operator, treated his slaves more kindly than others and did not whip; his servants were skilled craftsmen, which gave them negotiating power, perhaps enough to avoid the lash. But if Weaver did not whip his laborers, others might; a slave patrol lashed one of Weaver's bondsmen in the heat of the John Brown hysteria. In another part of the Valley a former slave, Bethany Veney, recalled a beating she received as a girl at the hands of a German-descended blacksmith. After behaving awkwardly around the forge, Veney's master whacked her with a nail rod so hard that she had trouble walking. Bethany's mistress noticed and must have spoken about it to her husband because the next day the blacksmith took Bethany into field and beat her again, commanding her to silence about her punishments. Masters physically disciplined their slaves with few second thoughts.[6]

Despite the best efforts of masters to control their slaves, or perhaps because of this, Valley slaves ran off, and advertisements seeking their return were commonplace. Notices also came from masters from other parts of the state who suspected that fugitives traveled through the Valley to the western mountains or to free territory to the north. Typical was Carson's owner, an Albemarle County master who advertised in Winchester and described his missing property as "a bright mulatto, pleasing countenance when spoken to, full head of hair, front teeth white and nice; several jaw teeth have been taken out." Masters claimed that altruism as well as self-interest motivated them to recover fugitives. One spokesperson for the master class rationalized the return of runaways by asserting that it restored these "poor deluded victims of mock-philanthropy to their abandoned wives and children" and, as a bonus, to a "milder and more congenial climate." But the prevalence of runaways testifies to the conditions of Shenandoah slavery. Joseph Taper, a former slave from Frederick County who fled to Canada, left little doubt about his distaste for wheat slavery. Although Tabor had kind words for "Mrs. Stevens," who during his illnesses "acted more like a mother than a mistress," he bitterly condemned a tormentor, "old Milla," whom Tabor assumed was destined for eternal damnation "where there are nothing but nasty, stinking black dogs a plenty." Tabor pointedly stated that he left Virginia as a "consequence of bad usage," but he assured a correspondent that in Canada he sat "by a good comfortable fire, happy, knowing that there are none to molest or make afraid." Even William Weaver's relatively well-treated slaves ran off.[7]

Slave sales, another burden born by bondspersons, divided families in the Shenandoah Valley just as they did elsewhere. Newspapers carried advertisements for local owners wishing to sell and for slave traders ready to buy. Masters such as William Weaver sold troublemakers down river, and coffles of slaves bound for the auction block moved south through the Valley. Jonas Graybill, an elder with the Dunkers, described the south-bound slaves as "handcuffed on the sides of a chain forty or fifty feet long" with each prisoner "given room enough to walk and to lie down at night to sleep." Occasionally owners refused to sell slaves out of the neighborhood, but more often advertisements for slave sales indicate that families could be split. A twelve-year-old boy advertized as a "good dining-room servant," and an advertisement offering cash for those between the ages of ten and twenty-five show an eagerness to buy children. Another announcement offered two women for sale, each aged twenty, each with two children. The owner offered to sell the women with or without their children, "as the purchaser may prefer." Given the age of the women, their children were likely very young. In another instance, Mary Patrick saw all three of her children sold off at a young age.[8]

In this environment slaves struggled to keep their families together. Mary Patrick's husband, a free black and a tenant farmer, bought her freedom for one thousand dollars. Lucretia, aged thirty-five, ran away from her owner in Bridgewater to join her husband in Virginia's Northern Neck, a region in the tidewater area. Polly Washington's master in Loudoun County suspected that she was hiding in the Valley near her father. Billy, or Will, escaped from Albemarle County, crossed the Blue Ridge, but suffered capture in Rockingham County. Billy had not seen his mother or other family members in over a decade and was headed for Winchester, his boyhood home. When he broke out of jail in Harrisonburg, whites expected him to continue to Winchester. Bethany Veney's master permitted her to hire herself out, which provided considerable independence as long as she gave her master regular income. But Veney's daughter was sold away, and several times her master threatened to sell her and separate her from a son. She found freedom when her employers, copper miners from Rhode Island working the Blue Ridge, bought her with the intention of taking her to Rhode Island and freedom. But she had to leave her homeland in the Valley forever. When Lucy Vesey's husband, Jerry, who lived seven miles away on the other side of the Blue Ridge, was sold, the slave trader offered to buy Lucy so that the husband and wife could remain together, but Lucy's master refused to sell. Jerry then ran off, but after a few days a slave dealer apprehended him. The slaver, seated on a horse, ordered his captive to mount behind him. So defeated was Jerry that the trader sat on the horse with his prisoner behind him in close physical intimacy, confident of his control. Before Jerry rode away, Lucy brought him his little bundle of clothes, stuck a testament and a catechism into it, and shook hands with her husband, never to see him again. Lucy and Jerry had been married for ten months.[9]

The Valley, then, was as typical on race and labor as any other Southern region. Though less dependent economically on bondage than other parts of the South, slavery was nonetheless ingrained in the Valley's economy, and conditions for slaves were more similar to the rest of the South than different. Given the variations within Southern slavery, ranging from Virginia tobacco fields, Carolina rice paddies, Louisiana sugar cane plantations, St. Louis docks, and Texas cotton fields, no region could claim to be truly representative. Bondage in the Shenandoah represents another variation on the theme of American slavery.

In politics as well as economics slavery in the Valley was not overtly overwhelming but nonetheless profoundly influential. On one hand, slavery held little sway over party identification, and by 1840, when the second party system (Whigs/Democrats) came of age, party loyalty in the Valley correlated more closely to ethnicity and religion than to slave ownership. Presbyterians were usually Whigs, and Germans, especially Lutherans but also those who became Baptists, tended to be Democrats. Consequently, Shenandoah Whigs and Democrats both possessed concentrations of strong support. Heavily Scots Irish Augusta and Rockbridge counties consistently gave large majorities to Whigs, yet Rockingham, just to the north of Augusta, and its predominantly German electorate routinely presented Democrats with even larger landslides. The Sixteenth Congressional District, which included Rockingham, Page, and Shenandoah, was almost ninety percent Democratic. Jefferson County, more ethnically diverse and including Catholics and "Yankees" employed by the Harpers Ferry armory, was more balanced politically with a small Whig majority but pockets of Democratic voters. Towns, i.e., Lexington, Staunton, Winchester, and Charles Town, were primarily Presbyterian and so voted Whig, with the exception of Harrisonburg and its Germans, which were Democratic. Besides religion and ethnicity, family connections and habit may also have been influential. In Augusta, for example, almost all of its mayors, justices, delegates to constitutional conventions, and legislative representatives had intermarried, and they were all Whigs.[10]

Yet if slavery and party label had little connection, the South's labor system still sharply influenced Virginia politics. Even before the passionate quarrels over territory captured from Mexico or the debates of the 1850s, Nat Turner's bloody slave uprising in 1831 in southeastern Virginia generated a statewide trauma that quickly entered politics. Turner's band slaughtered fifty-five whites, some of them axed to death. Most were women and children, killed and decapitated as they slept. In retaliation, whites indiscriminately took the lives of guilty and innocent blacks until the arrival of militia from Richmond ended the bloodletting. Fearing that more Turners lurked among their servants, most Virginians resolved to do something about their institution. Typical was Charles Faulker of Berkeley County, who lectured the House of Delegates that no one wanted to live where "such an evil" as slave insurrection might happen. Others suspected that slavery retarded economic growth by promoting inefficiency, discouraging innovation, or even demeaning honest work. Samuel McDowell Moore, who represented Rockbridge County in the House of Delegates, charged that slavery inevitably would "undermine and destroy everything like virtue and morality." Slavery even influenced the statewide political balance of power. Western Virginians detested large eastern planters who used slave-inflated population counts to malapportion the legislature. With these artificial majorities, they then denied badly needed internal improvements to the west. Many, but especially those in the west, including the Valley, concluded that in the long run the Old Dominion would be better off all-white.

On the other hand, some Virginians still objected to any tampering with their institution. Especially in South Side and the Tidewater, where slave populations ran high, masters opposed even the most gradual emancipation plans, and they considered any discussion of slavery as encouraging rebellion. They, too, liked the idea of a white Virginia, but they were more heavily invested in blacks than western Virginians. Easterners, therefore, favored natural emancipation through diffusion of slavery to the west through sales and migration, and they were willing to wait as long as necessary for that to happen. Until then, conservatives rigidly opposed even the smallest changes in their labor system. Slavery, rather than dividing Virginians by party affiliation, drove east apart from west.

In passionate House of Delegates debates after the Turner blood bath, Valley representatives usually sided with mountain Virginians from what is now the southwestern Virginia panhandle and West Virginia. In perhaps the most telling vote, Valley legislators supported a colonization plan to gradually remove slavery by settling free and manumitted blacks in Africa. This would disperse free black Virginians, allegedly the necessary first step towards a reduction in the overall black population and slavery. When the proposal went to the Senate it died, and Valley members in that body split over it, this time four to two against.[11]

Western Virginia's concerns continued beyond the Turner era. In 1847 Henry Ruffner, president of Washington College and an ordained Presbyterian minister, published a widely read pamphlet that repeated many of the familiar western arguments against bondage. Ruffner still chafed over representation issues, but he devoted most of his energies to economic arguments. In a comprehensive survey of agriculture, manufacturing, commerce, shipping, and education, he identified "the consuming plague of slavery" as the cause of Virginia's stagnation, noting that free Ohio and Pennsylvania had similar soil and climate to Virginia but enjoyed growth and prosperity while Virginia languished. In brief, slavery demeaned work, drove out free laborers, "and some of the best of them, too," and replaced them with blacks. Ruffner proposed *post-nati* emancipation west of the Blue Ridge that would leave the current generation in bondage but free the next when it reached adulthood. Nothing would change for at least twenty-one years, when the first slaves would qualify. Ruffner also would allow owners to protect their investment by moving south with their property or selling their slaves prior to emancipation, provided that they did not split families. For blacks Ruffner showed only contempt. He referred to slavery as "black vomit" and domestic female slaves as "black sluts." He thought slaves were "contented" and suggested that most runaways eventually regretted leaving behind a life of "ease and plenty." In Ruffner's view, slavery was a plague on whites, not blacks.[12]

All of this discussion, then, took place amidst an environment of fundamental support for the *status quo*. The debate centered on bondage's impact on white prosperity and security rather than its morality. Nobody demanded immediate abolition; the most radical proposal in the House debate proposed gradual emancipation in principal without spelling out details. More than likely, it would have evolved into a *post nati* plan like Ruffner's, which offered no hope for slaves currently alive, only for those yet to be born. None of the participants in this discussion urged anything that remotely helped those presently in bondage. Although Shenandoah politicians supported colonization and dreamed about a slaveless or all-white future, which differentiated them from slaveholders in more heavily enslaved Virginia or in the deep South, they only entertained schemes that left bondage untouched in the near future. Slavery, then, loomed large in popular politics, and as in slavery economics, the Valley's approach to slavery politics was a variation on the Southern theme.

Slavery's influence on Shenandoah religion was similarly Southern. Like politicians, religious commentators often intermingled energetic defenses of slavery with quibbles about their institution, but these doubts often sound perfunctory. Most Protestants did not include their "domestic concerns," a euphemism they used for slavery, in the definition of the sinful world.[13]

Religious supporters of slavery did, nonetheless, notice the harmful impact of bondage on slave marriages and families. The Baptist Ketoctin Association admitted that masters could break marriages "at their pleasure." Some Valley servants received wedding ceremonies, often simple affairs performed by black or white clergy and without licenses, but apparently not often enough to satisfy the Lexington Presbytery, which still urged performance of the rites of marriage for slaves and recommended that servants receive instruction on the "sacredness and perpetuity" of matrimony. The Lexington preachers and elders, however, voted down an expression of hope that in the afterlife blacks could honor the marriage covenant, an insinuation that in this life they could not. Socrates Henkel, an Old School Lutheran pastor who thought slave families important, responded with anger when a slave who tried to recover her children received a whipping. Apparently authorities pulled the anguished mother from a preacher's home in Tenth Legion, a nearby town and a hotbed of Jacksonian Democracy. Henkel's outrage flowed forth in a poem using the first person and his imitation of African-American vernacular. His concluding verse dripped with sarcasm:

> Tenth Legion is a braggy place
> Were none's to be a king
> Were 'spect is paid to ladies fair
> As you can see in old niggie's case.[14]

Henkel's ridicule reminded readers that blacks, especially "old niggie," did not share in egalitarian republicanism. Religious Shenandoans fretted, within limits, about slavery's potential to destroy black families.

The colonization movement emerged as a popular outlet for these misgivings. Founded in 1816 by influential clergy and quickly attracting support, the American Colonization Society hoped to resettle emancipated slaves or free blacks in a remote location, enabling them to build their own society, far from whites. As indicated by the movement's impressive list of endorsements, including political dignitaries like Henry Clay and Virginians James Madison, James Monroe, and John Marshall, the concept won widespread favor, and the Society managed to establish the colony of Liberia. But the overall transfer of population was small; in 1830, for example, only 259 free blacks resettled in Liberia. Significant change through colonization would be exceedingly slow, if at all.[15]

Despite this extreme gradualism, or perhaps because of it, colonization struck a chord in border areas like the Shenandoah Valley. Colonization proponents argued that blacks in America, whether slave or free, lived in deplorable conditions likely to worsen. Some in the movement doubted that blacks and whites would ever co-exist, but perhaps in Africa blacks could acquire full rights. Colonization also promised to help native Africans, who, according to a Virginia Dunker, lived in "total heathenism, barbarism, ignorance, and wickedness," by populating their continent with Americanized blacks who would spread civilization and Christianity. Moreover, colonization served the self-interest of slaveholders by removing free blacks, whom many whites considered unsupervised subversives. Finally, as sectionalism grew increasingly ominous, colonization provided Unionists with a thread of optimism. Slavery, the Baltimore Conference of Methodist preachers observed, gave extremists a pretext for disunion, but amidst this "rising storm cloud" with "fearful flashes" and the "forged bolt" of sectionalism and disunion, the ministers saw colonization as "a gorgeous bow of hope." In short, colonization had something for everyone; it would save the Union, evangelize what the Baltimore Conference of Methodists called a "continent of savage and barbarous men," bring relief to "degraded" American blacks, and remove an evil from American society, either slavery or free blacks, depending on one's point of view.[16]

Preachers, presbyteries, and conferences repeatedly endorsed colonization until the Civil War made it a moot point. Lewis Eichelberger, a Lutheran pastor in Winchester, published a sermon on colonization and donated the profits to the Society. His text, Deuteronomy 8:18-20: God gives humans the "power to get wealth," was hardly subversive to slavery. In 1819 the Presbyterian Synod of Virginia, meeting in Winchester, endorsed the scheme, and the Lexington Presbytery listened to addresses by agents for the American Colonization Society. After one such talk, the preachers resolved appreciation for the "excellent and eloquent" presentation and endorsed the plan with "full confidence," encouraging churches to contribute. Perhaps the Shenandoah's most energetic colonizer was Rufus W. Bailey, who served as an agent for the American Colonization Society from 1847 until 1851. Bailey, an ordained Congregationalist who taught in Staunton, longed to cleanse his territory of free blacks. To these ends, he lobbied the Virginian legislature for subsidies and goaded local authorities into cracking down on illegal free blacks and deporting them, hopefully to Liberia. In his most triumphant moment, he escorted fifty-five individuals to a ship in Norfolk after influential citizens in Lexington gave them a musical, poetic, and prayerful send-off. As late as the 1850s the Methodist Baltimore Conference annually adopted statements endorsing colonization, emphasizing its capacity to preserve the Union. The political shelf life of colonization was substantial.[17]

But popular opinion could embrace both colonization and slavery—the two were not incompatible—and many Shenandoah Christians confidently believed that their system was Biblical, part of God's divine plan. They amassed a substantial defense of it. Pro-slavery Protestants pointed out that Joseph's enslavement in the Old Testament became a blessing for himself and his family by saving them from starvation. Protectors or slavery were certain that the Bible commanded slaves to accept their situation and to be obedient, citing I Timothy 6:1-5, for example, as Scriptural support: "Let as many servants as are under the yoke count their own masters worthy of all honor" (v. 1, KJV). They observed that Jesus never complained about his hardships, instead he always yielded to authority. To defenders of slavery, the Apostle Paul's rebuke of persons who encouraged disobedience among servants sounded like a command to repudiate present-day abolitionists. Consequently, abolitionist appeals to a "higher law," i.e., the claim that God's law took precedence over civil or earthly law, won few supporters among Valley Protestants, and they denounced higher law advocates as contradicting the Bible's support for bondage. The Scriptures, after all, portrayed slavery as "an innocent relation," similar to marriage or a parental relationship.[18]

With a Biblical endorsement of bondage, most Valley Protestants, including Lutherans, Presbyterians, Methodists, and Baptists, owned other persons and maintained a free conscience. Of these four, Lutherans had fewer slaveholders (and slaves) in their pews,[19] and both national Lutheran periodicals serving the Valley, *The Lutheran Observer*, based in enslaved Baltimore, and *The Lutheran Standard*, from free Columbus, Ohio, were steadfastly noncommittal on bondage.[20] But Lutherans employed the common pattern of slaveholding among leadership. Slavery touched the Henkels, the extended family of influential Old School Lutheran preachers; Samuel Henkel rented one slave for

1860, and Socrates Henkel, who served several congregations in Page and Shenandoah counties, owned a twelve-year-old male bondsman. Two trustees of the Fremont congregation (named after the secular "pathfinder," John C. Fremont) in western Frederick County, near the Alleghenies, each possessed a servant. Owning servants, then, did not disqualify Lutherans from leadership, and considering their concentration in the lightly enslaved central Valley, they held slaves in patterns similar to their neighbors.[21]

Presbyterians, on the other hand, probably owned slaves at a rate higher than their neighbors. Scots Irish, among the earliest settlers in the Valley, had quickly become Southerners regarding labor. At least one of the first preachers on the Presbyterian frontier, John Craig, was a slaveholder; in 1763 a black man sued Craig for detaining him as a slave. (The court allowed the servant to return to his home county to gather evidence, and he came back with a deposition identifying him as the son of a free white woman, bound until age twenty-one, now of that age, and free.)[22] Nineteenth-century Presbyterians were no less involved, and slaveholding Presbyterians were common. Of the twenty-two persons who subscribed to support Winchester minister A.H.H. Boyd, only six did not own slaves, including two who were foreign born (Ireland and Scotland), two who were single, and one modest cashier for the Valley Bank. Boyd himself owned twenty bondspersons.[23] Jessie Wilson, a preacher's wife and a future president's mother in Staunton, confided that when her husband traveled, she felt secure in the manse because three slaves—two women and a man—stayed with her.[24] Further south in Augusta County Francis McFarland preferred to hire his slaves, but that still made him a master, and slaveholders filled the pews of his congregation.[25] The Lexington Presbytery candidly reported that many of its pastors, elders, and members held slaves by choice.[26]

Like Lutherans and Presbyterians, Baptists were part of the slavery mainstream. Just after the Revolution, their leadership encouraged an antislavery witness, but the membership resisted. In 1787 the Ketoctin Association, a Calvinist-leaning group consisting mostly of congregations in the northern Piedmont section plus several in the lower Valley, declared slavery a violation of divine law. When preachers and elders took their resolution home, members objected so much that the association backed down and took no further steps. In the next decade the association placed a plan for gradual abolition in the minutes and asked its member churches to respond, but the action went no further. Similarly, the General Committee, a national gathering, retreated from antislavery. In 1789 the Committee resolved to use "every legal measure to extirpate this horrid evil [of slavery] from the land," but two Virginia associations, both with congregations in the Valley, protested. The General Committee conceded that it had overstepped its bounds but attempted to rewrite the rules so that slavery would fall within its reach. This was so unpopular that Baptists dissolved the Committee, commenting that slavery was more appropriate for politics than church life. Apparently some Baptists, especially leadership, harbored misgivings about slavery, but grassroots affinity for bondage, especially in Virginia, more than offset this.[27]

By the nineteenth century Baptist slaveholding was common. Church books routinely refer to slaveholding members, and sometimes named slaves and their masters in the same congregation. The Buck Marsh membership list, for example, listed all blacks, except the one free man, by their owners, some of whom were members. The Berryville congregation, for example, noted that when "Bro. Nunn's servant Samuel" came before its council and told them that he belonged to another Baptist congregation, the assembled brothers and sisters considered his answers to their questions "satisfactory," and Brother Nunn saw his slave received into the fellowship.[28]

Brother Nunn's Samuel, Francis McFarland's hired bondspersons, and the vigorous Biblical justification of these relationships say volumes about the interaction between Shenandoah religion and slavery. On this issue, most Protestants swam in the secular mainstream.

Not surprisingly, then, many religious Shenandoans assisted with the preservation of traditional race relations. Although white-controlled religion, especially Methodism, included opportunities for African-American expression and esteem, it also carefully limited black autonomy.

Baptists eagerly included African Americans in their cherished spiritual families but withheld equality from them. On one hand, black Baptists were "brothers and sisters," equal at least in nomenclature to white members; this was strong language in a society based on race. When the Berryville Baptists received Brother Nunn's Samuel, the pastor extended to him the right hand of fellowship, a gesture of equality and physical familiarity in a society interlaced with racial caste lines. The Linville Creek whites allowed black members to sit among them during business sessions, although that the council deliberated this seating policy indicates that it was not assumed. Black brothers who believed that they could preach received the affirmation of white members. Thus, Phil, "the property of Maj. L. Butler, came forward and requested an opportunity to exercise his gift in exhortation." The "Brethren" were "unanimously pleased with his gift," but because attendance was so small that day, they requested Phil to preach some other time so that the rest of the congregation could hear him. Black brothers and sisters, just like whites, damaged the fellowship when they were in disharmony with it, and the spiritual family welcomed back blacks, such as "Dunlap's woman Edith," if they confessed and repented convincingly.[29]

Consistent with the terms of the spiritual family, white Baptists needed to be on good terms with black members of the fellowship. In one dramatic example, Margaret Harrison brought to the Linville Creek Baptists a grievance against "Mr. Moor's Joe," whom she accused of spreading a report about one of her family members. Joe was absent, but the charge seemed credible, leaving him with little defense, and the meeting suspended him. Two months later (the fellowship held monthly business meetings) they got around to hearing Joe's side of the story. His version sounded pretty good, too, so they suspended both him and Harrison and appointed a committee to resolve the dispute. In the end, Harrison consented to forgive Joe (the minutes never say that Joe did anything wrong, only that Harrison thought so), and she agreed that Joe could keep his place in the church. But Harrison exacted a price: Joe "shall not have the Previledge of her Wench Dine, as his wife." Joe and Harrison were then restored to full fellowship. Thus, Margaret Harrison, a white master, needed reconciliation with a black slave. African Americans enjoyed status in Baptist congregations that the larger society refused them.[30]

Yet, if citizenship in the Baptists' spiritual kingdom gave black Baptists rights denied in the democratic republic, it also furnished whites with another chance at control. Though blacks were brothers and sisters to whites, the relationship was hardly an association between equals. The Linville Creek committee that mediated between Margaret Harrison and Joe did not consult Joe, and the bargain struck denied him his choice of wife. Furthermore, black Baptists who pushed the bounds of racism encountered resistance. "Brother Daniel," for example, was in and out of trouble in the Waterlick congregation. Daniel managed his master's "affairs along the river," a mark of his abilities and independence, but when he sold a few pounds of bacon, someone brought a complaint to the council that this amounted to theft of his master's property. Despite Daniel's contriteness, he could not fully clarify the situation for the council because his right to sell his master's property was unclear. The church suspended him until one month later his master vouched for his behavior. By this time Daniel planned to preach for blacks, and although the council did not ban the meetings he led, it "advised [him] to be cautious" until the full membership had the opportunity to hear him. Two years later, Waterlick whites suspended Daniel and ordered him to stop the meetings. If white-dominated councils could affirm black sermonizing, they could also supervise black ministry.[31]

White Baptists found other ways to curb black self-reliance. Slaves who applied for membership sometimes appeared with notes of permission from their owners. Masters who planned to move out of the area asked for letters of dismission on behalf of their slaves, as they did for their wives and children, rather than allowing the bondspersons to appear on their own behalf. If blacks at Linville Creek sat among their white brothers and sisters, they did not vote. When "Black Joe" complained about a white brother seated among African Americans during services at Waterlick, perhaps seeking to preserve space free of whites, the council denounced him as abominable ("a balmable") and "gave him a word of admonition." Whites could sit where they wanted, and blacks had no right to challenge white independence. Baptists, then, showed fascinating inconsistency on race by extending the right hand of fellowship to African Americans but keeping them at arm's length.[32]

Presbyterians similarly used the church to regulate blacks. The Lexington congregation established a committee to study black participation in church life, and Stonewall Jackson, a professor at Virginia Military Institute, took this as seriously as anyone by spending his Sunday afternoons instructing African Americans. At three o'clock Jackson locked the doors to the meeting room, an expression of contempt for latecomers. Class began with a hymn, usually "Amazing Grace," the only one that he could sing decently, followed by prayer. Then Professor Jackson read a verse or two of Scripture and explained it, after which class members split into small groups for lessons, led by upper-crust whites. Under Jackson's tutelage, students were examined and graded on the lesson taught the previous week, with results recorded in a grade book, along with attendance and tardiness. Jackson also kept track of attendance and tardiness for teachers. At the close the class reassembled, sang, prayed, and underwent public examination on a few verses from a child catechism published by Presbyterians. Prompt dismissal came at 3:45 p.m. Participation averaged between eighty and one hundred but slumped in the summer when Jackson was away. Jackson's rigid and paternalistic approach notwithstanding, his concern for the spiritual life of African Americas seems genuine; but other Presbyterians were blunt about their use of religion to control race relations. One Lexington resident nervously noted unsupervised blacks lounging on street corners rather than attending Jackson's gathering and suggested that masters force them to attend. Clergy urged owners to bring their slaves to church as parents would their children and not allow them "to wander to other churches, and thus be removed from domestic and pastoral influences." Many whites, including those in the church, simply did not trust uncontrolled blacks.[33]

Sessions and their ability to discipline contributed to racial control. Jim, for example, had been publicly whipped by the magistrate for stealing. (White thieves were not whipped.) Despite Jim's claim of innocence, two members of his session had witnessed his trial and considered the case against him persuasive, so the session suspended him. "Drusilla, (Col. Norman)," appeared before Shepherdstown Presbyterians, accused of adultery. To be sure, Drusilla's behavior was provocative because without "the least sign of penitence" she boldly acknowledged the charges and told the elders that she no longer wished membership in their church. Replying for the session, the moderator condemned the "great criminality" of Drusilla's "wrong to herself, her husband, his family, to the church, to her savior and God," a statement whose strength is unmatched in session records. Bias had allegedly committed fornication and fathered an illegitimate child; for this his master sold him beyond the bounds of the session, but the elders suspended him anyway. "Big Ann," as she was commonly known, behaved so badly that she was sold; the session was confident that her conduct deserved censure and suspended her. Although suspension could not coerce slaves now absent, it had logic because it prevented miscreants from transferring membership to an unsuspecting congregation. Still, sessions pursued this with special vigor for slaves, and suspending slaves reinforced hierarchical race relations by emphasizing that whites controlled the church and that local religious institutions opposed misbehaving blacks as much as civil authorities.[34]

By the antebellum period, the spiritual families of Valley congregations increasingly resembled the stratified patriarchies of secular Southern households. They commonly segregated black worshippers in the galleries.[35] Baptist church books listed baptisms in racial hierarchy—whites first, followed by slaves. For example, a baptismal service on the first Sunday in April, 1842, in the chilly Shenandoah River, administered the sacrament first to "Bro. William C. Alexander," then to "Humphry a coloured Bro belonging to Richard E. Bird and coloured Sisters, Maria and Susan, Servants of Mrs. Burwell, and Fanny, servant of Sister Sarah Castleman, and Maria, Servant of Capt. Jno. Ship." Baptist council dismissed blacks with particularly harsh language. "E. J.

Smith's Nace," a longtime member, refused to commune with his congregation because he thought they had departed from the "Faith and Constitution" as it was thirty years earlier. The church listened to his explanation and deferred judgment, but three months later a committee examined him and recommended excommunication. He had, after all, withdrawn voluntarily from communion, but they sent him into the world "as an Heathen man and Publican." Berryville Baptists applied harsher sanctions against black absentees than white. They required whites who missed two church meetings in succession to clarify "voluntarily" their absence at the next meeting, but obliged blacks who missed communion to explain their "contempt." When this congregation decided to place "our coloured Brethren and Sisters" in the gallery for communion, they asked blacks who disagreed with this decision to stand. When none accepted the dare to challenge the master class so boldly, whites congratulated themselves on the "gratifying evidence that all present are satisfied."[36]

Even the spoken word became a form of control. In a collection of sermons, T. T. Castleman, the Anglican priest in Staunton, used the power of the pulpit to instruct slaves on their role, and, like other preachers across the South, Castleman counseled compliance. He told blacks not to steal from their masters, a chronic complaint of whites, and to obey even unkind owners, serving their earthly masters as if they "did it for God himself." Rewards for these propertyless outcasts would come in the afterlife when the faithful would receive "an inheritance in heaven which shall last forever." But only those who in this world served their masters and God would received the promised inheritance in the next world. The best way for this powerless class to acquire influence, Castleman suggested, was to become role models for amiable servanthood: With "no power to wield—no money to give—no learning to show," slaves, he believed, could "bring glory to God by setting a good example." In sum, for Castleman God's will for slaves was passiveness and obedience to masters.[37]

To be sure, Valley religion undoubtedly included opportunity for African Americans. It allowed slaves to make choices about the future of their souls, one of the few meaningful decisions available to them, and blacks affiliated with organizations that enjoyed much respect in the community. On Sunday morning slaves could decide which church to attend, and if Presbyterian anxieties are correct, apparently many of them parted ways from their earthly master on the Lord's Day. But if Valley churches gave blacks a taste of self-control, religion still helped whites manage them. Congregations reflected the inequality of Shenandoah society, and black independence in religious life made masters uneasy.

Regulating blacks also meant regulating white opinion, and Valley Protestants, like the secular mainstream throughout the South, had little patience with antislavery attitudes. Northern abolitionists naturally aroused a fiery response, often for their alleged misunderstanding of the situation. According to many Shenandoans, abolitionists failed to appreciate that slaves were unprepared for freedom and "unable or unwilling to sustain themselves by labor." Interference from these fanatics—the word most commonly associated with abolitionists—only prolonged slavery by causing so much alarm among Southerners that reasonable measures, such as gradual emancipation, could no longer be considered. Thus, pro-slavery sentiment concluded that abolitionists were the slaves' worst enemy. George Baxter predicted that if abolition ever actually happened, abolitionists would never feel its effects but Southerners would "face unforeseen calamity, including disunion, pillage, and a breakdown of law and order." The South could never let these "meddlers" or anyone else manage its slaves.[38]

Local critics, such as George Bourne, were just as objectionable as those from the North. Bourne, a Presbyterian pastor in Rockingham County, outraged colleagues with sharp criticism of bondage in untempered language. In 1815 he charged that slavery "doomed" its victims to "hopeless wretchedness without end," and he ridiculed slaveholders as hypocrites expecting a pardon for their sins but then kidnapping their "neighbor, his wife, his children, his ox, his ass and everything that is his!" Bourne demanded that the church expel "mansteelers," one of his terms for slaveholders, and he asserted that those who denied that slavery was theft were not real Presbyterians. He especially alienated his colleagues with allegations that several of them had abused slaves. Bourne claimed that one had driven slaves through a town and that another had tied an African-American woman, whom he had raised from childhood, to an apple tree, stripped her naked, whipped her till he was exhausted, and then washed her down with salt. (Jacob Gruber, the Methodist croaker described in the previous chapter, also told a version of this story: a local minister whipped his slaves on Sunday morning, leaving them tied in the cellar while he went off to preach.) Bourne's peers believed that this kind of talk embarrassed all clergy and thereby made him unfit to preach, so they expelled him.[39]

Bourne appealed his expulsion, humiliating his Presbytery on the national level by sharing his chilling accusation of the whip-wielding minister. He also asked for the General Assembly's advice on communing with slaveholders, which his congregation, he said, was unwilling to do. William Hill of Winchester happened to sit on the committee that received these "overtures," and it rebuffed both of them. Bourne nevertheless got one of his overtures to the floor of the Assembly, where Hill defended his home, saying that he just did not believe that a case like the whipping had ever occurred in Virginia.[40]

The affair dragged on for several years, through charges and counter charges.[41] During the controversy Bourne claimed that his security was in jeopardy and that his witnesses—black and white—were intimidated. "I dare not," he remarked, "appear in Virginia without risking my life." The Assembly asked the local Presbytery to reconsider his case. It did, found him guilty again, and in 1818 the Assembly upheld the decision and deposed him. Bourne found a congregation in Germantown, Pennsylvania, and became an active abolitionist. There was no room for him in the Valley.[42]

For Presbyterians defense of slavery was so important that it crept into the division of Old and New Schools. Proslavery Presbyterians liked the conservatism of Old School theology because it encouraged the preservation of traditional institutions like bondage, and Southern slaveholders also distrusted the fondness for abolition within the largely Northern New School. By expelling revivalists, Old School Presbyterians believed they purged the denomination of a dangerous influence on slavery. Indeed, New School Presbyterians in Virginia worried about the presence of antislavery among their Northern evangelical friends, and after the national schism became apparent, they met at Farmville, in the South Side section of Virginia, to affirm that slavery, a "civil and political institution," fell outside the church's sphere. Distaste for the new measures and disdain for abolition often went hand-in-hand and placed most Valley Presbyterians in the Old School.[43]

The Valley's Protestant mainstream, then, sometimes pondered slavery's harmful effects on black families and the Union, and they hoped that somehow colonization could improve the situation without impairing slavery. But most Protestants also considered bondage to be Biblical, used it in their personal lives, and employed the mechanisms of the church to protect it; they never thought of including bondage among the evils of the world. If one side of the coin was recognition of difficulties caused by slavery, the other side was anxiety over control, intolerance of criticism, and the overlap between religion and the interests of the master class. Increasingly this side was face up.

At the other end of the scale resided those who unequivocally labeled slavery as sinful. Sounding more confident, or at least more straightforward, than many of slavery's defenders, who often confessed their institution's evils before shifting into its vigorous defense, antislavery Protestants—Dunkers, Mennonites, Quakers, and United Brethren—avoided involvement with bondage and refused membership to slavemasters. In the growing heat of slavery politics, these fellowships became increasingly conspicuous minorities.

In most cases, tradition and guidance inherited from the national denomination influenced the Shenandoah Valley's antislavery fellowships. Quakers drew inspiration from their eighteenth-century Pennsylvania forebears who stood against bondage in public and inside the meetinghouse, and Mennonites looked to an even more slaveless past based more on practice than protest. (Both are described in chapter 2.) For Dunkers opposition to slavery extended from the previous century when in 1782 their Yearly Meeting had denied membership to slaveholders and participants in the slave trade, and seven years later again approved this policy by consensus. The 1789 decision equated slaves to white servants by allowing baptismal candidates to hold slaves long enough to recover the purchase price, and the stipulation that emancipated slaves were to receive a new suit of clothes, as "is given to a white servant," made the comparison explicit. Eight times between 1812 and 1860 the annual gathering reaffirmed or strengthened its opposition to slavery. Avoiding complex theology, the Dunkers simply concluded that slavery was sinful, that it was wrong to own and trade souls, and that slavery violated the golden rule. The United Brethren in the Valley relied on denominational disciplines enacted in 1821 that prohibited slaveholding "under any condition whatsoever," and their periodical, the *Religious Telescope*, detested slavery so much that it blasted colonization as a devious scheme to sustain bondage by removing free blacks and protecting the value of remaining slaves.[44]

Despite bold pronouncements against bondage at the national level, Valley members of the antislavery denominations fell short of complete egalitarianism. Joseph Funk, a prominent Mennonite hymnist, dismissed an African-American woman hired to help with the housework because he disapproved of her in the house "as a white woman." He thought that blacks should live separately from whites. For Dunkers the custom of greeting each other with a holy kiss and the intimacy of Love Feast, with feet washing and a holy kiss, presented a difficult racial barrier. Some white Dunkers withheld the kiss from their black brothers and sisters, prompting Yearly Meeting to consider the matter three times (1835, 1845, and 1849). The annual gathering criticized hesitant whites but counseled blacks to show patience with the "weak" Brethren, leaving no doubt about which party it considered in error. Yearly Meeting also warned congregations not to assign seating based on race or to deny admission to Love Feast "on account of colour," but in 1849 it allowed local congregations to decide for themselves how to relate to black members at communion, an apparent compromise. Yearly Meeting's policy indicates that those opposed to black participation in church life were a minority, but the appearance of these questions at the annual gathering, three times no less, suggests that the problems were real, i.e., that some Brethren stubbornly discriminated in seating and barred blacks from Love Feast.[45]

Neither did Valley United Brethren or Dunkers give unqualified endorsement to the abolitionism of their denominational policy. Local United Brethren worried about the inflammatory nature of the *Religious Telescope*, which one local newspaper flatly labeled an "abolition paper," and they decided to establish their own periodical. But the United Brethren may only have been concerned about the *Telescope*'s style rather than its antislavery substance, and they never published their own journal.[46] The Dunker preacher John Kline also distanced himself from the abolitionist wing of his denomination. He thought that Northern reformers who demanded immediate abolition were impractical because Virginia law forced newly emancipated slaves out of the state. Perhaps the recent efforts of Virginia Dunkers to emancipate a slave influenced Kline. The fortunate bondsman, Sammy Weir, received his freedom when his master, Andrew McClure, joined the Brethren, and his new spiritual community required him to free his servant. McClure declined an opportunity to sell Weir for fifteen hundred dollars, and Virginia law required Weir to leave. So Weir, also now a Dunker out of gratitude for those responsible for his freedom, departed for Ohio with a suit, horse, saddle, bridle, and cash given by his former master and with another brother riding as an escort, lest someone mistake him for a runaway or kidnap him. With this episode fresh in memory, Kline and other Valley Dunkers had first-hand evidence of the difficulties that Virginia created for emancipation.[47]

Nevertheless, despite hesitance about racial equality or immediate abolition, Dunkers, Mennonites, Quakers, and United Brethren were undeniable nonconformists on slavery. Quakers drew their mark early by leaving. Unwilling to live in a slave society or with slaveholders as neighbors, in the late eighteenth and early nineteenth centuries they separated from slavery by migrating. Shenandoah Quakers tended to inhabit the northern part of the Valley, and, therefore, their typical route west took them along the Potomac, the path later known as the National Road, and then overland to the Monongahela River, where keel-boats eventually floated them down the Ohio. They congregated with other Virginia Quakers in an area northwest of Wheeling and in 1813 established the Ohio Yearly Meeting. Migration devastated the Virginia and Shenandoah Quaker community. Over a period of forty years the South River meeting (Campbell County), for example, lost eighty-six families and forty-three single persons. So many members left Goose Creek (Bedford County) that it closed, or was "laid down." The Hopewell Monthly Meeting in Frederick County lost almost one quarter of its membership in the last decade of the eighteenth century. In 1829 the Virginia Yearly Meeting observed that Quaker membership in their state had dropped precipitously because of "the migration of Friends to other states, where slavery does not exist," and in 1844 the Virginia Yearly Meeting, which organized Friends east of the Blue Ridge, closed and joined Baltimore's. Although cheap land surely motivated Friends as it did other migrants, Quaker settlers avoided territories with bondage and left the impression that they had voted on slavery with their feet.[48]

Dunkers, Mennonites, and United Brethren remained in the Shenandoah Valley, maintaining antislavery convictions while living among slaveholding neighbors. Here too, Mennonites lacked denominational structure to provide guidance, but the only extant comments on bondage by Shenandoah Mennonites are antislavery. In 1837 Peter Burkholder, a bishop in the Valley, wrote that because "all are free in Christ," believers should not be slaveholders or participate in the slave trade. Joseph Funk linked a Presbyterian, slaveholding son-in-law, Jacob Baer, to worldliness, depicting him as someone who "seems to get along in the world fast, but [is] too much attached" to it. Baer's bondsman rebelled, nearly beat his master to death, was recaptured, and sold south. After this incident Funk exclaimed, "How much better it is never to meddle with slavery," and he denounced the slave trade as "a thing which I am very much opposed to—O the unhappy Negro Traffic!" Amidst military campaigns of the Civil War, Mennonites affirmed what they called their "creed and discipline" prohibiting slavery—it was informal and unwritten—and they added a refusal to hire slaves unless the servant received wages.[49]

Likewise, Dunkers and United Brethren also fell obviously out of step with the local mainstream on this issue. United Brethren congregations barred slaveholders from joining, though they allowed masters to recover the purchase price before manumitting, and those already within the fold received admonishment if they deviated from the policy. When Joseph Funkhouser bought and sold a child to a slave trader, the Conference reprimanded him in what one observer termed "an interesting session." Funkhouser does not appear on the list of Frederick County slaveholders for 1860, so either this transaction was all he wanted or could afford from slavery or else he took the words of his church to heart. Undoubtedly many United Brethren in the Valley agreed with the brother who summarized his antislavery lifestyle by observing that "living up to the Divine rule" was never dangerous.[50]

Among Shenandoah Dunkers, the most direct statement on slavery emphasized accord with their unrealistic Northern brothers and sisters and denounced slavery as "evil." In 1853 leaders of the Virginia Brethren had gathered to discuss pressure for abolition within the denomination and its impracticality in Virginia. With John Kline ready for "warfare with such that are of the Abolishionists," they took their concern to Yearly Meeting, which created a study committee to deal with the question of liberating Brethren-held slaves. In 1854 Yearly Meeting approved the committee report, a restatement of the traditional antislavery position, and the following year Virginia Brethren, this time gathering at Linville Creek in Rockingham County, accepted this. They resolved to remove slavery from their fellowship because it was divisive and "dangerous" for the denomination, which suggests yielding to the denomination for the sake of unity, but the short document also condemned slavery as "evil" three times. The gathering also disapproved of the growing practice of hiring slaves and requested members who still held servants to liberate them quickly or to provide for their freedom in a will. Reading between these lines suggests that a few Dunkers still held slaves, but they had a reputation in the area for avoiding slavery and no Dunker masters have emerged from the primary evidence. Complicating the search for Brethren and Mennonite slaveholders was their aversion to membership lists, but the names of their leaders are available and they did not own slaves.[51]

As the Valley's majority increasingly fell into step with slaveholders from other regions, Mennonites, Dunkers, Quakers, and United Brethren occupied the opposite pole by tagging this popular institution as part of the sinful world. They emphasized avoidance rather than reform; Valley members of these denominations understood that slavery was wrong but ordinarily did not march in the campaign to end it. But, they did not speak in harsh racist phrases, like Ruffner's "black sluts," and the antislavery fellowships were more progressive on race compared to the larger society, as suggested by Sammy Weir's treatment and the concern that hired slaves receive their wages. Given the potency of slavery in the Southern mainstream, the antislavery of Dunkers, Mennonites, Quakers, and United Brethren cast them as visible outsiders.[52]

Residing on ground between the poles of pro- and antislavery was nearly impossible, as Methodists demonstrated. The Baltimore Conference self-consciously constructed moderate restraints against bondage, but slavery politics were so intense that sooner or later they buried the Methodists' halfhearted measures.

Early Methodist leadership, beginning with Wesley and Asbury, spoke out strongly against slavery. Wesley denounced slaveholding and the slave trade as barbarous and unjust, and he compared slave owners to thieves, equating "men-buyers" to "men-stealers." Instead of coercing labor, Wesley encouraged gentleness, citing the Golden Rule, and in 1743 he placed a prohibition of buying and selling slaves in the General Rules. Asbury, too, frowned on slavery. He admired Quaker efforts to end bondage, and he specifically praised German areas of Pennsylvania for their absence of bondage. The Virginia legislature's antagonism towards abolitionists disturbed him, but he urged itinerants in the South to preach against slavery, and a trickle of manumissions in Maryland and Virginia encouraged him. Other Methodist leaders, including James O'Kelly and Ezekiel Cooper, criticized bondage, and in 1785 Methodists east of the Blue Ridge circulated petitions to the General Assembly that endorsed abolition. The petition, however, evoked a backlash so severe that the Assembly almost repealed a recent manumission law. The 1798 edition of the Methodist Discipline included a biblical argument against slavery written by the two Methodist bishops, Asbury and Thomas Coke.[53]

Like the Dunkers and Baptists, late eighteenth-century Methodist national gatherings imposed standards against slavery. The 1784 Christmas Conference, which organized American Methodism, adopted a discipline that expelled slaveholders from membership, but it took merely a year to rescind this, responding primarily to pressure from Southerners. Apparently significant numbers of masters already dwelled among the Methodist rank and file. The measure especially stirred anger in Virginia, home to almost half of all American Methodists, and in North Carolina. The General Conference's revised position expressed "the deepest abhorrence" of slavery and stated an intent to "seek its destruction by all wise and prudent means." In the next decade the General Conference banned participation in the slave trade, though allowing yearly conferences and quarterly meetings to establish their own rules on the subject. In the lower Valley circuit rider George Wells expelled two for selling slaves. In 1800 the General Conference required preachers to emancipate their slaves. Yet in the first decade of the nineteenth century the General Conference again straddled the fence on bondage. In 1804 it encouraged slaveholders to emancipate but did not mandate their expulsion, and it printed two versions of the Discipline; the one for states south of Virginia omitted any mention of slavery. At its next meeting in 1808 the General Conference gave ground once more by allowing the annual gatherings of regional conferences to make their own decisions on slavery, thereby giving local Methodists freedom to set their own course.[54]

Local conferences, then, assumed considerable latitude in developing slavery policy, and for much of the nineteenth century the Baltimore Conference, which included the Valley, Maryland, and southern Pennsylvania, took a middle position appropriate to its location, neither fully condemning nor condoning the peculiar institution. Like the Methodist Discipline, these border state clergymen always opposed the slave trade, but they never acted against slaveholding laity, objecting instead to slaveholding preachers. Perhaps a slaveless clergy would become role models, and the Conference needed to keep its ministry free of bondage, lest some of its members be unacceptable to its central Pennsylvania congregations.[55]

By the early nineteenth century, however, only a few Methodists in or near the Valley outwardly disapproved of bondage. One of the most outspoken was Jacob Gruber, who protested slavery as tactlessly as he did fashion. When a slaveholder developed a coughing spell during one of his services, Gruber told him to "cough up the niggers" and his breathing would improve. In 1818, after preaching against slavery to a camp meeting in western Maryland (Washington County) that included blacks, authorities arrested Gruber for encouraging rebellion. Gruber's lawyer, Roger B. Taney, a future chief justice of the United States Supreme Court, won acquittal by arguing that Methodist opposition to slavery was well-known and masters who allowed their slaves to attend the service were fully aware of this. According to Taney, given this, the service could hardly have been subversive. Taney added that it was unlikely that Gruber attempted to incite slaves to violence with 3,000 whites in attendance at the meeting. Although Gruber's passion made him unusual, Taney's defense implied that itinerants still supported antislavery. Later generations of Baltimore Conference ministers lacked anyone with Gruber's zeal for opposing slavery.[56]

To the contrary, the Baltimore Conference, and especially its members in the Valley, grew increasingly supportive of the South's institution. Valley Methodists owned slaves in proportion to the general population; in Harrisonburg, for example, class leader Peachy Harrison and Mayor Isaac Hardesty both possessed servants.[57] John Kline noticed the affection of Virginia Methodists for slavery. After preaching to a Methodist congregation on Sunday, July 4, 1847, he concluded that worldly desires blinded "seemingly good and reasonable people" who justified owning slaves, sometimes even using Scripture. "Seeing," he complained, "they see not, and hearing they understand not."[58]

With few restrictions against slavery among the laity, it became increasingly difficult to keep the clergy unsoiled by bondage. Sometimes clergy or candidates for the ministry became slave-holders through marriage or inheritance. The Baltimore Conference gave these unintentional masters a year to dispose of their bondsmen and women. When Alexander Compton, for example, was elected to deacon's orders, he told the Conference that he expected to inherit slaves in the coming year, but he pledged to put them at the disposal of the district, an acceptable response. Clergy who possessed slave children kept them until maturity, but Conference demanded immediate execution of a deed of manumission. When in 1841 Layton J. Hansberger acquired a family of slaves through marriage, he apologized to the Conference and promised to free the children, if "practicable," after the boy, currently fifteen years old, was twenty-five and the two girls, currently twelve and nineteen, were twenty-three. With this pledge, the ministers agreed to ordain Hansberger after he arranged for the children's emancipation, and they also specified that any children born to the two girls would be freed with their mother. The Conference took this opportunity to reaffirm, by a vote of 142-5, that its members should be untouched by slavery. But despite Conference's wishes, occasionally the web of slavery became too complex to disentangle. Elderly servants, for example, unlikely to have the means of self-support, could not be emancipated. The father and mother in Hansberger's family were sixty and fifty-three years old, respectively, both beyond the age of emancipation. Benjamin F. Steward owned two slaves, one over sixty and the other born blind, bought for one cent each as an act of charity. They could not be emancipated according to Virginia law, and he was elected to deacon's orders. The clergy's accidental acquisition of slaves through marriage or inheritance suggests the depth of slavery's penetration into the laity, and it hints that as Methodist clergy married, more and more they married into bondage.[59]

Sometimes preachers challenged their Conference's policy. In 1840 the Westmoreland Circuit of the Conference complained to the General Assembly that denial of ordination only on the basis of slaveholding was unfair. A committee of the Assembly found that the Conference had the right to choose its own members but that slaveholding alone did not disqualify a candidate for ordination. In 1844 the case of Francis Harding, a Maryland cleric who refused to emancipate his slaves, went to the floor of the General Conference. Harding argued that the servants were not his but his wife's and that their emancipation would force them out of Maryland, separating them from their families. Harding lost. By a large majority the national gathering upheld Baltimore's contention that ministers were subject to Conference and could not do as they pleased. For the first time Southern Methodists tasted defeat in an important vote.[60]

But if Baltimore Conference preachers kept themselves free from slavery, more or less, they increasingly refused to advocate abstinence for anyone else. As Northern antislavery conferences in the 1840s and 1850s intensified pressure for immediate emancipation, Baltimore rejected their circular letters unanimously. In 1844, the same year that it stood up to Harding and his slaves at the General Assembly, all 148 delegates to the Conference's annual meeting refused to receive one of these circulars, and in 1855 an even two hundred Baltimore Conference clergymen unanimously voted against an abolitionist appeal. The Conference was self-consciously moderate and viewed itself as exerting a "conservative influence upon the conflicting extremes" in the denomination.[61] As mentioned earlier, they endorsed colonization annually. But if in 1818 Roger Taney claimed to a jury that Methodist opposition to slavery was common knowledge, by 1850 this assertion was much less realistic.

As Valley Methodists began to think more like Southerners, alarm grew over the significant number of African Americans within their societies. Overall, blacks were approximately twenty percent of the total, which roughly imitated the ratio of blacks to whites in the overall population. Although black Methodists in the Shenandoah did not have independent societies in the Valley, just as white Methodists wished, they formed large majorities in several congregations, such as Shepherdstown, where one in three members was African American.[62] Concerning the few independent black preaching stations in Baltimore or Alexandria, the Baltimore Conference instructed traveling clergy, not local black preachers, to conduct all discipline, love feasts, and classes. Conference bluntly urged traveling ministers, always white, to give these potential trouble spots as much attention as possible in order to maximize guidance and dissuade blacks from developing their own leadership. Discipline of black preachers further reinforced race. The Quarterly Conference at Winchester delegated two of its number to deal with two black preachers who had criticized each other from the pulpit rather than have the entire Conference consider the matter, as was often done with white preachers in trouble. The wisdom of individual whites was more than adequate for black matters. Also, the Conference listed black preachers in attendance separately, as "also present," and without the title of "brother." Methodists further disapproved of black Sunday School leadership. By the 1850s Methodists increasingly paralleled the Baptists or Presbyterians and considered blacks a permanent "source of ungovernable and angry excitement," whether in the body of believers or the body politick. The assumption that blacks represented a control problem and the growing impatience with abolitionists demonstrate that fighting slavery was a rear-guard action in the Baltimore Conference.[63]

Valley Methodism's drift towards slavery was also evident in its reaction to the Methodist schism. When in 1844 American Methodism divided over slavery, the Baltimore Conference stayed with the Methodist Episcopal North, and most Valley preachers kept their congregations in the fold. Only a few societies dissented, and Harrisonburg split; the majority affiliated with the South and defiantly named their new building the Andrew Chapel, in honor of the slaveholding bishop, James O. Andrew from Georgia, whose human property precipitated the crisis. Baltimore denounced its wayward congregations as "violent and revolution-ary" and classified them as "interior charges," meaning that according to the borders separating the two denominations, these churches remained inside the Conference. But the Virginia Conference, which represented Methodists east of the Blue Ridge, was steadfastly Methodist Episcopal (ME), South and probed the Baltimore Conference for congregations with weak ties to the ME, North. Baltimore pastors feared that Virginia preachers who passed through their territory to reach the congregation in Harrisonburg would spread subversion. Indeed, despite the loyal-ty of ministers to their conference, many laypersons in the Valley sympathized with the new Southern fellowship, and between 1841 and 1860 white membership in the Winchester and Rockingham circuits declined significantly, indicating defections to the ME, South, while black numbers held steady.[64]

Black and White Membership
Winchester and Rockingham Circuits, 1841 and 1860[65]

	Whites	*Blacks*	*Total*
Rockingham			
1841	4031	740	4771
1860	2840	732	3572
Winchester			
1841	4598	984	5582
1860	3834	1020	4854

For a few years in the late 1840s the flashpoint for these ten-sions was a small society of Methodists at Swift Run Gap, in the shadow of the Blue Ridge, the border between the Baltimore and Virginia conferences and their denominations. The class at Swift Run Gap voted to go with the South, but the losers challenged the legitimacy of the vote, charging that the seceders' faction had held a rump vote without notifying all members. The Baltimore faction claimed twenty-six signatures of the forty members. The Virginia Conference backed the seceders by accusing the local preacher of neglecting the class and then innocently asserting that it filled a void at Swift Run Gap, nothing more. The minister, for his part, admitted an illness but maintained that the class had always functioned. Baltimore supporters equated Swift Run Gap to a Methodist Thermopylae through which Virginia Conference intruders would have to pass to reach the Valley, and here they made a stand, refusing to surrender the little class.[66]

A few years later last ditch resistance to Southern influence seemed improbable. In 1854 Valley laity complained about the antislavery attitudes of the denominational periodical, the *Christian Advocate and Journal*,[67] and soon the frustrated Baltimore Conference established its own publication. Pressure from Northern Methodists to deny membership to slaveholders further exasperated Baltimore. Finally, in 1860 it threatened to leave the denomination if it ever lost the longstanding ability to enforce the discipline within its bounds, particularly the supervision of slaveholders. On one hand, conference worried about the impact of its secession on the federal Union; if Christians divided, what did that portend for the nation? But despite this appeal for union, the Conference declared out of bounds any criticism of the "motives underlying the relations of master and slave." The church's only mission, the Conference unanimously asserted, was to proclaim the Gospel and save souls, not to question slavery.[68]

At this point, no Valley Methodists argued that bondage belonged to the world that obedient laity needed to avoid. While early American Methodism had been mildly nonconformist on bondage, this emanated primarily from clergy and ended by the first decade of the nineteenth century. For much of the antebellum period, Shenandoah Methodists were content with slaveless clergy, but this became increasingly difficult to maintain. By the 1850s the Baltimore Conference had become so much like the secular majority that the chief protagonists were no longer ME, South infiltrators but abolitionists from the North. If the nation could not exist half slave and half free, neither could the Baltimore Conference, and with each passing year its guardianship of slavery grew.

At first glance, then, Methodists appear to have restructured their position on slavery, but closer inspection unearths a foundation of continuity. The Methodist position on bondage never required anything from laity; only clergy had carried a daily cross. Perhaps even in the early stages of the debate, when the General Conference had been critical of slaveholders, Methodist layperson owned enough persons to put the denomination, or at least its laity, in the mainstream on this issue. Because Methodism had never required laity to differ from the mainstream on slavery, they responded like other Southerners when sectionalism became the dominant political issue. To be sure, slaveholding had grown among the clergy. But, Baltimore Conference ministers also felt pressure from the rank-and-file to tilt south on slavery, and in many ways, the southernization of Baltimore was a bottom-up movement generated by members who had always been comfortable with the South's institution.

The dark storm clouds and lightning bolts that gathered and crashed on the horizon, alarming the Baltimore Conference Methodists, symbolized the growing dominance of slavery in a public debate that became increasingly bipolar. As the storm gathered in intensity, most Valley Protestants accepted the conventional Southern defense of its institution. Although the majority Protestant viewpoint disliked slavery's impact on black families and fretted over slavery's baneful effect, most Protestants rarely dissented from non-religious viewpoints. Many Shenandoans supported colonization and gave blacks a place in the church, but it was usually in the galleries, and the master class ruled in church as it did in temporal life. Its definition of the sinful world never included slavery, and bondage never made the oft-cited lists of sins that described the world. Presbyterians were heavy slaveholders, and Lutherans, although they were not, never objected to slavery in principal nor to masters in their midst. Early Methodists and Baptists flirted with the fringe on slavery, but the uncertain separation they created between the world and themselves wilted when faced with slavery's power. At one point, the Methodists' shift on slavery resembled their altered definition of fashion: just as they never abandoned the war on fashion—they merely redefined it so that laity no longer were effected—so their emphasis on slave-owning clergy left laity free to own other persons. But as sectionalism intensified and slavery increasingly dominated popular politics, the Southern sympathies of Valley Methodists heightened. By 1860 even the Valley's Methodist clergy were ready to secede. Presbyterians, Baptists, Lutherans, and Methodists did not consider slavery a worldly temptation, and so they became nearly indistinguishable from secular currents.

As the majority rallied to slavery's defense, Quakers, German Anabaptists, and the United Brethren confirmed their traditional resistance to this aspect of popular culture and the political economy. For Quakers and Anabaptists antislavery was an old line against the world, first drawn in the eighteenth century, before it became a consuming issue. In the hothouse environment created by the sectional crisis, their opposition to slavery became even sharper, placing them unmistakably on the outside. The times changed, but they held their ground. With one of every five residents of the Valley an African-American slave, interaction with slaves must have been fairly commonplace, and each contact would have reminded those opposed to bondage that on this issue they were a minority. Fellowships most inclined to define outsiderness in daily life were again on the margins.

The South's Revolution, II:

The Civil War

In every place of resort; on 'change, and in the counting-room—
in the shop and on the farm—in the houses of the rich and in the
cottages of the poor—the troubles of the country form the topic of
conversation.

Lutheran Standard, November 11, 1860.[1]

AS THE SOUTH EDGED CLOSER TO REVOLUTION to protect its
system, the parameters of outsiderness changed. In
December, 1859, shortly after John Brown's raid on
Harpers Ferry, Virginia, Levi Pitman, a Republican activist and a
United Brethren, felt the shifting landscape. The local post office
held Pitman's newspapers, including his denominational periodical, "on suspicion," and a few months later Pitman complained
that on another trip to the post office, one "Co. Albert" assaulted
him over slavery "in a violent manner."[2]

Soon all Shenandoans felt these rising temperaments, and
eventually when Confederates and Yankees marched up and down
the Valley, they routinely drew civilians into the conflict, leaving
few bystanders. Enemies were no longer far-off, mysterious abolitionists; now foes appeared, often literally, at the doorstep. The
cause was no longer an idealistic, largely verbal and political
defense of the South's institution but a bloody and increasingly
desperate stand by the nation-state. For individual Shenandoans
this undertaking was traumatizing, and on the community level
the Civil War polarized the populace far more than anything felt
in peacetime. Nonconformists still opposed slavery or dressed

oddly, but after the Valley went to war, these tendencies became secondary. Instead, resistance to popular politics and defiance of political authority pushed outsiders to margins heretofore unseen.

Many Shenandoans recognized that 1860 was not a normal election year. Fractious Democrats met in Charleston, South Carolina, for their national convention and took the unprecedented step of adjourning without a nominee. Stephen Douglas held the support of a small majority, but Southerners denied him the two-thirds margin required for nomination because he refused to endorse federal support for slavery in the territories. Douglas had made popular sovereignty his singular issue, giving inhabitants the power to determine the status of slavery in their territory, and the Southern proposal for federal protection would have gutted this. Delegates from several Southern states bolted the convention, and the deadlocked gathering reconvened six weeks later in Baltimore. At this second assembly Southerners again walked out, this time over a credentials dispute, and the left-overs nominated Douglas. The next day Southern delegates met across town and selected John C. Breckenridge to carry their banner. Meanwhile, Republicans, comprised almost exclusively of Northerners, rallied around Abraham Lincoln, a consistent critic of slavery. Yet another party, the Constitutional Union ticket, a compromise, pro-Union movement built on the remnants of Southern border Whigs and nativist Know-Nothings, nominated John Bell. To most, it was obvious that the survival of the Union teetered on the outcome of this bitterly contested election.[3]

In this four-way contest Shenandoans divided their loyalties threefold. They agreed on little except for Unionism, though that varied in degree, and they held a near-consensus that the first priority was Lincoln's defeat. Nearly all voters believed that Republicans were awash with abolitionism, and they feared that their victory would menace the South with tangible danger. Valley newspapers routinely denounced Lincoln's supporters in racist terminology as "Black Republicans" or sometimes as the "Black Republican John Brown Party of the North." Although Lincoln's great uncle, John Lincoln, had been an elder for Separate Baptists in eighteenth-century Rockingham County before the family moved west, Honest Abe's political base was solidly Northern, and in the Shenandoah he was a non-factor. But after shunning Black Republicans as political untouchables, Shenandoans splintered. Bell and Douglas campaigned on preservation of the Union, denouncing Breckenridge as carrying a secessionist banner for the Deep South cotton-belt, and both portrayed themselves as reasonable alternatives to Breckenridge and Lincoln extremism. Bell supporters, appealing to traditional or "Old Line" Whigs, spoke charitably of Douglas's Unionism but dismissed his candidacy as unwinnable because he had no chance of carrying a Southern state. This was probably true. Additionally, Bell Unionists scorned popular sovereignty, which they denounced for allowing a "handful of squatter" sovereigns to deny citizens their property rights. Douglas's scheme, they alleged, gave "Northern cutthroats and escaped penitentiary convicts" the power to determine what property a "Southern man of wealth and respectability" could hold in a territory. Southern elites had no intention of yielding to the middling sort, whether it held a majority or not. Douglas backers in the Valley said little about popular sovereignty, which was too soft on slavery's defense to appeal to the Shenandoah mainstream. Instead, they focused on traditional Democrats, who were uncomfortable with Breckenridge's deep South ties, and German-Americans, who were uneasy with the nativism of Bell's Whig base. One editorialist labeled Breckenridge's wing of the Democratic Party as the "sofa" party, suggesting that common workingmen had little in common with these genteel politicians. Breckenridge represented the Democratic Party's ardent deep South, proslavery defenders although some local party organizations in the upper South, including Shenandoah County, also backed him. To appeal to upper South voters, his organizers in Virginia cast him in a Unionist hue and downplayed his association with secessionists, but their protection of slavery remained passionate. In Richmond, Breckenridge's men maintained that Lincoln's election would be cause enough to secede, and in the Valley one of Breckenridge's spokespersons accused "Stephen Arnold Douglas" of betraying the party to the Black Republicans.

Valley voters, then, faced a choice between Bell's Whig-based Border South Unionism, Douglas's Unionism with popular sovereignty based in the Democratic Party, or Breckenridge's unabashed appeal to Southern rights.[4]

For Shenandoans Stephen Douglas's visit provided perhaps the brightest moment of the campaign. Although other candidates followed precedent and said little, instead deploying legions of surrogates to talk for them, Douglas broke with tradition and undertook heavy personal campaigning at great risk to his poor health. In early September he came to the Valley, traveling by a special stagecoach, and gave speeches before large and receptive crowds in Staunton, Harrisonburg, New Market, Strasburg, and Winchester. In Staunton the Staunton Artillery, commanded by John B. Imboden, a future Confederate general, greeted Douglas with a multi-gun salute and escorted the "Little Giant" to the courthouse, where a large crowd listened to a speech that mentioned only one topic: slavery in the territories. A Whig newspaper in that town complimented the Northern Democratic nominee as "very plausible and shrewd" but remained unconvinced "that a little squad of squatters from New England, settled in one corner of a large territory," had the right to exclude slave holders from it forever. (This referred to popular sovereignty in Kansas, which the Douglas-authored Kansas-Nebraska Act specified. The editor's opinion notwithstanding, antislavery forces possessed the majority in Kansas.) In Winchester a large crowd escorted Douglas to his hotel, and their cheers drowned out the band.[5]

Douglas's visit exuded rare good will in an otherwise ill-natured campaign, and Shenandoans felt the nation's distress as much as other Americans. In October the Lexington Presbytery detected "political rancor and sectional jealousy" and blamed it on a "spirit of worldliness," noting that only one revival had been reported and that giving had declined. The Presbytery suggested a day of fasting. The growing crisis sent Francis McFarland, the slave-owning Presbyterian preacher in Augusta County, to the polls to vote for president for only the second time in his life. In 1840 McFarland had supported William Henry Harrison, and this time, feeling "great anxiety" over the election, he cast a ballot for Bell, which he pronounced as a "duty."[6]

Francis McFarland, a well-dressed, slave-hiring, ordained
Presbyterian Whig who seceded reluctantly but resolutely.
Source: Howard McKnight Wilson, *The Lexington Presbytery
Heritage* (The Presbytery of Lexington, 1971). Published with per-
mission of the Shenandoah Presbytery.

Despite the reconfigured party system and anxiety-soaked
political landscape, many Shenandoans voted according to normal
political loyalties. Breckenridge, allegedly the Southern extremist,
carried the lightly enslaved but traditionally Democratic
Shenandoah County, while Bell not surprisingly took Augusta and
Rockbridge, Whig bastions. McFarland's duty-bound ballot for a
former Whig was routine for a Presbyterian in one of the most

Whiggish counties in the state. On the other hand, Bell took
Rockingham and Page, normally Democratic, indicating the
beginning of fissures in the party system. Local newspapers did
not include Lincoln's vote totals in their reports. Overall, Bell
handily defeated his two opponents in the Valley, garnering fifty-
one percent to Breckenridge's thirty-one percent and Douglas's
eighteen percent. Bell carried the state by .1% over Breckenridge.[7]

Results of the Election of 1860
Shenandoah Valley Counties[8]

	Bell	Breckenridge	Douglas
Augusta	2558 (66%)	218 (6%)	1094 (28%)
Clarke	288 (43%)	335 (50%)	49 (7%)
Frederick	963 (41%)	1315 (56%)	66 (3%)
Jefferson	959 (52%)	458 (25%)	440 (24%)
Rockbridge	1201 (55%)	344 (16%)	643 (29%)
Rockingham	1349 (47%)	876 (30%)	667 (23%)
Page	937 (81%)	141 (12%)	75 (7%)
Shenandoah	412 (19%)	1598 (75%)	134 (6%)
Warren	276 (56%)	141 (29%)	75 (15%)
Totals	8943 (51%)	5426 (31%)	3243 (18%)

With Lincoln's election and the quick secession of deep South
states, beginning with South Carolina soon after the election,
Valley residents discerned the winds of war gathering momentum.
On November 20 McFarland went to Staunton to "pass off" ten-
dollar notes from North and South Carolina banks because they
had depreciated. John Clark, the Primitive Baptist from Front
Royal, also worried about the value of paper money and asked
subscribers to the *Zion's Advocate* to pay in Virginia bank notes,
gold coin, or postage stamps. John Kline assumed that "secession
means war, and war means tears and ashes and blood." He was
convinced that the coming conflict would bring suffering for the
Brethren.[9]

Denominational journals that for years had avoided sectionalism could no longer escape the issue, evidence of the new heights

of divisiveness achieved by slavery politics. The *Lutheran Standard* worried about "fratricidal" civil war and division that might come to the church. It censured abolitionists but emphasized prayer's ability to overcome demagoguery and pull the nation through this crisis. The *Standard's* New School rival, the *Lutheran Observer,* could not resist pointing out that those who participated in the excitement of a political gathering had no business complaining about enthusiasm in worship, but it nevertheless concluded with the *Standard* that too many expected God to intervene and prevent the violence.[10]

Most in the Valley agreed with the Lutheran journals and hoped for a peaceful solution to the crisis, but they remained unwilling to budge on slavery. A.H.H. Boyd, a New School Presbyterian minister in Winchester, sounded like a fire-eater—a Southern zealot—as he clarified the situation for his congregation in a Thanksgiving sermon. He blamed the mess directly on Northern extremists. He passionately denounced abolitionists— "wretched" fanatics he called them—for using their numerical majority to elect a president with no qualifications except open hostility to slavery, and he charged that Northerners attacked the Constitution by subverting the fugitive slave law, which he claimed was designed to "carry out the spirit and letter of the Constitution." If the North would only cease its attack on the fugitive slave law and "its unreasonable and maddened assaults upon our domestic relations," i.e., the John Brown raid, Boyd predicted that fraternal relations with the North would return. But he also warned that if runaways continued to be a problem, then he preferred "peaceful separation" to the "humiliating, degrading position" of vassalage to a Northern majority that ignored "constitutional obligations."[11]

Stonewall Jackson, with calmer but no less determined words, similarly hoped for peace with slavery. He opposed secession for the moment but warned that if the free states continued to deny basic Constitutional rights—if the North attempted to "subjugate" the South and "thus excite slaves to servile insurrection"— then war became the only option. He remained hopeful that Northerners were more committed to the Union than to "their peculiar notions of slavery." Jackson left no doubt that he was committed to his notions of slavery.[12]

In February, 1861, Virginia inched closer to separation from the Union with local elections to select delegates to a state convention on secession. McFarland, until recently a self-proclaimed unpolitical man, now braved snow to attend a local political gathering. In late January he traveled to Staunton in a sleigh—it was "not good sleighing," he reported, despite over six inches of snow on the ground—to hear candidates for the state convention. McFarland described the crowd as the largest he had ever seen in Staunton. The statewide results of the special election demonstrated the reluctance of most Virginians to secede at this moment; less than one-third of the elected delegates supported disunion, and only the Tidewater and Southside counties, with large slave populations, voted for candidates favoring immediate secession. In the Valley only heavily Democratic Shenandoah County showed a majority for withdrawal from the Union. That a county with so few slaves sent immediate secessionists to the convention suggests that opinion had not yet fully hardened and that traditional party loyalties still counted for something. Most in the Valley yet hoped to preserve both slavery and the Union, but they viewed these goals as increasingly incompatible.[13]

As the nation drifted towards destruction, Valley Christians turned to prayer. McFarland "rejoiced" at lame duck President James Buchanan's call for a day of prayer and fasting on Friday, January 4, 1861. McFarland held a service, which was well-attended, and noted approvingly that four elders had prayed "appropriately." In Lexington the *Valley Star* endorsed Buchanan's request and urged businesses to close between ten o'clock and two o'clock so that citizens might express "their anxiety for the public peace and welfare." John Clark, on the other hand, criticized Buchanan's request as improper interference by the government in worship, but he nevertheless urged cooperation. Clark considered the situation so grave that the "nation should be clothed in sack cloth and ashes," regardless of whose idea it was.[14]

While the Old Dominion waited before withdrawing from the Union, Valley Methodists, meeting in Staunton, adopted their own version of secession several weeks prior to Fort Sumter. The final straw for many in the Baltimore Conference came over an ordination issue. When a candidate for the ministry objected to a recent antislavery resolution passed by the General Conference, which met in Buffalo, New York, Baltimore Conference Bishop Levi Scott then refused him ordination. Scott explained that he could not ordain anyone who took exception to any portion of the Discipline, slavery or otherwise. The matter was delegated to a committee, which recommended withdrawal from the denomination. The committee complained that the action of the General Conference had censured "many pious members of our church holding slaves, and slandered the memories of the pious dead." Public opinion also weighed heavily on the Conference. Simply put, preachers tied to a Northern denomination increasingly struggled to win the hearts and minds of laypersons who were Southern. The Baltimore preachers complained that since the Methodist schism in 1844 slavery agitation had made mission work and cooperation with other Methodists in Virginia more difficult. Several times the committee's resolution mentioned that withdrawal would better enable preachers to perform their duties, a point underscored by memorials to Baltimore from angry proslavery laity. Lay activity like this was uncommon, emphasizing the depth of feeling, and this time a lay gathering met concurrently with Annual Conference. With pressure from both laypersons and national events, the meeting must have been emotional. Conference sang the "Doxology" to give thanks for a unanimous vote to receive the committee's report, but Bishop Scott refused to put the withdrawal resolution on the floor so the Secretary performed this parliamentary chore. The final vote to withdraw from the ME, North passed with eighty-seven votes against only one in the negative, but forty-three preachers voted "present." A minority protested the decision but the minutes do not include their words, and the minutes took the unusual step of listing by name the recorded vote.[15]

Thus, Shenandoah Methodists left their denomination over a secular cause. As the nation focused its attention on a beleaguered federal outpost in Charlestown harbor, sectionalism loomed larger than any previous markers that had identified religious tradition or separated outsiders from popular culture.

The events feared by Clark, McFarland, Kline, the Lutheran periodicals, and so many others occurred quickly after the bombardment of Fort Sumter, a turning point that contemporaries recognized immediately. "Civil war was inaugurated today at Fort Sumter," one diarist matter-of-factly concluded.[16]

Lincoln's call for volunteer troops to subdue the rebellion promptly pulled the Valley's mainstream squarely behind the Confederacy and its war effort. A few days after the conflict's first shots, John Clark, mixing prophetic observation with financial self-interest, blamed "the powers that be" for making war all but inevitable and begged those who owed him for a subscription or hymnal to pay promptly due to the uncertainty of the mail. Six days after Sumter, Francis McFarland's son received orders to march to an unknown destination. "O God, watch over my dear son," the anxious father prayed. His son wound up at Harper's Ferry. That same afternoon McFarland, along with a Methodist preacher, prayed for other people's sons when a company of troops marched out of Lexington, tears flowing freely. Meanwhile, Levi Pitman was arrested and taken before the magistrate on suspicion of being an abolitionist. Pitman was an obvious target; he voted for Lincoln, served as a Republican elector, and attended the inauguration where he met the president and Vice President Hannibal Hamlin. No charges were brought, but the magistrate advised Pitman to leave the state within several days. Instead, the next day Pitman went to a lawyer to take an oath of allegiance, which included a pledge never to "agitate directly or indirectly the subject of abolition."[17]

On April 17 the Virginia convention passed a secession ordinance, and in late May Virginians went to the polls once more to ratify the convention's decision. The 1860 presidential election and the early 1861 selection of convention delegates had disappointed secessionists, but this time they won overwhelmingly. The entire Confederate government had already arrived in Richmond, so the outcome of the election was hardly in doubt. The Valley, heretofore hesitant about disunion, now gave it large, sometimes unanimous, majorities. McFarland cast his ballot for secession, "the most painful vote" ever for him, but he felt that Lincoln's use of force against the South left him with little choice. He confided that "I mourn in bitterness over the state of things, but Virginia did all she could for peace." Widespread intimidation forced the few remaining Unionists into staying home and made the voters' verdict appear nearly unanimous. One non-voter complained that secessionists returning from the polls cursed him as a "damned black Republican and other like names," and many Dunkers and Mennonites reported threats, usually hanging, if they did not "vote the Secesh" ticket. A few Mennonites and Dunkers cast anti-secession votes, but armed men brought them back to the polls to change their ballots. Pitman managed to vote against secession but went into hiding after a warning that his ballot placed him in danger. He stayed with friends and relatives for two weeks before returning home.[18]

Now Valley Protestants responded to the calls for days of fasting and prayer from Jefferson Davis rather than a federal president. At a special Thursday prayer service in June, McFarland found his congregation "uncommonly large" with a gallery filled with African-American slaves. He called it a "solemn meeting," and normal business was suspended. Later that afternoon McFarland attended another service nearby, which was also full, while other worshippers met at a schoolhouse in the neighborhood.[19]

After years of relative silence on slavery, John Clark exploded. No war hawk, Clark dreaded the coming conflict and appealed for peaceful separation, similar to that between Abram and Lot, rather than war. Clark's home in Front Royal, only thirty-five miles from Harper's Ferry and the Potomac River, was a likely battleground, and he understood that the war's winner would gain little. Clark was also concerned about losing Northern subscribers, and he called for new patrons to replace them, paying in advance. For causing the catastrophe, he laid blame squarely on two devils: benevolent institutions and Yankees. For several decades, he declared, Primitive Baptists had identified benevolent institutions, especially mission societies, as evil; and now that another of them—abolitionism—gained political power, the government faced destruction and calamity hovered on the horizon. At fault, according to Clark, was the "Puritan spirit of New England," the same fanaticism that "burned and hung Baptists and Quakers and banished Roger Williams," a fellow Baptist. Now the current version of this zealotry, "abolitionized Yankees," again attempted "to dictate what other people should believe." But Clark also reflected public opinon on slavery. The Republican Party, he further charged, violated the spirit of the Constitution and was willing to employ any means, including war, to achieve its goals. He accused the governor of Massachusetts of approving John Brown's attempted "murder" of Virginians, and Clark predicted that Lincoln would wage a war of extermination against the South and give confiscated property to "land pirates and robbers." Bent on the oppression of free men, these "incarnate devils" left little choice but resistance. Clark suggested a China-like wall, so that Virginians would "never again have any intercourse with Yankeedom." Suddenly, the Primitive Baptists seemed much more mainstream.[20]

Dunkers, too, learned that the crisis quickly involved them. Coincidentally, they had scheduled their 1861 Yearly Meeting for the Shenandoah during the traditional time of late April, or Pentecost. But as the gathering approached, their national periodical questioned the safety of meeting in the South and suggested a change of venue. Angry Virginia leaders, writing in late February, conceded the "excitement that exists in the government" but refused to relocate the meeting. They accused the editor of fomenting sectionalism among the Brethren and denied that the Valley was unsafe, pointing out that it would be just as dangerous for them to travel north as for Northern Dunkers to journey south. Therefore, soon after Methodists met in Staunton to withdraw from the Methodist Episcopal, North, 3500 Dunkers held their Yearly Meeting in Rockingham County, but only four northern congregations sent representatives.[21]

Departed sons, election fraud, prayer days, endangered subscriptions, and a controversial conference disrupted life almost immediately. It would get worse.

Once the war began, the Southern cause shifted from defending its way of life to defending its national life, and the demands of a nation-state clinging to survival displaced cherished pre-war concepts, such as states' rights and agrarianism. The Confederacy no longer embodied a sectional movement but had become a nation with its own set of laws, officials, heroes, and obligations, including taxes, wartime economic management, and conscription. Even slavery took a backseat to the nation-state when, late in the war, Confederate officials considered offering abolition in exchange for English intervention or emancipating slaves who volunteered to serve as Confederate soldiers. Life-and-death defense of the cause, i.e., Confederate nationalism, exacted a frightful price on all Shenandoans, both center and periphery, and stretched the gap between outsiders and mainstream wider than ever.[22]

The Shenandoah was an active front throughout the war. It was the most productive wheat area in the Upper South, and three major east-west railroads cut across the area. For previous generations the Shenandoah had served as a natural artery for immigrants, and during the Civil War it became a highway for invaders, allowing Southern troops to threaten Washington and Yankees to jeopardize supply lines to Richmond. Armies fought hundreds of skirmishes, a dozen major battles, and two major campaigns there.

Perhaps the best-known campaign occurred in 1862 when Stonewall Jackson launched a series of diversionary attacks in the Valley to prevent Union troops from reinforcing the Richmond front. In an oft-studied series of battles against divided but larger forces, Jackson employed quick marches and clever tactical retreats to win battles in the mountains west of Staunton and at the head of the Valley near Front Royal and Winchester. President Lincoln ordered federal armies to converge on the troublesome Confederates, but Jackson speedily retreated back up the Valley, escaping a trap through battles at Port Republic and Cross Keys and then crossing the Blue Ridge to join General Robert E. Lee's forces at Richmond.

Winchester suffered another battle in June of 1863, but the middle and upper Shenandoah gained a breathing spell that summer as Lee marched into Pennsylvania. In 1864, however, the dogs of war returned when Northern troops attempted to prevent Confederate troops in the Valley from interfering with a planned assault on Richmond. Southern troops, reinforced by cadets from the Virginia Military Institute in Lexington, repulsed the Northern invaders at New Market, but the enemy soon returned and moved quickly up the Valley, looting and burning much along the way, including VMI. Lee dispatched an army under Jubal Early, who drove the intruders into West Virginia. With the Valley now barren of Yankee troops, Early attempted to replicate Jackson's 1862 campaign by marching into the northern Shenandoah. He crossed the Potomac and menaced the outer defenses of Washington, D. C. before retreating. Several weeks later, Early again ventured into Union territory, this time burning Chambersburg, Pennsylvania. General Ulysses S. Grant ordered Philip Sheridan after Early, and he drove the Confederates back up the Valley.

In the war's final stages, terror rose to new levels. As Sheridan moved south, chasing Early deeper up the Shenandoah, guerrilla bands harassed his column from both sides. Some attackers belonged to recognizable units in the Confederate army—the best known was Major John Mosby's 43rd Virginia—but others were bushwackers who shot stragglers or soldiers who wandered too far from camp and attacked lightly defended wagon trains. Union soldiers were outraged that sometimes these irregulars cut down men who attempted to surrender or hung Yankees caught burning houses. An angry Sheridan ordered the death of all bushwackers and guerrillas, including anyone in civilian clothes with a weapon when captured, making no distinction between Confederate partisans and freelancers who were little better than outlaws. At one point both sides took the lives of several prisoners in a tit-for-tat exchange. In one of the most tragic scenes, federal troops executed Henry C. Rhodes, a seventeen-year-old resident of Front Royal who just that morning had borrowed a neighbor's horse to join in the adventure. The teenager was captured in a fight that claimed the life of a Yankee officer, who was probably shot while trying to surrender. Angry Yankees killed six prisoners, including Rhodes, as revenge. Rhodes's captors dragged him into town terrified and nearly unconscious between two horses, then into a pasture where a cavalryman emptied a revolver into him as his frantic mother watched. This was war without restraint.[23]

By this point, food had become a strategic commodity, and Grant directed Sheridan to turn the Valley into a desert. "Do all the damage to crops you can," Grant instructed. Previous invading Northern armies had largely ignored agricultural produce, but now Grant ordered Sheridan to "carry off stock of all descriptions, and negroes, so as to prevent further planting." If the war continued another year, Granted wanted the Valley to "remain a barren waste." Sheridan followed his orders. Eyewitnesses reported "great columns of smoke rising like dark clouds almost from one mountain to the other" and "a dense blanket of smoke and fog." With the Valley in ashes and his mission accomplished, Sheridan withdrew north, and except for guerrilla activity, the campaign ended on October 19, 1864, when Sheridan all but destroyed Early's army at Winchester. The Valley's last battle was fought on March 2, 1865, at Waynesboro. It was, one Michigan trooper observed, a "hard war."24

Because the home front and military front commingled so closely, the war became an especially searing experience for Shenandoans. Endangered sons, invading armies, plundering soldiers, and scorched earth policies disrupted life for countless civilians in the Shenandoah Valley.

Little could be done about the torn lives and damaged property, but religion often offered spiritual balm for the tattered nerves. Prayer meetings were common and provided solace for the weary of heart. During the 1864 campaign season Lexington Presbyterians prayed every afternoon at 4 :00 p.m. in well-attended services. Lucy Buck, a teenager in Front Royal, noted several sermons that soothed her soul. At a funeral, for example, with cannon audible in the distance, the preacher spoke on "I will patiently bear the indignation of the Lord for I have sinned against Him and He will deliver me." On another occasion Lucy attended church just after Confederates had evacuated the town but before the Yankees arrived. Prior to the service, a cousin leaned over the pew to share the latest rumor: the Union military governor of the region had ordered the arrest, imprisonment, and possible execution of all able-bodied men who refused service in the cause of the Union. Lucy confided that this proved "one drop too many" in her "cup of sorrow," and when the congregation sang the opening hymn, "How Firm a Foundation," a childhood favorite, she wept. But Lucy composed herself and listened to a "comforting" sermon on "Let not him that girdeth on his armor boast as him that putteth it off," a defiant message of support for those who might resist the latest Yankee outrage. Buck "felt quite calm" by the end of the service.[25]

Nonetheless, it must have been particularly unsettling when the fighting suddenly intruded on worship. In May, 1863, for example, news of recent fighting quickly ended a service. Lexington's residents were aware that a major battle had just been fought, but they knew little else except that Generals Jackson and A. P. Hill had been wounded. Almost everyone had a son in the battle—wherever it was—and many families had several sons involved. The town spent a few days in suspense waiting for news. The mail finally arrived just as Presbyterians began a service (Sunday mail?), whereupon the preacher dismissed the congregation. A few months later in the same congregation an announcement that women must go home and immediately make 250 haversacks halted another service.[26]

Sons serving on the front lines were not especially distant, and the close proximity of children in danger brought the war home in a unique way. Occasionally, parents made the trip to aid wounded sons or to retrieve their bodies, sometimes with hearses. When James Preston received the news that his son, Frank, had been severely wounded at a battle at Winchester, he left within two hours, knowing only that his child had a broken arm and a ball in his side. After hitching a ride to Winchester in an ambulance, he found Frank, now an amputee with his arm gone at the shoulder. Advancing federal troops left Preston only about thirty-six hours with his son, and he was obliged to leave Frank behind, soon to be a prisoner of war. This story, however, ended on a happy note; two and one-half weeks later Frank surprised everyone by walking into the Preston dining room while the family was at dinner. The Yankees had treated him kindly and operated on him again. Then they sent him to a residence outside the lines to recover, and the women who nursed him arranged for his escape.

But one family member was absent from this joyous home-coming. Another son, Willy, had answered a call-up two or three hours before Frank's arrival, and soon the family heard that Willy had been mortally wounded at Manassas. Again Preston left home quickly, planning to travel all night in order to catch a train in Staunton ("take the cars tomorrow morning"). When Preston reached the northern Virginia battlefield, he learned that Willy had been buried for five days. Uncertain as to Willy's grave, he had one dug up. When he opened the blanket and unwrapped the body, the face was so disfigured that identification was impossible, but he opened the shirt and found "W. C. Preston" where his wife had written it. An attempt to cut a lock of hair failed when the memento crumbled to the touch. Unable to remove the body, he marked it for later retrieval.[27]

Jacob Hildebrand, a Mennonite from Augusta County, had a similar experience. Hildebrand's son, Gideon, joined the Confederate army. In the dying days of the war a friend brought Gideon's horse home and informed the family that six days previously Gideon had been wounded behind the lines near Petersburg, Virginia, by an accidental shot. The friend had stayed with the younger Hildebrand for a day, then left to escape the advancing Yankees. Hildebrand went for his son, but upon arrival he learned that Gideon had died two weeks earlier, the day after he was injured. Gideon was buried without a coffin, so Jacob dug him up, made a coffin, and reburied him. Two weeks later, Hildebrand recovered Gideon's body again and brought it home for a funeral and burial in the Mennonite graveyard.[28]

When invaders appeared in the neighborhood, rendering the home front and the military front indistinguishable, Valley residents came face-to-face with the war. In these times plunderers added to the trauma of war. In Harrisonburg neighbors gave their valuables to a Unionist, Mary Lamb, for safekeeping. Lamb, an immigrant, was a community charity case. Her husband was an invalid with an illness that left him blind, crippled, and frequently deprived of his mental capacities, and Mary supported her family, including two children, as a housekeeper. Both sides showed her compassion. Others, however, were much less fortunate. During the 1862 campaign German American troops serving in the Union army earned an especially ugly reputation for robbing civilians. A Union officer admitted that they straggled from their units "for miles on each side of the road" and pillaged "every house, smokehouse, milk house, chicken house, kitchen, barn, corncrib, and stable and clean out everything, frequently opening drawers, trunks, bureaus, etc., leaving women and children crying behind them." Their standard reply to all complaints was "*Nix forstay*" [*nichts versteh*—I don't understand]. By the end of the war invading troops of all stripes, not just the ill-disciplined Germans, were a pestilence. When units encamped on farms, officers some-times posted guards at the house, but the barn, smoke house, and stock often fell prey to plunderers. But in the worst situations, which became increasingly commonplace as the war continued, plunderers roamed the house, rummaging kitchens, cupboards, clothing, trunks, and whatever else attracted their attention, tak-ing what they wanted, and invading privacy at will.[29]

For the master class, runaways added to the property loss and social upheaval. To be sure, some slaves assisted whites in protect-ing their homes and property from the blue scourge; one slave woman, for example, concealed a five-pound sack of sugar under her clothing. Many slaves, however, took advantage of the near-ness of Union armies to escape. David and Susan Coiner had eight slaves on their Augusta County farm when the war started, but by 1864 six were gone. In Rockingham County Joseph and Abigail Coffman lost all eleven of their slaves, who before running off told the Yankees where to find the Coffmans' stock. (Abigail Lincoln Coffman was Abraham Lincoln's first cousin once removed; her father and Lincoln's grandfather were brothers.) Reunion with family members served as a powerful motivation for some run-aways. William Braxton, who was already free, sent the Yankees to a farm to retrieve his family. Sometimes masters recognized the impending danger and took steps to protect their slave property. Isaac Hardesty's slaves lost any chance of quick emancipation when he moved to Georgia, taking his six bondspersons with him. Early in the war Frank B. Jones, who served on Jackson's staff, wrote home expressing hope that his overseer would manage effec-tively because if his slaves grew "dissatisfied," Jones expected them to attempt escape, and he feared that they would succeed. But many slaves caught their owners by surprise. One morning in June, 1863, Lucy Buck, a teenager in Front Royal, woke up to find no fire, no water, and no "movement whatever below stairs." All the slaves had run off that night with their best clothes and the Bucks' three horses, effectively concealing their intentions from the whites. The loss of slave labor forced the Bucks into performing much of their own labor, an arduous adjustment: "Oh such a weary time as we had of it," Lucy complained that day to her dairy, "the stove *wouldn't* get hot, the bread *would* not bake, and the cows *would* run" (Lucy's emphasis). William Mason Buck, Lucy's father, estimated his loss at $16,000, including the horses and the slaves. When he found the runaways in Winchester, they explained that they left after overhearing conversation that they would be sold south. (The Bucks vehemently denied this.) Buck recovered two of his horses, but Union authorities gave the other to the fugitives as compensation for wages owed, and his slaves eventually settled in Chambersburg, Pennsylvania. The end of slavery was far from traumatic for all Shenandoans—for some it meant freedom—but slaves were a large investment and the property loss their departure created was high.[30]

The war's ferocity reached its zenith during Sheridan's mission to take the Valley out of the war. Sheridan's troops routinely burned barns, outbuildings, and crops and drove off or killed farm animals. At the Peter Blosser farm, soldiers went through the house, taking anything of value, and Jonas Blosser, Peter's thirteen-year-old son, watched a Yankee "with a drawn pistol in his hand" walking behind his mother and forcing her to reveal where she kept her bacon. Blosser's father salvaged "a few pieces by throwing them out the garret window into a patch of weeds." Soldiers shot all the hogs, taking the best meat and leaving the rest behind. The chickens and sheep also suffered slaughter. "It was bang bang all day," Jonas recalled.[31]

An unfortunate incident in Rockingham County provoked the war's most severe attack on Shenandoah civilians. When Confederate scouts shot Lieutenant John Meigs, a close aide to General Sheridan, just outside Dayton, an outraged Sheridan blamed bushwhackers rather than regular military units, and as retaliation he ordered the burning of every building, including barns, outbuildings, and houses, in Dayton and the surrounding area. Ironically, many antislavery Dunkers and Mennonites lived there. Some Yankees balked at making war on civilian property, especially houses, but others were eager to repay the locals for alleged atrocities. Yankees believed that civilians took captured soldiers into the woods, strung them up by their heels, and slit their throats. A last-minute appeal to Sheridan from the commander of the unit assigned to fire Dayton saved the little town; the townsfolk and the regiment had befriended one another. But nothing spared the outlying area, and the destruction was extensive. Sometimes the burners plundered the homes before torching them. Other times Yankees helped residents carry personal property onto the yard and posted pickets to protect the belongings, but then they fired every room in the house. Sometimes widows, the ill, or Masons received mercy and had their homes spared; sometimes not. According to legend Abigail Lincoln Coffman stood on her porch and told the soldiers to leave her house alone because she was the president's cousin. The dwelling survived (but not the outbuildings), though according to some accounts it was because General George Armstrong Custer took it for his headquarters or because the officer ordered to burn it was a Mason and found a Masonic apron inside. Some Yankees, before riding off, threatened to return and shoot anyone who doused the flames. Reuben Swope, with a wife and three grown daughters at home, ignored this warning and threw water on his burning house as soon as the burners had disappeared from sight. The Swopes extinguished the flames, but remembering the threats, they had second thoughts and reset the fires, completing the destruction of their home. At the Blosser farm, "old Uncle Abraham" attempted to douse the fire, but family and neighbors persuaded him to just let it burn, lest the Yankees return and physically harm them. Mennonite bishop Lewis Heatwole remembered spending the night in the open, as did nearly all the other families in the area, with burning buildings throughout the neighborhood. In the morning a thick fog and smoke filled the air.[32]

When armies departed the Valley, surreal landscapes reminded residents of the carnage. Those passing through the Port Republic battlefield noticed that hogs had rooted at bodies of Yankees buried in the shallow graves, leaving human bones scattered in the road. A few months after the war hikers enjoying the scenery on "three top mountain" stumbled on breastworks and skeletons. They took home a bone as a souvenir.[33]

War weariness, not surprisingly, set in early and provides further evidence of the impact of the war on individual Shenandoans. In April, 1862, a Lexington resident bemoaned, "I loathe the word—War," and she complained that after Jackson's death at Chancellorsville, few spoke of victory. At one depressing moment in 1863 Hildebrand entered in his diary:

> This is Christmas day. There are many who were alive one year
> ago who are now in their graves, many of whom died of disease,
> others were killed in battle and were denied burial in this most
> unrighteous and desolating war and we don't know what God has
> laid up in store for us.

Later Hildebrand prayed simply that "God may speed the day when we have peace once more." Others similarly tired of the conflict. Lucy Buck suffered depression for nearly a year. Margaret Preston hid a wounded, seventeen-year-old VMI cadet in her home in Lexington. She feared that if the Yankees discovered the boy, they might kill him or burn her house, but she finally showed the cadet to a guard she trusted. The compassionate Yankee offered to sit up with the boy at night and talked so kindly that the cadet shed tears. Then Preston's daughter wept, and after watching for a moment, the guard remarked, "Well, in the other world there will surely be somebody made to suffer for all this!" As Southern hopes faded, prayers for peace rather than victory became more prevalent.[34]

By the end of the war some insiders began to feel like outsiders. Sermons invoked the classic underdog tale of David and Goliath to celebrate "the superiority of the physically weak," who rely on God, compared to the strong, "who confide entirely in their own strength."[35] Destroyed farms, disrupted families, and shattered lives created an upside-down world for all Shenandoans and left many feeling powerless before a fierce, alien antagonist.

For nonconformists, for those who neither embraced the ideals of the Confederacy nor joined in its defense, the war brought additional trauma, though they often suffered from burners or plunderers along with their Confederate neighbors. Always outsiders because of their views on slavery, now the nonviolence and Unionism of Dunkers, Mennonites, United Brethren, and Quakers placed them further on the margins than ever. Although antislavery had been odd, from a mainstream point of view, outmigration diminished the Quaker presence, and the soft-spoken and hard-working Germans created little commotion. But as the majority defended its nation and eventually its home and hearth, it was in no mood to tolerate dissenters. The bitterness of the war and its high cost further diminished the majority's capacity for forbearance, and refusal to defend the Confederacy resulted in persecution. Before the war broke out, John Kline confidently predicted that young Brethren men would die rather than violate their nonviolent convictions, and this resolute defiance of the nation-state, even more than the politics of slavery, marginalized them during the South's "Great Cause."[36]

Religious outsiders faced an aroused mainstream just as willing to uphold the new Confederate nation as it had the old South, maybe more. Francis McFarland believed that God blessed the Confederacy, and he credited the Divine with the South's victory at Manassas. In the fall of 1861 the Lexington Presbytery withdrew from the national General Assembly after it endorsed a resolution supporting the Union. The Lexington preachers and elders described the federal government's subjugation of the South as "cruel," "unjust," and "unconstitutional." In 1862 Methodists affirmed their secession of the previous year, and at an Annual Conference Methodist clergy enthusiastically endorsed the "Staunton platform," i.e., Baltimore's separation from the ME, North. According to an eyewitness, when one diminutive minister voted, he stood on tip-toes and responded, "Mr. President, I wish I could not only say aye with my lips, but deep down in my heart aye," perhaps suggesting lingering uncertainty. Later that year thirty-two preachers of the Virginia section of the Baltimore Conference met in Harrisonburg and pledged their loyalty to Dixie. An unnamed Valley Lutheran, a soldier gone to war, left little doubt that he considered the war one of national self-defense: "The time will soon come, Oh how long will it be/ When from union and Yankees our country will be free." William E. Baker, another Presbyterian, sermonized to encourage resistance to "oppression" and "enemies." Borrowing from the Scriptures, he urged his Presbyterians to take up the trowel to build the church and the sword to destroy enemies. "We will not behold the very jewels of the republic about to be trampled under by swine," he declared.[37]

Even in the darkest days of early 1865 when many privately saw the handwriting on the wall, popular opinion tolerated only public expressions of support. On February 27 a public meeting held in Staunton, typical of many held across the state, reaffirmed loyalty to the Confederacy and denounced reconstruction as "but another name for submission to tyranny." Local gentlemen pledged financial assistance and donated food for local relief efforts. Though Shenandoans wearied of the awful conflict, most never doubted its righteousness, even unto the end.[38]

As might be expected, some members of the antislavery denominations, usually young, unmarried men not yet baptized into the fellowship, enlisted in the cause to defend the South. One of the commanders of the Stonewall Brigade, John Francis Neff, was the son of a Dunker preacher. Before the war Neff left his Dunker home to pursue an education at the Virginia Military Institute, and when the war broke out, he became a Confederate. The Brigade elected him colonel, but he died at Second Manassas, and his father brought his body home (another parent retrieving a son's body). An entire Mennonite congregation in Augusta County supported the Confederacy, honoring Jefferson Davis's calls for days of prayer and asking God to assist them in the national "struggle for liberty and independence." One of its preachers, shedding his pacifism, declared support for "our" army and prayed for deliverance from "our enemies," whom he called "Lincoln's hireling tools." After hearing reports that Northern authorities had sent Yankee soldiers back to Washington in irons, he surmised that they must have "refused to fight any longer for the Nig." Not all members of dissenting traditions followed their faith community to the fringes.[39]

On the other hand, many Anabaptist congregations held firm to their nonviolent convictions. According to tradition, the Dunkers would not allow Colonel Neff's burial in their cemetery because of his military service (he had never been a member). Mennonite societies refused to baptize members who enlisted, and expelled those who did. Gabriel Shank, a Rockingham County Mennonite who joined a volunteer company within a week of Fort Sumter, applied to an emergency meeting of a nearby Presbyterian session because his Mennonite fellowship "virtually excluded" him. He wanted membership prior to marching off with his unit the next day, and the session admitted Shank. He became a lieutenant in the Valley Guards, was captured at Chancellorsville, and died in prison.[40]

While loyalty to tenets, especially nonviolence, maintained traditional nonconformity, in the environment of a nation-state at war this outsiderness quickly destroyed previously amicable relations with neighbors. After the American Revolution petitioners seeking exemption from militia duty had stirred up opposition, especially in Frederick County, from those lacking sympathy with the Quaker position, but subsequent generations of pacifists had grown accustomed to tolerant treatment of their nonviolent principles. Antebellum conscientious objectors had quietly paid modest fines of fifty or seventy-five cents for refusing to muster on militia days and enjoyed the trust of their neighbors. In January, 1861, the *Rockingham Register* praised local Germans for "orderly and honest lives," and one month later, as Virginians prepared to vote for a secession convention, its editor defended German neighbors from accusations that they were "not sound on slavery." The commentator reported that "we have mingled" with Germans for years and asserted that "a people more loyal to the

Constitution and the laws cannot be found anywhere." Dunkers and Mennonites, he noted, were "a worthy and loyal community" that abstained from slaveholding despite their prosperity, but also withheld criticism of slaveholders and did not interfere with slavery, code words implying that they did not assist runaways. Antebellum Anabaptists had enjoyed the respect of the mainstream despite their avoidance of it.[41]

The war ended that. Anticipating problems, in January, 1861, John Kline wrote to Virginia's governor, John Letcher, seeking relief for young Mennonite and Dunker men. Letcher agreed to Kline's suggestion of modest fines for conscientious objectors, observing that "enough others take pleasure in the performance of such duties."[42] But during the winter of 1861-62 when pressures for manpower became more intense, patience with nonresistance ebbed. In March, 1862, authorities arrested a group of Mennonites and Dunkers that had fled into the mountains of western Virginia rather than take up arms. Some were held in Harrisonburg, and others taken to Richmond. The arrival of the pacifist prisoners in Richmond surprised authorities, who were even more puzzled to learn that the objectors were cooperative and had ignored opportunities to escape. Although the resisters broke no law—neither the Confederacy nor Virginia had yet enacted draft legislation—they paid a fine of $500 and were released.

In Harrisonburg, however, the prisoners, including two Mennonite ministers, remained detained in the jury room of the courthouse. Soon Kline, in his sixties, joined them in confinement, arrested for his advocacy on their behalf. Rain, snow, and occasional sleet continued outside for three days, lowering the room's temperature. The fire was inadequate, Kline complained, and he developed hoarseness and a heavy cough. Kline and some of the other prisoners passed the time by composing a hymn. "The world may at us look, As though we too much undertook," their words confessed, but they acted "for conscience sake, [and] did not wish God's laws to break." The impasse ended when authorities freed the prisoners as Union troops advanced up the Valley.[43]

Those who said they could not break God's laws reached temporary peace with the temporal government when Virginia granted exemptions to those in nonresistant faiths. The price of accommodation was fines of $500 plus two percent of property value. But the Confederate Congress quickly assumed authority for conscription, making Virginia's recent state legislation irrelevant, and the national law allowed Friends, Dunkers, Mennonites, and Nazarenes to provide substitutes or pay a tax of $500. Some Confederate officials ignored fees that Brethren and Mennonites had already paid to Virginia. Sometimes resisters paid in gold and silver, but one objector used inexpensive Confederate money and another had his confiscated horses offset his fine. On the other

Dunker women, dressed in nonconformist garb and bundled against the cold, deliver food to John Kline and other conscientious objectors imprisoned for nonconformist religion.
Source: S. F. Sanger and D. Hays, *The Olive Branch of Peace and Good Will to Men: Anti-War History of the Brethren and Mennonites, the Peace People of the South, During the Civil War, 1861–1865* (Elgin, IL: Brethren Publishing House, 1907).

hand, many paid assessments for those who could not afford them in addition to meeting their own obligations.[44]

Furthermore, the law did not cover new converts, so young men who reached draft age during the war had no protection. Conscientious objectors subsequently employed a variety of schemes to maintain their scruples, including bribing recruiting officers, feigning illness, or simply hiding. Levi Pitman's son, Henry Clay Pitman, a United Brethren, went to Hagerstown, Maryland, and then on to Ohio to flee the draft. A few hired substitutes, and one Mennonite secured an exemption by purchasing a mail route from a handicapped Methodist preacher. When public reaction objected to a healthy man obtaining exemption by taking a disabled man's place, he acquired a second route and carried mail for four years. Many hid in the Alleghenies, beneficiaries of a network, referred to by participants as an "underground railroad," that directed hundreds of men into the mountains. Guides escorted resisters, usually Dunkers and Mennonites but sometimes Confederate deserters, along a network of private homes and a Mennonite church located near the mountains, then into the hills. Typically, they stayed in seclusion at each stop for several days. John Garber, for example, a Dunker, accompanied his younger brother, who came of age in 1865, along the route for several nights. Garber "had just got him started" when Richmond fell and the war ended. In Augusta County, Mary Patrick, a former slave, sheltered and fed men escaping the army. (Patrick was likely a political rather than religious Unionist; she noted, "I was always glad when the Union army was whipped.").[45]

Some served against their will. Early in the war Jonas Blosser hired a substitute, who failed to serve. Then, in early December, 1861, the army impressed Blosser and his team, and for the next several months Blosser hauled clothing, corn, harnesses, ill soldiers, and ammunition through snow, rain, and sleet in the wintry Valley and the western mountains. Apparently this was more than enough military experience for the Mennonite farmer because he was among the draft evaders caught in Petersburg, but he slipped away from his captors and hid at home for five weeks. When it became possible to pay a fine, Blosser came out of hiding, paid his levy, and stayed at home for the duration of the war. Anecdotal accounts describe conscripted Mennonites who refused to shoot or aim, and Stonewall Jackson confirmed that Mennonites, Dunkers, and Quakers could "be made to fire but can very easily take bad aim." He believed that because members of these faiths were "careful with property," they had more value as teamsters than combat soldiers. He proposed organizing them into units without officers, thereby releasing soldiers for combat and improving the care of horses, but apparently little came of his innovative solution to the problem of soldiers who would not shoot.[46]

Nonresistance was an old marker of nonconformity now more significant, but Unionism was a new line and it incurred the wrath of the mainstream. Unionists had little luck in hiding their affiliation because their identity was common knowledge. Even those who were politically quiescent could not conceal their loyalties, and one resident claimed to know all the Unionists within a ten- to fifteen-mile radius. George Snapp, a young United Brethren minister and a determined Unionist, was held prisoner in the Bethlehem meeting house in Augusta County; later in the war he returned to this building to preach but kept silent to the congregation about his previous experience in their house. Snapp referred to Dunker preachers with whom he had been incarcerated as his "guard house friends." Several times Levi Pitman feared that he would be detained. Once he reported that cavalry were "riding up and down the back road threatening to arrest all 'union men.'" Someone tipped him off that he was on the list, and he managed to evade the dragnet. But Pitman knew of others who were seized. In 1864, after traveling to Annual Conference in Indiana, John Kline confided to a congregation that he considered his return to Virginia dangerous, and he disclosed to friends around a dinner table that he had been threatened.[47]

Quakers were more aggressive Unionists. Friends also were jailed and several died in captivity. Mary Joy Jackson, a Winchester resident, spirited a captured Union flag out of a Confederate camp by wearing it as a petticoat, and she smuggled military information to General Sheridan, wrapped in tin foil and hidden in the mouth of an elderly African American. After the war, Sheridan rewarded her with a gold watch and Jackson wore it proudly. But her neighbors noticed it, and eventually she had to move. Scars created by the war did not heal quickly. [48]

Just as the mainstream embraced spiritual comfort for its tribulations, so outsiders found Scriptural encouragement for their position on the Confederate fringe. They thanked God, rather than government officials, for their draft exemptions, and preached on texts such as Hebrews 12:11, which encourages steadfastness in time of discipline, and Matthew 11:28, "come unto me all ye that are weary and heavy laden." John Kline reminded Dunkers of Jesus' teaching that "my kingdom is not of this world" and that the peace brought by Jesus was "not as the world giveth." He denounced as worldly those who sought "national greatness, in which the rich and powerful" oppressed the "poor and weak." During his imprisonment in the county courthouse, Kline preached on the Apostle Paul's appearance before the magistrate Felix and exhorted his fellow captives to obey God's law rather than civil or human law, even if it brought "tribulation." As a rain/snow mix fell outside, Kline reminded the prisoners of Jesus' assurance that his "yoke is easy and [his] burden is light."[49]

The experience of the nonviolent, antislavery Unionists reveals several lessons. Unionism's emergence as a marker of outsiderness shows that sometimes one firmly held boundary against the world can unexpectedly lead to another; determined antislavery resulted in opposition to Confederate nationalism. Secondly, boundaries of little notice can quickly become critical in new circumstances; nonviolence in peacetime was a little-noticed marker, but it brought persecution when the nation-state desperately struggled for life.

The war near its close possessed a remarkable ability to disrupt life in a variety of ways. By the end of 1864 George O. Conrad, a Rockingham Methodist, was leading prayer meetings at Fort McHenry in Baltimore, where he was a prisoner of war. In August Conrad had enlisted as a forty-year-old private in the 14th Virginia Cavalry; he was wounded twice before being captured by Sheridan's men at Cedarville. In October, Michael Shank, a Mennonite from Dayton, Virginia, became an exile; after

Sheridan's troops burned his farm, including every last outbuilding, he and hundreds of other Dunkers and Mennonites accepted Sheridan's offer of a team and a wagon to Unionists desiring to leave the Valley. Shank recounted that his family departed after dark in a heavy rain, "some of the children crying to go to bed, and some for bread, neither of which could be granted under the circumstances." But John Kline was dead, assassinated just a few miles from his farm by Confederate irregulars, who suspected him of being a spy.[50]

This chaotic era confirms the ability of a changing environment to alter relationships with the center. The hyper-polarizing atmosphere of war not only affected persons in daily life, almost an understatement, but created life-jolting traumas. Thus, the secession crisis and its war lodged some Protestants more deeply than ever in the mainstream. Baptists, Methodists, and Presbyterians hardly thought twice about defending slavery, and assemblies of their clergy implemented their own versions of secession. Primitive Baptists, most recently outsiders for their staunch resistance to revivalism, were indistinguishable from the secular majority on slavery. The war completely overwhelmed their nonconformity and swept them into the mainstream. Protestant slaveholders, once hesitant to break with the Union, now engaged in war to defend their new nation and suffered the consequences.

But the war's greatest impact was on the outsiders. Now those on the margins—Dunkers, Mennonites, Quakers, and United Brethren—became pariahs rather than oddities. While antislavery and nonviolence were always minority positions, for decades their advocates suffered little. But in the grotesque world of the Valley at war these beliefs now marked Dunkers, Friends, Mennonites, and United Brethren as enemies. As the Valley's mainstream defended its nation, it lost tolerance for nonconformists, who suffered exile, imprisonment, and harassment for defiance of political authority and popular thought. During the South's revolution daily crosses become more literal and less symbolic.

Conclusions

The lines have fallen unto me in friendly places.
Yea, I have a goodly heritage—Psalm 6:2

IT WAS A COOL, CLEAR, LATE AUGUST EVENING in 1997 as the South Atlantic ("Sally") League season wound down. With geese gliding over the outfield, a sure sign of summer's end, the Hagerstown (Maryland) Suns hosted the Cape Fear Crocs in aging Municipal Stadium.

A busload of boys from a nearby summer camp for orthodox Jews emptied into the ballpark, and the young fans quickly established their presence with loud, enthusiastic cheering. "Rabbi-rabbi Schwa-artz; Rabbi-rabbi Schwa-artz," they chanted. Their rabbi waved. Then it was "Mister-mister Ka-ash." Kash Beauchamp, the Crocs' firstbase coach and probably not Jewish (and definitely not Orthodox), looked into the stands from the coach's box and smiled. An inning later the young men turned their attention to a figure in the Suns dugout: "Mister-mister Be-ell; Mister-mister Be-ell." George Bell, 1987 American League Most Valuable Player and now a minor league hitting instructor, turned around, smiled, and waved. The boys adopted the Suns' center fielder as their favorite player, and he responded by signing autographs between games of the doubleheader and with three hits in the nightcap. These young men followed the game closely and cheered almost continually.

They also were conspicuously Jewish. All wore yarmulkes, whether tucked underneath a baseball cap or in the open, and all had prayer belts. At several critical moments in the game the boys slid into Yiddish folk melodies, then just as naturally back to traditional baseball yells. They clearly enjoyed each other's company, and they participated in the game as a group. As the Psalmist might say, their lines fell in friendly places.

The young fans also carried daily crosses into the ballpark. Although their demeanor indicated that they considered their nonconformity a blessing, not a burden, and as Jewish Americans they would have categorically rejected the cross metaphor, they unabashedly and publicly expressed their nonconformity, particularly with folk music and distinctive garb.

As Shenandoans settled the Valley, disestablished Anglicanism, argued over revivalism, experienced a changing economy, defended slavery, and waged war, they demonstrated the necessity for successful outsiders to separate themselves sharply from the majority. Like the young ball fans in Municipal Stadium, the most successful nonconformists define the mainstream so that they encounter it in daily life.

Conversely, fellowships with vague or distant concepts of the world and without daily crosses had little hope of remaining outsiders and sooner or later became part of the center. The long lists of sins—adultery, fornication, witchcraft, murder—used so often to define the world, fall into this category because the transgressions often lacked day-to-day nonconformity. Surely these misbehaviors are unbiblical, but secular individuals and nonchristians also condemned these behaviors, which left them as ineffective boundaries against the world. The Methodist supplication to avoid fashion also lacked definitions that lay persons could apply in daily life, and Methodist men, especially, found few restrictions. Likewise, markers in distant locations contributed little towards nonconformity. Avoiding the theater was a far-off example of worldliness that required neither discipline by congregations nor self-discipline by individual believers in the largely theaterless Valley. Presbyterian outsiderness concentrated on opposition to the Anglican establishment rather than a daily cross, and after tax-supported religion ended in Virginia, Presbyterians struggled to locate the mainstream. Consequently they joined it. Imprecise or distant markers against the world lack potency.

Moreover, small walls between outsiders and the mainstream are not much better than no walls because they provide minimal contrast with the center. The adage that "half a loaf is better than none" does not apply to outsiderness. The half-way covenants of the Methodists against slavery and fashion could not keep their laity out of the world, as croakers so bitterly complained. Non-slaveholding was only for clergy, not laity, a modest wall that gradually eroded, and the redefinition of worldly fashion as unhealthy, outlandish, or impractical diminished another boundary between the faithful and the larger society. Presbyterian opposition to dancing, sexual immorality, and drunkenness plus support for the Sabbatarrian and colonization movements did not add up to nonconformity because of the diminutive stature of these lines. Sabbath-keeping and avoidance of dancing were distinct markers against the world, but Sabbatarianism only worked on Sundays and laity responded lukewarmly to the call to abstain from dancing. Endorsement of colonization and calls for public sobriety and sexual morality did little to separate the laity from the world because they closely resembled secular attitudes. The total is less than the sum of the parts if most parts are half loaves.

Modernity often makes bearing the daily cross more difficult because of its power to intrude in daily life. Plainness, for example, became more complicated. Outsiders in the pre-market economy used vague definitions of simplicity because fashion was less accessible; we know that nonconformists dressed plainly and were noticeable, but the specifics are unclear. The market revolution left this ambiguity obsolete by making fashion much more available with many more options. Consumers now needed less wealth and exerted less effort to acquire it, and fellowships wishing to remain plain needed more specific lines. Dunkers employed Yearly Meeting to counsel membership on avoidance of many of the latest products of the market revolution, especially in apparel, but Methodists, who did not increase their endeavors against fashion, slid into the center. Another aspect of modernity, the nation-state pressured opponents with prison and fines during the Civil War.

These blunt encroachments into private life meant a higher than ever cost to outsiderness and forced nonconformists further out on the margins. Modernity, then, in its economic and nationalistic versions, changed the terms of outsiderness and required greater nonconformity of those who remained outside the center.

Given the ineffectiveness of half-hearted measures and the pressures of modernity, outsiders with lasting power recognized well-marked, multiple boundaries. The success of the Methodist Revolution was so overwhelming that resistance to this form of popular religion became obvious nonconformity. Mennonites exhorted against it, Dunkers prohibited members from participating in the movement, and Primitive Baptists made a crusade of their anti-mission beliefs. While evangelicals once had been the outsiders, sometimes a persecuted minority, by the early nineteenth century it was their opponents, especially Primitive Baptists, who felt like a remnant, crying alarm in the wilderness. John Clark, speaking for Primitive Baptists, used biting language to sharpen further their line against jewelry, and Dunkers were specific about hoops, mustaches, jewelry, bonnets, and other items. Plainness amidst plenty worked because it forced laity to confront rather than avoid the market revolution and because it put them at odds with popular culture. Strong antislavery beliefs likewise positioned individuals counter to popular culture and popular politics. Dunkers, Mennonites, and United Brethren barred slaveholders from the fellowship, and Quakers moved out of the Valley. Moreover, plainness, anti-revivalism, and antislavery all were clear lines for laity in their daily lives. Revivalism and slavery were so vital to popular culture that those with a contrary position were out of step with their neighbors, and simplicity made individuals obviously different. Sometimes they literally wore their religion on their sleeves.

In addition to clear limits, numerous ones are also vital, considering the tendency of single lines to rise and fall in importance. Presbyterianism and political nonconformity illustrate this point. Sometimes resistance to the political center results in unmistakable outsidersness, as it did for Presbyterians under the establishment and for Unionists during the Civil War. But with fewer lines than other outsiders, Presbyterians had too many eggs in the anti-establishment basket, and, therefore, when the statute for religious freedom left them with one less boundary against the world, the center suddenly pulled more powerfully. On the other hand, some limits that seem non-essential in one context become surprisingly important as circumstances change. For example, during the Civil War, after decades of unobjectionable nonconformity, Dunkers and Mennonites suddenly suffered persecution, perhaps the ultimate definition of outsiderness, for their commitment to nonviolence and Unionism. As times change, those with multiple lines stand the best chance of remaining on the margins.

In short, plain dress, nonviolence, alternate communities, plain meetinghouses, conflict with revivalism, nonconformity to conventional race relations, and opposition to slavery were among the markers that built high walls. Faith communities who practiced these beliefs were the strongest outsiders, and for those with these numerous boundaries, the total was greater than the sum of the parts.

Daily crosses make outsiders. Had Peter Nead, the Dunker preacher who suggested that living faith swims upstream but that dead fish float with the stream, sat in front of the Jewish boys at the ballpark, he probably would have been disappointed with their repudiation of Christ and their lack of baptism. But he would have recognized live fish.

Notes

Notes to Preface

[1]Carl F. Bowman, *Brethren Society* (Baltimore, MD: Johns Hopkins University Press, 1995).

Notes to Introduction

[1]George Baxter Papers (Washington and Lee University), Box 1, folder 15.

[2]Walter H. Conser, Jr., and Sumner B. Twiss, eds., *Religious Diversity and American Religious History: Studies in Traditions and Cultures* (Athens: University of Georgia Press, 1997), xi–xiv; The old debate about the causes of the weakness of American socialism also provides a model for my project because it, too, examines flaws within the movement; see Eric Foner, "Why Is There No Socialism in the United States?" *History Workshop: A Journal of Social Historians* 17 (1984): 57–80.

[3]Conser and Twiss, *Religious Diversity and American Religious History*, xiii–xiv; R. Laurence Moore, *Religious Outsiders and the Making of Americans* (New York: Oxford University Press, 1986), 208–9; Nathan Hatch, *The Democratization of American Christianity* (New Haven, CT: Yale University Press, 1989), 3–16, 210–19. I also owe much to Rosabeth Moss Kanter's sociological inquiry into the internal mechanisms used by nineteenth-century communes to maintain commitment because I am interested in the internal characteristics of religious communities; see Kanter, *Commitment and Community: Communes and Utopias in Sociological Perspective* (Cambridge, MA: Harvard University Press, 1972).

[4]Bowman, *Brethren Society*, 414–17; James C. Juhnke "Recent Trends among Mennonites," in Emmert Bittinger, ed., *Brethren in Transition: 20th Century Directions and Dilemmas* (Camden, ME: Penobscot Press, 1992), 113–19; Donald R. Fitzkee, *Moving Toward the Mainstream: 20th Century Change Among the Brethren of Eastern Pennsylvania* (Intercourse, PA: Good Books, 1995), 37–311; Donald B. Kraybill, *The Riddle of Amish Culture* (Baltimore: Johns Hopkins University Press, 1989), 17–23; Kraybill, "A Response: Patterns of Cultural Transformation in Four Denominations," in Bittinger, ed., *Brethren in Transition*, 133–38. For a similar but non-Anabaptist perspective on the loss of identity through assimilation into the

mainstream see Thomas D. Hamm, "Separation, Discipline, and Nineteenth-Century Quakers," in Bittinger, ed., *Brethren in Transition*, 123–32; and Hamm, *The Transformation of American Quakerism: Orthodox Friends, 1800–1907* (Bloomington: Indiana University Press, 1988).

[5]Donald G. Mathews, *Religion in the Old South* (Chicago: University of Chicago Press, 1977), 81–135; Christine Leigh Heyrman, *Southern Cross: The Beginnings of the Bible Belt* (Chapel Hill: University of North Carolina Press, 1997); Cynthia Lynn Lyerly, *Methodism and the Southern Mind, 1770–1810* (New York: Oxford University Press, 1998), 176–86; John H. Wigger, *Taking Heaven By Storm: Methodism and the Rise of Popular Christianity in America* (New York: Oxford University Press, 1998), 175; Dee E. Andrews, *The Methodists and Revolutionary America, 1760–1800: The Shaping of an Evangelical Culture* (Princeton, NJ: Princeton University Press, 2000), 229–32; Robert M. Calhoon, "'Inescapable Circularity': History and the Human Condition in Revolutionary Virginia," *Reviews in American History* (March 1983): 38–41. For other discussions of evangelical assimilation into the mainstream see Anne C. Loveland, *Southern Evangelicals and the Social Order, 1800–1860* (Baton Rouge: Louisiana State University Press, 1980), 91–129; and Russell E. Richey, *Early American Methodism* (Bloomington: Indiana University Press, 1991), 55–58.

[6]Rhys Isaac, *The Transformation of Virginia, 1740–1790* (Chapel Hill: University of North Carolina Press, 1982), 88–114, 161–77; Hatch, *The Democratization of American Christianity,* 14, 199–200; Mathews, *Religion in the Old South,* 97; William Henry Williams, *The Garden of American Methodism: The Delmarva Peninsula, 1769–1820* (Wilmington, DE.: Scholarly Resources, Inc., 1984), 179–80; Wigger, *Taking Heaven By Storm,* 192–95.

[7]Emory M. Thomas, *The Confederate Nation: 1861–1865* (New York: Harper and Row, 1979), 221–23.

[8]Baxter Papers, Box 1, folder 15; "Die Klage eines Sparsamen," *Die Virginische Volksberichter und Neumarketer Wochenschrift* 1 (October 12, 1808); Lewis Eichelberger, "A Sermon on the Death of the Rev. Ebenezer G. Proctor, Late Pastor of the Lutheran Churches Constituting the Smithfield Charge," (Winchester, VA: Hervey Brown's Book and Job Office, 1851), appendix; "The Simplicity of the Religion of Jesus Christ," *Gospel Visiter* 1 (February 1852): 184; "A Word to Parents," *Lutheran Observer* 26 (April 9, 1858): n. p.; "Extracts of a Letter to a Young Lady," *Christian Journal and Advocate* 2 (January 11, 1828): 76; William Graham Papers (Washington and Lee University), Box 1, folder 2; Peter Burkholder, *A Treatise on Outward Water-Baptism,* trans. Abraham Blosser (Dale Enterprise, VA: 1881; originally published Harrisonburg, VA: Lawrence Wartman, 1816), 13, 43; Burkholder, *Confession of Faith, of the Christians Known by the Name of Mennonites, in Thirty-three Articles; with a Short Extract from their Catechism* (Winchester, VA: Robinson and Hollis, 1937), 315; untitled sermon (June 1853), Henkel Family Papers (James Madison University), Box 1, folder 6; "The Fraternity of German Baptists," *Gospel Visiter* 1 (June 1851): 39. For other examples see William Hill, "A Sermon Upon the Subject of Confirmation" (Winchester, VA: Samuel H. Davis, 1830, preached at

Winchester, First Presbyterian Church, June 27, 1830), 21; "On the Character of Jesus Christ as Exhibited by the Evangelists," *The Virginia Evangelical and Literary Magazine* 1 (March 1818): 102; Benjamin Funk, ed., *The Life and Labors of Elder John Kline, the Martyr Missionary* (Elgin, IL: 1900) 14, 45-46; Christopher Keyser to the Editor, *Zion's Advocate* 2 (April 7, 1855): 102-3; J. G. Shepperson, "On the Nature and Importance of a Christian Profession, and Its Connexion with Membership in the Visible Church," *Southern Presbyterian* 6 (April 1853): 492, 502.

9 "Marks of Religious Declension," *Zion's Advocate* 7 (October 6, 1860): 289–90; J.M.G., "The End of the Perfect Man," *The Lutheran Observer* 27 (September 9, 1859): n. p.; "Fashionable Christianity," *Lutheran Standard* 12 (March 9, 1855): 12; Hill, "A Sermon Upon the Subject of Confirmation," 21; "The Simplicity of the Religion of Jesus Christ," *Gospel Visiter* 1 (February 1852): 184. J.M.G. was from Harrisonburg.

10 1 Timothy 2:9 (KJV).

11 For other models of outsiderness, such as abstinence, movement, defense of doctrine, and community, see Kantor, *Commitment and Community*, 75–125; and Jonathan D. Sarna, ed., *Minority Faiths and the American Protestant Mainstream* (Urbana: University of Illinois Press, 1998), 5–10.

12 This is Webster's Second of March speech, in which he decried the schism within the Methodist Church, quoted in C. C. Goen, *Broken Churches, Broken Nation: Denominational Schisms and the Coming of the American Civil War* (Macon, GA: Mercer University Press, 1985), 149. For Webster's morality see Robert V. Remini, *Daniel Webster: The Man and His Time* (New York: W. W. Norton, 1997), 9, 184–85, 306–9, 508, 569, 682–83.

Notes to The Valley

1 David Hackett Fischer and James C. Kelly, *Bound Away: Virginia and the Westward Frontier* (Charlottesville, VA: University Press of Virginia, 2000), 101–3; Edward Porter Alexander, ed., *The Journal of John Fontaine; An Irish Huguenot Son in Spain and Virginia, 1710–1719* (Williamsburg, VA: Colonial Williamsburg Foundation, 1972).

2 The phrase "winter does not really set in" is quoted in Elizabeth Preston Allan, *The Life and Letters of Margaret Junkin Preston* (Boston and New York: Houghton, Mifflin and Company, 1903), 50. The weather data is from New Market, Virginia, a central location in the Valley. See the Weather Channel website at www.weather.com. See also Robert D. Mitchell, "'From the Ground Up': Space, Place, and Diversity in Frontier Studies," in Michael J. Puglisi, ed., *Diversity and Accommodation: Essays on the Cultural Composition of the Virginia Frontier* (Knoxville: University of Tennessee Press, 1997), 31–36; John Edwards Caldwell, *A Tour Through Part of Virginia in the Summer of 1808*, ed. William M. E. Rachal (Richmond, VA: The Dietz Press, 1951), 15; Chris Bolgiano, *The Appalachian Forest: A Search for Roots and Renewal* (Mechanicsburg, P: Stackpole Books, 1998), 206–9.

3 Lincoln MacVeagh, ed., *The Journal of Nicholas Cresswell, 1774–1777* (New York: Dial

Press, 1924), 48–50, 60–61; P. B. Price, *The Life of the Reverend John Holt Rice, D. D.* (Richmond: The Library of Union Theological Seminary in Virginia, 1963), 94–95.

[4]Mitchell, "From the Ground Up," 25–29; Alexander, *Journal of John Fontaine*, 105–6; John Craig, "Autobiography of John Craig," Records of the Lexington Presbytery, Reel 94; Arista Hoge, *The First Presbyterian Church, Staunton, Virginia*, (Staunton, VA: Caldwell-Sites) 5.

[5]Warren R. Hofstra, *A Separate Place: The Formation of Clarke County, Virginia* (Madison, WI: Madison House Publishers, 1999), 3–6.

[6]Turk McCleskey, "Rich Land, Poor Prospects: Real Estate and the Formation of a Social Elite in Augusta County, Virginia, 1738–1770," *Virginia Magazine of History and Biography* 98 (July 1990): 449–86.

[7]Warren R. Hofstra, "'The Extension of His Majesties Dominions': The Virginia Backcountry and the Reconfiguration of Imperial Frontiers," *Journal of American History* 84 (March 1998): 1281–1300; McCleskey, "Rich Land, Poor Prospects," 486.

[8]Hofstra, "The Extension of His Majesties Dominions," 1305; J. Susanne Schramm Simmons, "The African American Presence in Frontier Augusta County," in Puglisi, *Diversity and Accommodation*, 163, 166.

[9]Fred Anderson, *Crucible of War: The Seven Years' War and the Fate of Empire in British North America* (New York: Alfred A. Knopf, 2000), 16–41, 50–65; Francis Jennings, *Empire of Fortune: Crowns, Colonies, and Tribes in the Seven Years War in America* (New York: W. W. Norton and Company, 1988), 8–70; Robert Leckie, *"A Few Acres of Snow": The Saga of the French and Indian Wars* (New York: John Wiley and Sons, 1999), 269–76; James Titus, *The Old Dominion at War: Society, Politics, and Warfare in Late Colonial Virginia* (Columbia: University of South Carolina Press, 1991), 20–23, 52–54; Harry M. Ward, *Major General Adam Stephen and the Cause of American Liberty* (Charlottesville: University Press of Virginia, 1989), 7–12; John F. Zirkle, "Buckskin Imperialists: Some Activities of the First Virginia Regiment, 1754–1758" (M. A. Thesis: James Madison University, 1981), 41–42, 46.

[10]Anderson, *Crucible of War*, 108–9.

[11]Samuel Kercheval, *A History of the Valley of Virginia* (Harrisonburg, VA: C. J. Carrier Company, 1981, fourth ed.; originally published in 1833), 102–3. For other examples of Indian raids in the Valley see Kercheval, 72–108.

[12]Anderson, *Crucible of War*, 158; Titus, *Old Dominion at War*, 94; Zirkle, "Buckskin Imperialists," 83, 85, 96.

[13]Washington quoted in Titus, *Old Dominion at War*, 111. See also id., 22, 24–25, 32–33, 52, 111–112.

[14]"Autobiographical Sketches of the Revd. Dr. William Hill" (William Hill Papers, Records of the Synod of Virginia, Winchester Presbytery), 24; Craig, "Autobiography of John Craig"; "Mossy Creek Church," John Marshall McCue Papers, Records of the Synod of Virginia, Lexington Presbytery, 5. See also "Covenant Statement," (August 6, 1756), Smith's Creek and Lynville Creek Church Book (Masanutten Regional Library).

[15]Howard McKnight Wilson, *The Lexington Presbytery Heritage: The Presbytery of Lexington and its Churches in the Synod of Virginia, Presbyterian Church in the United States* (McClure Press), 35–36; Wilson, *The Lexington Presbytery Heritage*, 39, 42; Carlton Jackson, *A Social History of the Scotch-Irish* (Lanham, MD: Madison Books, 1993), 103.

[16]Nancy L. Rhoden, *Revolutionary Anglicanism: The Colonial Church of England Clergy during the American Revolution* (New York: New York University Press, 1999), 11–14, 26–36; Isaac, *The Transformation of Virginia*, 58–65, 186–92.

[17]George Maclaren Brydon, *Virginia's Mother Church and the Political Conditions Under Which It Grew: The Story of the Anglican Church and the Development of Religion in Virginia, 1727–1814*, 2 vols. (Philadelphia: Church Historical Society, 1952), II:117–26; Katherine Hoge Davidson, "Anglicanism in the Valley of Virginia" (M. A. Thesis: University of Virginia, 1941), 62–65; Hofstra, *A Separate Place*, 12; Nancy Sorrells, Katherine Brown, Susanne Simmons, *"Conformable to the Doctrine and Discipline": The History of Trinity Church, Augusta Parish, Staunton, Virginia, 1746–1996* (Staunton, VA: Lot's Wife Publishing, 1996), 5–11, 16, 18–19, 22–25, 35–38.

[18]Warren R. Hofstra, "Ethnicity and Community Formation on the Shenandoah Valley Frontier, 1730–1800," in Puglisi, *Diversity and Accommodation*, 59–81; Richard K. MacMaster, "Religion, Migration, and Pluralism: A Shenandoah Valley Community, 1740–1790," id.; Russell Duncan, ed., *Blue-Eyed Child of Fortune: The Civil War Letters of Colonel Robert Gould Shaw* (Athens: University of Georgia Press, 1992), 194–95; George Tucker, *The Valley of the Shenandoah, or Memoirs of the Graysons*, intro. Donald R. Noble, Jr. (Chapel Hill: University of North Carolina Press, 1970; reprint, 1966), 49–54. Shaw's letter is dated April 19, 1862, Near New Market, Virginia; after leaving the Valley he became the commander of the fifty-fourth Massachusetts, one of the early African-American units and subject of the film, "Glory."

[19]Catherine L. Albanese, *America: Religions and Religion* (Belmont, CA: Wadsworth Publishing Company, 1981), 88; Stephen L. Longenecker, *Piety and Tolerance: Pennsylvania German Religion, 1700–1850* (Metuchen, NJ: Scarecrow Press, 1994), 1–2, 84–86; Edward L. Queen II, Stephen R. Prothero, and Gardiner H. Shattuck, Jr., "Lutheranism," *The Encyclopedia of American Religious History* (Boston: Facts on File, Inc., 1996), I:371–72.

[20]Albanese, *America*, 88–90; "The Refomed Tradition," *Encyclopedia of American Religious History*, II:550–51; "Confessions," *The Oxford Encyclopedia of the Reformation*, ed. Hans J. Hillerbrand (New York: Oxford University Press, 1996), I: 278.

[21]C. W. Cassell, W. J. Finck, and Elon O. Henkel, eds., *History of the Lutheran Church in Virginia and East Tennessee* (Strasburg, VA: Published by the Lutheran Synod of Virginia, 1930), 4, 43–45.

[22]Cassell, *A History of the Lutheran Church in Virginia and East Tennessee*, 3–4, 48–49, 64–65, 82–83; Klaus Wust, *The Virginia Germans* (Charlottesville: University Press of Virginia, 1969), 135–41.

[23]J. Silor Garrison, *The History of the Reformed Church in Virginia, 1714–1941* (Winston-Salem, NC: Clay Printing Company, 1948), 39, 41, 49–50, 59, 62, 68–72, 385–86; Wust, *Virginia Germans*, 142–43.

[24]*The Mennonite Encyclopedia: A Comprehensive Reference Work on the Anabaptist-Mennonite Movement*, 4 vols. (Hillsboro, KS: Mennonite Brethren Publishing House, 1954–1959) II:832–3; Longenecker, *Piety and Tolerance*, 8–9; Richard K. MacMaster, *Land, Piety, Peoplehood: The Establishment of Mennonite Communities in America, 1683–1790* (Scottdale, PA: Herald Press, 1985), 116–17, 124, 133–36; Wust, *Virginia Germans*, 138–39.

[25]Donald F. Durnbaugh, ed., *The Brethren Encyclopedia*, 3 vols. (Philadelphia: Brethren Encyclopedia, 1984), II:1307. The definitive histories of the Dunkers are Bowman's *Brethren Society* (Baltimore: Johns Hopkins University Press, 1995) and Donald F. Durnbaugh, *Fruit of the Vine: A History of the Brethren, 1708–1995* (Elgin, IL: The Brethren Press, 1997).

[25]Roger E. Sappington, *The Brethren in Virginia: The History of the Church of the Brethren in Virginia* (Harrisonburg, VA: Committee for the Brethren History in Virginia, 1973), 31, 33–34, 57.

[26]Barry Levy, *Quakers and the American Family: British Settlement in the Delaware Valley* (New York: Oxford University Press, 1988), 5, 11–14, 241–42; John W. Wayland, *Twenty-Five Chapters on the Shenandoah Valley, to Which is Appended a Concise History of the Civil War in the Valley* (Harrisonburg, VA: C. J. Carrier Company, 1976; first ed., 1957), 89–95; Stephen B. Weeks, *Southern Quakers and Slavery: A Study in Institutional History* (New York: Bergman Publishers, 1968), 97–100.

[27]David Hackett Fischer, *Albion's Seed: Four British Folkways in America* (New York: Oxford University Press, 1989), 610, 635–42; Robert Bell Woodworth, Clifford Duval Grim, and Ronald S. Wilson, *A History of the Presbyterian Church in Winchester, Virginia, 1780–1949* (Winchester, VA: Pifer Printing Company, 1950), 15.

[28]Robert F. Hunter, *Lexington Presbyterian Church, 1789–1989* (Lexington, VA: Lexington Presbyterian Church, 1991), 3, 7–8.

[29]Gregory A. Wills, *Democratic Religion: Freedom, Authority, and Church Discipline in the Baptist South, 1785–1900* (New York: Oxford University Press, 1997), 6–7.

[30]Eldon G. Ernst, "The Baptists," in Charles H. Lippy and Peter W. Williams, eds., *Encyclopedia of the American Religious Experience: Studies of Traditions and Movements* (New York: Charles Scribner's Sons, 1987), I:556, 558; Janet Moore Lindman, "A World of Baptists: Gender, Race, and Religious Community in Pennsylvania and Virginia, 1689–1825" (Ph.D. diss.: University of Minnesota, 1994), 57–59; Smith's Creek/Linville Creek Church Book (August 6, 1756); Reuben Edward Alley, *A History of Baptists in Virginia* (Richmond, VA: Virginia Baptist General Board, n. d.), 55.

Notes to The American Revolution

[1]Quoted in Marilyn J. Westerkamp, *Triumph of the Laity: Scots-Irish Piety and the Great Awakening, 1625–1760* (New York: Oxford University Press, 1988), 60–62.

[2]Morgan Edwards, *Materials Towards A History of the American Baptists, in XII Volumes* (Philadelphia: Crukshank and Collins, 1770).

[3]Janet Moore Lindman, "A World of Baptists," 82–83, 206; Buck Marsh Church Book (December 1787, April 1788, April 30, 1796, and May 4, 1804); Smith's Creek Church Book (October 6, 1792, April 5, 1792, January 2, 1796, and April 30, 1796); Bowman, *Brethren Society*, 62; MacMaster, 194–95.

[4]Lindman, "A World of Baptists," 82–83, 206; Thomas Hamm, *The Transformation of American Quakerism*, xx; Levy, *Quakers and the American Family*, 131–32; Minutes of the Hopewell Monthly Meeting (February 2, 1777); Jack D. Marietta, *The Reformation of American Quakerism, 1748–1783* (Philadelphia: University of Pennsylvania Press, 1984), 4–10; Alexander Mack, Sr., *Rights and Ordinances: A Brief and Simple Exposition of the Outward but Yet Sacred Rights and Ordinances of the House of God* (Schwarzenau, Germany: 1713), in Donald F. Durnbaugh, *European Origins of the Brethren: A Source Book on the Beginnings of the Church of the Brethren in the Early Eighteenth Century* (Elgin, IL: The Brethren Press, 1958), 370–76; Sander Mack to John Preiz (February 14, 1776), in Durnbaugh, *The Brethren in Colonial America: A Source Book on the Transportation and Development of the Church of the Brethren in the Eighteenth Century* (Elgin, IL: The Brethren Press, 1967), 238–39.

[5]Edwards, *Materials Towards A History of the American Baptists*, 66–67; Durnbaugh, *The Brethren in Colonial America* 221; Durnbaugh, *Fruit of the Vine*, 110–12; Hamm, *The Transformation of American Quakerism*, 8; Longenecker, *Piety and Tolerance*, 59–60; MacMaster, *Land, Piety, Peoplehood*, 196–97.

[6]Hamm, *The Transformation of American Quakerism*, 8; "Covenant Statement," Linville Creek; Linville Creek Church Book (September 1773, June 1774, August 13, 1774, and March 13, 1777); Henry Schlingluff et al., to Christopher Sauer II (August 1764), and Sauer II to John Priez (December 13, 1775), in Durnbaugh, *Brethren in Colonial America*, 202–7; MacMaster, *Land, Piety, Peoplehood*, 201–2.

[7]The phrase "knit citie" is quoted in William H. Brackney, *The Baptists*, foreword by Henry Warner Bowden (Westport, CT: Praeger, 1994), 23. See also Edwards, *Materials Towards A History of the American Baptists*, 66–67; Bowman, *Brethren Society*, 73, 85–92; Brackney, *The Baptists*, 44–47, 72–74, 79–83; Marietta, *The Reformation of American Quakerism*, 4–8; MacMaster, *Land, Piety, Peoplehood*, 202–4; Gregory A. Wills, *Democratic Religion*, 6–7.

[8]Lindman, "A World of Baptists," 91–92; Durnbaugh, *Fruit of the Vine*, 199-220; Brackney, *The Baptists*, 69.

[9]Hamm, *The Transformation of American Quakerism*, 4–5, 7–8; Levy, *Quakers and the American Family*, 58.

[10]Isaac, *Transformation of Virginia*, 161–77; Smith/Linville Creek Church Book (June 1757). Jewel L. Spangler, "Becoming Baptists: Conversion in Colonial and Early National Virginia," *Journal of Southern History* 68 (May 2001): 243–86 became available too late to be incorporated fully into this study, but her thoughtful work endangers previous scholarship that reemphasized Baptist hostility to social elites.

[11]"True Christian Faith," 1541, in *The Complete Writings of Menno Simons, c.*

1496–1561, ed. John Christian Wenger, trans. Leonard Verduin (Scottdale, PA: Herald Press, 1956), 377, 386; Thomas Hughes, June 27, 1780, *A Journal by Thos. Hughes: For His Amusement, and Designed Only for His Perusal by the Time He Attains the Age of 50 if He Lives So Long (1778–1789)* (Port Washington, NY: Kennikat Press, 1947, reissued 1970), 88–89; Edwards, *Materials Towards A History of the American Baptists,* 94–95; MacMaster, *Land, Piety, Peoplehood,* 176–77; Durnbaugh, *The Brethren in Colonial America,* 174; J.B.S., "The Alert Traveler," id., 122; Durnbaugh, "Religion and Revolution: Options in 1776," *Pennsylvania Magazine of History and Biography* 1 (July 1978): 8.

[12]Hamm, *The Transformation of American Quakerism,* 5–7.

[13]Marietta, *The Reformation of American Quakerism,* 274–78; Longenecker, *Piety and Tolerance,* 142–44.

[14]Linville Creek Church Book (April 1788; May 1788; June 7 and 8, 1794).

[15]Brackney, *The Baptists,* x, 3–10, 23–25; Eldon G. Ernst, "The Baptists," in Charles H. Lippy and Peter W. Williams, eds., *Encyclopedia of the American Religious Experience: Studies of Traditions and Movements* (New York: Charles Scribner's Sons, 1987), I:555–56; Patricia U. Bonomi, *Under the Cope of Heaven: Religion, Society, and Politics in Colonial America* (New York: Oxford University Press, 1986), 66, 162–67; William G. McLoughlin, *Isaac Backus and the American Pietist Tradition* (Boston: Little, Brown, and Company, 1967), 116–20; Stephen A. Marini, *Radical Sects of Revolutionary New England* (Cambridge, MA: Harvard University Press, 1982), 23–24.

[16]Levy, *Quakers and the American Family,* 86.

[17]Claus-Peter Clasen, *Anabaptism, A Social History, 1525–1618: Switzerland, Austria, Moravia, South and Central Germany* (Ithaca: Cornell University Press, 1972), 110–16; MacMaster, *Land, Piety, Peoplehood,* 20–24, 24–25; Durnbaugh, *Fruit of the Vine,* 51–52; Mack, *Rights and Ordinances,* 365–68; Longenecker, *Piety and Tolerance,* 7–25.

[18]Marietta, *The Reformation of American Quakerism,* 98–105, 108–21, 127–28.

[19]Edwards, *Materials Toward a History of the American Baptists,* 103–4, 189; "Covenant Statement," Smith's Creek and Linville Creek; Lewis Payton Little, *Imprisoned Preachers and Religious Liberty in Virginia: A Narrative Drawn Largely from Official Records of Virginia Counties, Unpublished Manuscripts, Letters, and Other Original Sources* (Lynchburg, VA: J. P. Bell Co., 1938), 220–21, 518; Robert B. Semple, *A History of the Rise and Progress of the Baptists in Virginia,* revised and extended by G. W. Beale (Richmond, VA: Pitt and Dickinson, Publishers, 1894), 243–44; James Ireland, *The Life of the Rev. James Ireland, who was, for many years, Pastor of the Baptist Church at Buck Marsh, Waterlick and Happy Church in Frederick and Shenandoah Counties, Virginia* (Winchester, VA: Printed by J. Foster, 1819), 158–59, 164–65, 182–84; Smith/Linville Church Book (June 1757); Kercheval, *A History of the Valley of Virginia,* 66.

[20]Leigh Eric Schmidt, *Holy Fairs: Scottish Communions and American Revivals in the Early Modern Period* (Princeton, NJ: Princeton University Press, 1989), 22–29;

Westerkamp, *Triumph of the Laity,* 21–22, 26–31.

[21] Schmidt, *Holy Fairs,* 79, 80–81, 84–86, 108–12; John Craig, "Autobiography of John Craig," *Records of the Lexington Presbytery,* Reel 94. It is not clear that Craig's sermon came during communion, but its tone is typical of those preached prior to the Eucharist. See also John Craig, "Sermon" (Records of the Lexington Presbytery, Synod of Virginia).

[22] Fischer, *Albion's Seed,* 623–28; Schmidt, *Holy Fairs,* 11–21; Westerkamp, *Triumph of the Laity,* 20–21.

[23] Schmidt, *Holy Fairs,* 22–31, 32–41; Westerkamp, *Triumph of the Laity,* 21–22, 26–31, 38–39, 58.

[24] Fischer, *Albion's Seed,* 629–32; Westerkamp, *Triumph of the Laity,* 60–73.

[25] Craig, "Autobiography."

[26] John Luster Brinkley, *On the Hill: A Narrative History of Hampden-Sydney College, 1774–1994* (Farmville, VA: Hampden-Sydney College, 1994), 15–17; Wilson, *The Lexington Presbytery Heritage,* 35–36. The college does not use the same spelling the Mr. Sidney did.

[27] David Hackett Fischer, *Paul Revere's Ride* (New York: Oxford University Press, 1994), xvii, 14–29; Alan Taylor, *William Cooper's Town: Power and Persuasion on the Frontier of the Early American Republic* (New York: Alfred A. Knopf, 1995), 58–59; Gordon S. Wood, *The Radicalism of the American Revolution* (New York: Alfred A. Knopf, 1992), 169–89.

[28] Scholars still struggle to explain why Virginia's planters, apparently entrenched atop the social pyramid with strong self-interest in the *status quo,* became revolutionaries. Most explanations suggest that the gentry's position was not as secure as it might appear and focus on planter indebtedness to Scottish and English merchants, which had grown to alarming proportions, potentially rebellious slaves, and growing insubordination among small farmers, the backcountry, or evangelicals. See T. H. Breen, *Tobacco Culture: The Mentality of the Great Tidewater Planters on the Eve of the Revolution* (Princeton, NJ: Princeton University Press, 1985); Woody Holton, *Forced Founders: Indians, Debtors, Slaves, and the Making of the American Revolution in Virginia* (Chapel Hill: University of North Carolina Press, 1999), xvii–xxi, 206–13; Isaac, *The Transformation of Virginia,* 264–69; Bruce A. Ragsdale, *A Planters' Republic: The Search for Economic Independence in Revolutionary Virginia* (Madison, WI: Madison House, 1996), 283–86.

[29] The timing of the Valley's response to the Revolution seems typical; see Taylor, *William Cooper's Town,* 59.

[30] Paul A. W. Wallace, *The Muhlenbergs of Pennsylvania* (Philadelphia: University of Pennsylvania Press, 1950), 116–22.

[31] Don Higginbotham, *Daniel Morgan: Revolutionary Rifleman* (Chapel Hill: University of North Carolina Press, 1961), 23–24, 27–54, 135–55; Higginbotham, *The War of American Independence: Military Attitudes, Policies, and Practice, 1763–1789* (New York: Macmillan, 1971), 110–14.

[32] E. M. Sanchez-Saavedra, *A Guide to Virginia Military Organizations in the American*

Revolution, 1774–1787 (Richmond: Virginia State Library, 1978), 54–56, 81, 109, 121–22, 144–45; Freeman H. Hart, *The Valley of Virginia in the American Revolution, 1763–1789* (New York: Russell and Russell, 1971, originally published by the University of North Carolina Press, 1942), 79–101; Holton, *Forced Founders*, 171; Higginbotham, *Daniel Morgan*, 25-26; Ward, *Major General Adam Stephen*, 108–10, 194–202; Sorrells et al., *"Conformable to the Doctrine and Discipline,"* 24–25; Albert H. Tillson, Jr., *Gentry and Common Folk: Political Culture on the Virginia Frontier, 1740–1789* (Lexington: University Press of Kentucky, 1991), 78–82, 87, 120–21, 139–40.

33 Tillson, *Gentry and Common Folk*, 96-97; "Biographical: A Memoir of Rev. William Graham," *The Virginia Evangelical and Literary Magazine* 6 (May 1821): 259–60.

34 Stephen L. Longenecker, *The Christopher Sauers* (Elgin, IL: The Brethren Press, 1981), 137–41; MacMaster, *Land, Piety, Peoplehood*, 256–57, 279; Jay Worrall, Jr., *The Friendly Virginians: America's First Quakers* (Athens, GA: Iberian Publishing Company, 1994), 209–13.

35 Tillson, *Gentry and Common Folk*, 79–80; Thomas J. Curry, *The First Freedoms: Church and State in America to the Passage of the First Amendment* (New York: Oxford University Press, 1986), 134–48.

36 Thomas E. Buckley, S. J., *Church and State in Revolutionary Virginia, 1776–1787* (Charlottesville: University of Virginia Press, 1977), 106, 109–11.

37 In 1779 a petition from Augusta County agreed to a bill "establishing the privaleges of the several denominations" which, it said, would lay a "permanent foundation" for liberty; petition from Augusta County, October 20, 1779, Religious Petitions to the General Assembly.

38 Presbyterian Memorial to the General Assembly (June 3, 1777); The Presbytery of Hanover to the Assembly (October 1784), in Charles Fenton James, *Documentary History of the Struggle for Religious Liberty in Virginia* (New York: Da Capo Press, 1971; originally published 1900), 231–35; The Humble Petition of Dissenters from the Ecclesiastical Establishment of Tuscarora Congregation, Berkeley County (October 25, 1776); The Petition and Memorial of John Todd and John B. Smith (November 18, 1784); The Petition of Sundry of the Inhabitants of Rockingham County (November 18, 1784); From the Inhabitants of Rockbridge County (November 2, 1785). See also Inhabitants of Augusta and Rockbridge Counties (November 12, 1785); Inhabitants of Frederick and Berkeley Counties, November 12, 1785; Presbyterians of Frederick County (November 15, 1785); Petition of Tuscarora Congregation, Berkeley County, Virginia (November 18, 1785); The Memorial and Petition of the Freemen of Rockbridge County (December 1, 1784); From the Ministers and Lay Representatives of the Presbyterian Church in Virginia, Assembled in Convention (November 2, 1785); From the Ministers and Lay Representatives of the Presbyterian Church in Virginia, Assembled in Convention (November 2, 1785) Religious Petitions to the General Assembly.

39 The Memorial of the Committee of the County of Augusta to the Honorable President and Gentlemen of the Convention of the Colony of Virginia, November

9, 1776, id.; Petition from Augusta County, October 20, 1779, id.; Buckley, *Church and State in Revolutionary Virginia*, 106, 109–11. See also From the Dissenters from the Ecclesiastical Establishment in the Commonwealth [10,000 name petition], October 16, 1776, Religious Petitions to the General Assembly.

40Curry, *The First Freedoms* 134–48.

41Thomas J. Buckley, S. J., "After Disestablishment: Thomas Jefferson's Wall of Separation in Antebellum Virginia," *Journal of Southern History* 61 (August 1995): 446–80.

Notes to The Methodist Revolution

1Thomas O. Summers, ed., *Autobiography of the Rev. Joseph Travis; A.M., A Member of the Memphis Annual Conference* (Nashville, TN: Southern Methodist Publishing House, 1856), 36–37.

2John Wesley, "Friendship with the World," *The Works of the Rev. John Wesley, A.M.* (London: 1872), VI: 459; J.C.D. Clark, *The Language of Liberty, 1660–1832: Political Discourse and Social Dynamics in the Anglo-American World* (New York: Cambridge University Press, 1994), 147; Harry S. Stout, *The Divine Dramatist: George Whitefield and the Rise of Modern Evangelicalism* (Grand Rapids, MI: Eerdmans, 1991), 19–21; Williams, *The Garden of American Methodism*, 19–21.

3"A Camp-Meeting," *Rockingham Register* (August 11, 1825); "Camp Meeting," *Lexington Gazette* 1 (July 31, 1835); Andrews, *The Methodists and Revolutionary America*, 28, 93–94, 226–27; Terry D. Bilhartz, *Urban Religion and the Second Great Awakening: Church and Society in Early National Baltimore* (Rutherford, NJ: Fairleigh Dickinson University, 1986), 34–35, 86–89; Lyerly, *Methodism and the Southern Mind*, 14-15; Richey, *Early American Methodism*, 1–7, 24–30; Wigger, *Taking Heaven by Storm*, 80–87, 94–97.

4See, for example, John Nevin, *The Anxious Bench: A Tract for the Times* (Reading, PA: Daniel Miller, 1892).

5Wigger, *Taking Heaven by Storm*, 15–20; Hatch, *The Democratization of American Christianity*, 34–40, 130–41, 146–79; Summers, *Autobiography of the Rev. Joseph Travis*, 22–26; Louis Fechtig Sermon Book (June 16, 1818; August 4 and 5, 1819), United Methodist Historical Society—Lovely Lane Museum), 77, 160; Journal of George Wells (August 11, December 3, and December 6, 1791), Lovely Lane.

6Wesley, "Concerning Dress," *Works*, X:434–6; Robert Emory, *History of the Discipline of the Methodist Episcopal Church* (New York: G. Lane and C. B. Tippett, 1845), 34.

7The phrase "superfluous ornaments" is in Emory, *History of the Discipline of the Methodist Episcopal Church*, 36. The phrase "man and a queu" is in James E. Armstrong, *History of the Old Baltimore Conference from the Planting of Methodism in 1773 to the Division of the Conference in 1851* (Baltimore: King Brothers, 1907), 98. See also Emory, *History of the Discipline*, 37; Francis Asbury, *Journal and Letters of Francis Asbury*, ed. Elmer Clark, 3 vols. (Nashville, TN: Abingdon Press), I:706, II:49n24; Journal of George Wells (October 18, November 9, December 8, 1791; April 14, April 24, June 23, 1792 (United Methodist Historical Society—Lovely

Lane Museum, Baltimore, MD); Lyerly, *Methodism and the Southern Mind*, 19–22; Wigger, *Taking Heaven by Storm*, 101–2.

[8]D. Berger, *History of the Church of the United Brethren in Christ* (New York: The Christian Literature Company, 1894), 340–54; J. Bruce Behney and Paul H. Eller, *The History of the Evangelical United Brethren* Church (Nashville, TN: Abingdon Press, 1979), 48–49; *Doctrine and Discipline of the United Brethren in Christ* (Hagerstown, MD: Gruber and May, 1819), 21; Abram Paul Funkhauser, *History of the Church of the United Brethren in Christ, Virginia Conference*, ed. Oren F. Morton (Dayton, VA: Virginia Conference of the United Brethren in Christ, 1931), 51; Donald K. Gorrell, "'Ride a Circuit of Let It Along': Early Practices That Kept the United Brethren, Albright People and Methodists Apart," *Methodist History* 25 (October 1986), 9, 11; J. Steven O'Malley, *Pilgrimage of Faith: The Legacy of the Otterbeins* (Metuchen, NJ: Scarecrow Press, 1973), 176–78, 182; Francis Asbury and William McKendree to the Conference of the United Brethren, *Minutes of the Annual and General Conferences of the Church of the United Brethren in Christ, 1800–1815*, ed. and trans. A. W. Drury (Dayton, OH: United Brethren Historical Association, 1897), 45–47; Klaus Wust, *The Virginia Germans*, 143.

[9]Richey, *Early American Methodism*, 47–64.

[10]Christian Newcomer, *The Life and Journal of Christian Newcomer, Late Bishop of the Church of the United Brethren in Christ*, ed. John Hildt (Hagerstown, MD: F. G. W. Kapp, 1934), 30–31, 56–57, 98–100, 171–73, 263, 276, 319; Wust, *The Virginia Germans*, 134–35, 143.

[11]Wigger, *Taking Heaven by Storm*, 3, 5, 175, 180; Mark A. Noll, "Methodism Unbound," *Reviews in American History* 29 (June 2001): 196.

[12]Asbury, *Journal and Letters of Francis Asbury*, I:648, 759, 760; II:15, 360, 446, 718; Armstrong, *History of the Old Baltimore Conference*, 30–31, 86, 97.

[13]Comparisons of membership growth in the Valley are difficult both because Methodists did not count members every year and because boundaries shifted with the addition of new circuits and stations. Minutes of the Baltimore Conference (1819) 121; (1828) 213; (1841), 361–62; United States Census, 1820, 1830, 1840.

[14]United States Census, 1860.

[15]Journal of George Wells (October 11, 1791); Mathews, *Religion in the Old South*, 188–97; Williams, *The Garden of American Methodism*, 111–18.

[16]Wigger, *Taking Heaven by Storm*, 53–54.

[17]John Wesley, "An Urgent Appeal to Men of Reason and Religion," in Timothy L.Smith, ed., *Whitefield and Wesley on the New Birth* (Grand Rapids, MI.: Francis Asbury Press, 1986), 140–51. See also Smith's introduction, 139–40. "Love Divine, All Loves Excelling," *Hymns for the Use of the Methodist Episcopal Church* (New York: Lane and Scott, 1849), #498, 300.

[18]Scholars will quickly notice that appeal to women is conspicuously absent from my list of reasons for Methodist growth. Although I agree that the egalitarianism of free will conversion must have appealed to women living in a heavily patriarchal society, non-evangelical groups seem heavily female as well, and I am not convinced that

women participated in greater percentages in evangelical than in other groups. See Heyrman, *Southern Cross*, 161–71; 101–10; Williams, *Garden of American Methodism*, 107–11.

[19]The account of mission trips is in *Third Annual Report of the Lexington Missionary Society*, October 14, 1820, (Lynchburg, VA: Published by the Society, October 14, 1820, in *Reports of Interest, Records of the Synod of Virginia, Lexington Presbytery*), 4–7, 9, 14. The phrase "painful sense of duty" appears in Minutes of the Mossy Creek Session (April 20, 1844), 92–93. See also Wilson, *The Lexington Presbytery Heritage*, 79. Baker had studied with William Hill in Winchester, a New School leader; see Woodworth et al., *A History of the Presbyterian Church in Winchester, Virginia*, 34.

[20]Joseph Funk, ed., *Harmonia Sacra: A Compilation of Genuine Church Music, Comprising a Variety of Metres, All Harmonized for Three Voices; Together with a Copious Elucidation of the Science of Vocal Music* (Winchester, VA: J. W. Hollins, printer, 1832); Benjamin Funk, *Life and Labors of Elder John Kline, the Martyr Missionary* (Elgin, IL: Brethren Publishing House, 1900), 123, 205; Daniel Good, "Manual for Ministers and Bishops" in Harry Anthony Brunk, *History of Mennonites in Virginia*, 2 vols. (Harrisonburg, Va.: published by the author, 1959), I:64, see also I:79–83; Newcomer, *The Life and Journal of Christian Newcomer*, 41, 55, 63, 99, 145, 149, 165, 182, 315; *Journal of George Wells* (June 8, 1792) United Methodist Historical Society—Lovely Lane Museum, Baltimore; MacMaster, *Land, Piety, Peoplehood*, 211; John R. Hildebrand, ed., *A Mennonite Journal, 1862–1865: A Father's Account of the Civil War in the Shenandoah Valley* (Shippensburg, PA: Burd Street Press, 1996), 8.

Funk, the compiler of the *Harmonia Sacra*, was not a typical Mennonite. While he remained a lifelong member of this fellowship and contributed to published defenses of his denomination in the pamphlet wars with Dunkers, in other ways he occupied a position in the outer orbits of Mennonitism. For example, he married outside the church, and none of his children became Mennonites.

[21]Minutes of Special Meeting (January 26, 1828), Henkel Family Papers; Funk, *Life and Labors of Elder John Kline*, 344; Preston to wife, Winchester (December 1, 1861), in Allan, *The Life and Letters of Margaret Junkin Preston*, 121.

[22]Brunk, *History of Mennonites in Virginia*, I:79–83; Christian Burkholder, "Third Address," *Useful and Edifying Address to the Young on True Repentance, Saving Faith in Christ Jesus, Pure Love, etc.* (Lancaster, PA: John Baer and Sons, 1857), 221–22. For his account of Frederick Rhodes, Brunk relied on the memory of Bishop Peter Burkholder's daughter, Margaret Burkholder Blosser, who was a young woman during the dispute.

[23]"Report on the State of Religion, Classis of Virginia" (1840), in Garrison, *The History of the Reformed Church in Virginia*, 67; Hatch, *Democratization of American Christianity*, 164–67; Longenecker, *Piety and Tolerance*, 128–29; Nevin, *The Anxious Bench*, passim.

[24]Ernest Trice Thompson, *Presbyterians in the South, Volume One: 1607–1861* (Richmond, VA: John Knox Press, 1963), 405–6; Woodworth et al., *A History of the*

Presbyterian Church in Winchester, Virginia, 36; Wilson, *The Lexington Presbytery Heritage*, 103, 105, 109–10; Minutes of the Lexington Presbytery, (September 9, 1737, September 15, 1838, and December 26, 1738).

[25] Samuel Simon Schmucker, *The American Lutheran Church*, Religion in America Series (New York: Arno Press and The New York Times, 1969; originally published 1851), 19–20, 90–119.

[26] Minutes of Special Meeting (January 26, 1828), Henkel Family Papers, Box 1, folder 11; "The Lutheran Observer," *Lutheran Standard* 15 (May 27, 1857). See also "The Observer at the Anxious Bench," id., 14 (May 30, 1856). Examples of doctrine from sermons are in Henkel Family Papers, Box 1, folder 6, which includes a collection of sermons from the 1850s.

[27] Abdel Ross Wentz, *A Basic History of Lutheranism in America* (Philadelphia: Muhlenberg Press, 1955), 100; Wust, *The Virginia Germans*, 138; Minutes of Special Meeting (January 26, 1828), Henkel Family Papers, Box 1, folder 11.

[28] William Edward Eisenberg, *The Lutheran Church in Virginia, 1717–1962* (Roanoke, VA: Trustees of the Virginia Synod, Lutheran Church in America, 1967), 166, 183–84; Schmucker, *The American Lutheran Church*, 216, 219; Wust, *Virginia Germans*, 137. Schmucker had filled a pulpit in the Valley before moving to Gettysburg, Pennsylvania, to lead the Lutheran Seminary there. He conceded that Reformation-era Lutherans believed in the bodily presence in the elements, but he asserted that this had been "universally rejected by our church in the present age."

[29] *Classified Minutes of Annual Conference of the Brethren: A History of the General Councils of the Church from 1778 to 1885* (Mt. Morris, IL: The Brethren Publishing Company, 1886), 139–41, 143; Peter Nead, *Theological Writings on Various Subjects; or a Vindication of Primitive Christianity, As Recorded in the Word of God* (Dayton, OH: 1866; reprinted Youngstown, OH: Dunker Springhaus Ministries, 1997, intro. William Kostlevy), 31, 396, 401. Nead's book is a collection of his writings between 1834 and 1845, and the volume first appeared in 1850.

[30] Emily Painter to editor, 3 (May 17, 1856): 157; Julia Sprinkel to editor, 7 (January 21, 1860): 59; Lambert, "Predestinating Grace," 2 (July 21, 1855): 222—all in *Zion's Advocate*. For other accounts of conversion see "The Old School Baptists," id., 1 (April 1, 1854): 97; untitled, id., 1 (March 18, 1854): 82. See also "The Confession of Faith of the Regular Baptist Church Called Brock's Gap," Brock's Gap Church Book (February 18, 1843); "Election! 'Tis a Joyful Sound," *The Ebenezer Selection of Hymns and Spiritual Songs, with an Appendix Consisting of Miscellaneous Pieces*, ed. John Clark (Philadelphia: Henry B. Ashmead, 1858), #105, 86.

[31] "Arianism—What Is It?" 1 (February 4, 1854): 40; Samuel Williams to the editor, 1 (February 18, 1854): 54. "The World and the Church," 7 (February 7, 1857; reprinted from the *Religious Herald*.): 33–34; "The Man of Sin," 7 (August 18, 1860): 241; J. Axford, "The Present Excitement on Religion," 7 (April 17, 1858): 114–16; Christopher Keyser to the editor, 2 (March 3, 1855): 102-3—all in *Zion's Advocate*.

[32] "The Confession of Faith of the Regular Baptist Church Called Brock's Gap," Brock's

Gap Church Book, (February 18, 1843); Christopher Keyser to the Editor, *Zion's Advocate* 2 (April 7, 1855): 102–3; Keyser to editor, id. 2 (March 3, 1855): 102–3.

Notes to The Market Revolution

[1] Benjamin Funk, ed., *Life and Labors of Elder John Kline, the Martyr Missionary*, 110.

[2] Karin Calvert, "The Function of Fashion in Eighteenth-Century America," in Cary Carson, Ronald Hoffman, and Peter J. Albert, eds., *Of Consuming Interests: The Style of Life in the Eighteenth Century* (Charlottesville: University Press of Virginia, 1994), 252–83; Jack P. Greene, *Pursuits of Happiness: The Social Development of Early Modern British Colonies and the Formation of American Culture* (Chapel Hill: University of North Carolina Press, 1988), 31–35, 107–10; Greene, *Imperatives, Behaviors, and Identities: Essays in Early American Cultural History* (Charlottesville: University Press of Virginia, 1992), 192–94, 221–23; Neil McKendrick, John Brewer, and J. H. Plumb, *The Birth of a Consumer Society: The Commercialization of Eighteenth-Century England* (Bloomington: Indiana University Press, 1982), 10–11; Jack Michel, "In a Manner and Fashion Suitable to the Degree: A Preliminary Investigation of the Material Culture of Early Pennsylvania," *Working Papers from the Regional Economic Research Center* 5 (1981): 25; Charles Sellers, *The Market Revolution: Jacksonian America, 1815–1846* (New York: Oxford University Press, 1991), 14–15.

[3] Paul E. Johnson, *A Shopkeeper's Millennium: Society and Revivals in Rochester, New York, 1815–1837* (New York: Hill and Wang, 1978), 38–48; Bruce Laurie, *Artisans into Workers: Labor in Nineteenth-Century America* (New York: Noonday Press, 1989), 15–112; Sellers, *The Market Revolution*, 23–28;152–57; Carol Sheriff, *The Artificial River: The Erie Canal and the Paradox of Progress, 1817–1862* (New York: Hill and Wang, 1996), 96–97, 126–27; Merritt Roe Smith, *Harpers Ferry Armory and the New Technology: The Challenge of Change* (Ithaca, NY: Cornell University Press, 1977), 254–56, 271–73.

[4] Kenneth E. Koons and Warren R. Hofstra, eds., *After the Backcountry: Rural Life in the Great Valley of Virginia, 1800–1900* (Knoxville: University of Tennessee Press, 2000), xxiv; Robert D. Mitchell, "The Settlement Fabric of the Shenandoah Valley, 1790–1860: Pattern, Process, and Structure," in Koons and Hofstra, *After the Backcountry*, 46; Charles B. Dew, *Bond of Iron: Master and Slave at Buffalo Forge* (New York: W. W. Norton, 1994), 5.

[5] Hofstra, *A Separate Place*, 28–29; Kenneth E. Koons, "'The Staple of Our Country': Wheat in the Regional Farm Economy of the Nineteenth-Century Valley of Virginia," in Koons and Hofstra, *After the Backcountry*, 4–5.

[6] "Prices Current," *Winchester Republican* (May 19, 1821); Kenneth W. Keller, "The Wheat Trade on the Upper Potomac, 1800–1860," in Koons and Hofstra, *After the Backcountry*, 23–26; Koons, "'The Staple of Our Country,'" 6; Sellers, *Market Revolution*, 15–16.

[7] Hofstra, *A Separate Place*, 28–30, 94–97; Keller, "The Wheat Trade on the Upper Potomac," 23–25; Koons, "The Staple of Our Country," 6; Dew, *Bond of Iron*, 136,

248; William G. Shade, *Democratizing the Old Dominion: Virginia and the Second Party System, 1824–1861* (Charlottesville: University Press of Virginia, 1996), 43, 45–46.

8"Early Fall Goods" (August 11, 1825); "New and Cheap Goods" (January 19, 1933); "Fall Fashions of Hats and Caps" and "Fall and Winter Goods" (October 13, 1949)—all in the *Rockingham Register*; "New Goods" (September 1, 1836); "Fresh Garden Seed" (April 4, 1844); "New Goods" (April 11, 1844)—all in the *Staunton Spectator*; "Fashionable Hats" and "Mrs. Thomas Respectfully Announces" (July 10, 1839); "Spring Goods" (June 20, 1828)—all in the *Winchester Virginian*; Robert D. Mitchell "'From the Ground Up,'" 39–40.

9"Hathaway Patent Cooking Stoves," *Staunton Spectator* (April 4, 1844); "Stoves," *Winchester Virginian* (November 27, 1839); Paul E. Johnson and Sean Wilentz, *The Kingdom of Matthias: A Story of Sex and Salvation in 19th-Century America* (New York: Oxford University Press, 1994), 110; "Paper Hangings," *Winchester Republican* (February 3, 1831); Daniel Walker Howe, "The Market Revolution and the Shaping of Identity in Whig-Jacksonian America," in Melvyn Stokes and Stephen Conway, eds., *The Market Revolution in America: Social, Political, and Religious Expressions, 1800–1880* (Charlottesville: University Press of Virginia, 1996), 259–77; Stuart M. Blumin, *The Emergence of the Middle Class: Social Experience in the American City, 1760–1900* (New York: Cambridge University Press, 1989), 140–63; Patricia C. Click, *Spirit of the Times: Amusements in Nineteenth-Century Baltimore, Norfolk, and Richmond* (Charlottesville: University Press of Virginia, 1989), 34–56; "Yesterday was Valentine's Day," *Rockingham Register* (February 15, 1861); Leigh Eric Schmidt, *Consumer Rites: The Buying and Selling of American Holidays* (Princeton, NJ: Princeton University Press, 1995), 39–104; Scott C. Martin, *Killing Time: Leisure and Culture in Southwestern Pennsylvania, 1800–1850* (Pittsburgh, PA: University of Pittsburgh Press, 1995), 50–56; Daniel Feller, "Market Revolution Ate My Homework," *Reviews in American History* 25 (September 1997): 408–15. For another example of Valentines, see *Winchester Republican* (February 11, 1859). Some scholars, especially Sellers, have argued that the market revolution came abruptly, particularly in the 1820s and 30s, but in the Valley commercialization seems more creeping than forceful.

10"Carpet Traveling Bags" and "Hardware," *Winchester Virginian* (July 17, 1839); "Umbrellas and Parasols," *Winchester Republican* (August 4, 1831).

11Registry of Baptisms for the Staunton Mission, 1844–1885; Staunton Mission Registry of Marriages; Confirmation and First Communions, St. Francis of Assisi, Staunton, Virginia; Hampton H. Hairfield, Jr., Elizabeth M. Hairfield, and Jane F. Smith, *A History of St. Francis of Assisi Parish, Staunton, Virginia: Celebrating 150 Years, 1845–1995* (Bridgewater, VA: Good Printers, 1995), 7–11.

12John Craig, "Autobiography of John Craig," *Records of the Lexington Presbytery*, Reel 94; Samuel S. Schmucker sermon (January 26, 1828), Henkel Family Papers, Box 1, folder 11; "Circular Letter," Minutes of the Ketocton Baptist Association (Winchester, VA: Hervey Brown's Cheap Book and Job Office, 1851). See also John

Craig, "Sermon" (Records of the Lexington Presbytery, Synod of Virginia); "Circular Letter," Minutes of the Thirtieth Anniversary of the Ebenezer Baptist Association (Front Royal: Printed at the office of *Zion's Advocate*, 1857).

13The phrase "lower passion" is found in "Amusements," *Lutheran Observer* 20 (November 5, 1852): 816; "every vice in fashion" and "true religion and good morals" are found in Senior, "On the Theater," *Virginia Evangelical and Literary Magazine* 5 (1822): 72. See also "Theatricals," *Central Presbyterian* 3 (March 20, 1858): 46; "A Commendable Reply," *The Lutheran Observer* 20 (January 9, 1852): 627; "On the Inconsistencies of Christians," *Virginia Evangelical and Literary Magazine* 1 (June 1818): 268–69; "The Simplicity of the Religion of Jesus Christ," *Gospel Visiter* 1 (February 1852): 184.

14Address No. 2nd, "To Young Gentlemen," George Baxter Papers, Box 1, Folder 15; "The Late Duel," *Central Presbyterian* 3 (September 25, 1858): 154. See also "The Taber Duel," *Central Presbyterian* 2 (January 1, 1857): n.p., a reprint from the *Southern Presbyterian*; John D. Blair, "A Sermon on the Impetuosity and Bad Effects of Passion, and the Most Likely Means of Subduing It" (Richmond: printed by Lynch and Southgate, 1809); Steven Stowe, *Intimacy and Power in the Old South: Ritual in the Lives of Planters* (Baltimore: Johns Hopkins University Press, 1987). Christine Leigh Heyrman believes that clergymen, aspiring to genteel status but prohibited by their faith from dueling, substituted theological debates for ritual violence; see Heyrman, *Southern Cross*, 246–47.

15Abzug, *Cosmos Crumbling*, 111–16; Richard John, "Taking Sabbatarianism Seriously," *Journal of the Early Republic* 10 (Winter 1990): 517–67; Steven Mintz, *Moralists and Modernizers: America's Pre-Civil War Reformers* (Baltimore: Johns Hopkins University Press, 1995), 70–71.

16 The phrase "idle hour" is found in "The Savior and the Sabbath," *Central Presbyterian* 3 (March 20, 1858): 45. See also *Minutes of the Lexington Presbytery* (October 18, 1834); "Sunday Visits and Recreations," *Central Presbyterian* 3 (February 20, 1858): 30; Summers, *Autobiography of the Rev. Joseph Travis*, 15–16; T. J. Jackson to J.T.L. Preston (December 22, 1862), in Allan, *The Life and Letters of Margaret Junkin Preston*, 152–53. For other examples see *Minutes of the Lexington Presbytery* (June 21 and October 18, 1832, August 29, 1836); "The Sabbath," *Lutheran Observer* 20 (June 4, 1852): 729. "Profaning the day of the Lord" also violated the Methodist Discipline; see *History of the Discipline*, 129.

17Minutes of the Shepherdstown Session (March 1, 1854); and Minutes of the Bethel Session (September 13, 1823; August 8, 1835). For another Presbyterian congregation's support of the Sabbath see Minutes of the Kent St. Session (February 13, 1860).

18"Memoir of Randolph Barton" and "Address of Randolph Barton," (1912), in Margaretta Barton Colt, *Defend the Valley: A Shenandoah Family in the Civil War* (New York: Crown Publishing, 1994), 54–56; Frank E. Vandiver, *Mighty Stonewall* (New York: McGraw-Hill Book Company, 1957), 85, 87–88; Byron Farwell, *Stonewall: A Biography of General Thomas J. Jackson* (New York: W. W. Norton and Co., 1992), 104–5, 124; Thomas Jackson Arnold, *Early Life and Letters of General*

Thomas J. Jackson, "Stonewall" Jackson, by his nephew, Thomas Jackson Arnold (Richmond: The Dietz Press, 1957; originally published 1916), 315. I am indebted to one of my students, Jeremiah Hawkins, for bringing this aspect of Jackson's life to my attention.

[19]The phrase "bewhiskered villains" appears in "Fashionable Dancing," *The Lutheran Observer* 23 (May 4, 1855): 75. See also Charles Porterfield Krauth, "Popular Amusements: A Discourse Delivered in the Evangelical Lutheran Church, Winchester, Va., on the Afternoon of Whitsunday, June 8th, 1851" (Winchester, VA: The Republican Office, 1851); "Dancing," *Central Presbyterian* 3 (October 16, 1858): 155; "Fashionable Dancing," *Lutheran Observer* 23 (May 4, 1855): 75; "The Way to Spoil Girls," *Lutheran Observer* 28 (December 20, 1860): n. p.; "Amusements," *The Lutheran Observer* 20 (November 5, 1852): 816; Amicus Feminarum, "Female Influence," *The Lutheran Observer* 20 (June 4, 1852): 729; Hildebrand, *A Mennonite Journal*, 64, 32; Elizabeth R. Baer, ed., *Shadows on My Heart: The Civil War Diary of Lucy Rebecca Buck of Virginia* (Athens: University of Georgia Press, 1997), 314.

[20]Many Episcopalians sat in Krauth's congregation on this Sunday because their church was closed. Adolph Spaeth, *Charles Porterfield Krauth*, Religion in America Series, 2 vols. (New York: Arno Press, 1969), I:144–47. For clerical support of Krauth's published sermon see J. A. Seiss to Krauth (July 22, 1851), in Spaeth, *Charles Porterfield Krauth*, 148–49. In 1851 Seiss was in Cumberland, Maryland, but previously he had served several Valley congregations; see C. W. Cassell, et al., *History of the Lutheran Church in Virginia and East Tennessee*, 107–8, 255.

[21]Prior to being born again as a college professor, I had a small career as a high school teacher and consequently accept as natural the tendency of adolescents to spin aggressively their version to older authority figures.

[22]"Autobiographical Sketches of the Revd. Dr. William Hill" (William Hill Papers, Record of the Synod of Virginia, Winchester Presbytery), 28; Francis McFarland Diary (December 25 and 31, 1856); Martin, *Killing Time*, 22, 112–13.

[23]*Minutes of the Lexington Presbytery* (April 24, 1841). For another example of dancing among the faithful see *Minutes of the Lexington Presbytery* (October 15, 1842); and I. Taylor Sanders, II, *Now Let the Gospel Trumpet Blow: A History of New Monmouth Presbyterian Church, 1746–1980* (Lexington, VA: New Monmouth Presbyterian Church, 1986), 48–49. Youth had begun a dance in the home of an elder despite his opposition. See also Wills, *Democratic Religion*, 121–23.

[24]*Minutes of the Lexington Presbytery* (May 1, 1826), 349–50; Minutes of the Bethel Session (April 25, 1857), 72; Minutes of the Cooks Creek Session (July 18, 1846), 138; and October 9, 1846, 140–41. For another example of discipline for dancing see *Minutes of the Lexington Presbytery* (October 15, 1842), 576; Sanders, *Now Let the Gospel Trumper Blow*, 47–49. The presbytery overruled a session that disciplined an elder for dancing done in his home although it was done without his permission. For an example outside the Valley of a preacher eager and a session reluctant to discipline for dancing, see Loveland, 99–101.

[25]Ronald G. Walters, *American Reformers, 1815–1860* (New York: Hill and Wang, 1976), 123–25; Mintz, *Moralists and Modernizers*, 72–76; Abzug, *Cosmos Crumbling*, 81–104. It would be convenient to accept the argument that temperance was a tool of the middle class seeking to restore the control over the working classes that they had lost during the market revolution (see Johnson, *Shopkeeper's Millennium*), but I find William J. Rorabaugh's *The Alcoholic Republic: America 1790–1840* (New York: Oxford University Press, 1979) more convincing; he suggests that temperance was a reaction to rising consumption of alcohol. See also Daniel Walker Howe, "The Market Revolution and the Shaping of Identity in Whig-Jacksonian America," in Melvyn Stokes and Stephen Conway, eds., *The Market Revolution in America: Social, Political, and Religious Expressions, 1800–1880* (Charlottesville: University Press of Virginia, 1996), 271.

[26]W. P. Strickland, *The Life of Jacob Gruber* (New York: Carlton and Porter, 1860), 59–60; "The Evangelical Lutheran Synod of Virginia," *Lutheran Observer* 20 (November 5, 1852): 816; "How It Works," *Lutheran Observer* 23 (May 4, 1855): 75; Wilson, *The Lexington Presbytery Heritage*, 108; "Christmas in Bridgewater," *RR* (January 11, 1861). See also Rebecca E. Derr (Philadelphia) to the Editor, *Zion's Advocate* 2 (March 17, 1855): 84–86; Minutes of the Baltimore Conference (1851); "Thoughts on the 'Times,'" *Virginia Evangelical and Literary Magazine* 2 (October 1819): 471.

[27]"Come out and separate" quoted in "Theoklitus," *Gospel Visiter* 1 (May 1852): 243. See also Burkholder, "Third Address"; Theron F. Schlabach, *Peace, Faith, Nation: Mennonites and Amish in Nineteenth-Century America*, Mennonite Experience in America Series, II (Scottdale, PA: Herald Press, 1988), 167–69; *Minutes of the Annual Meeting*, 1842, 76; 1862, 207; 1867, 262. The 1867 statement claims that the Brethren have a history of "opposing intoxicating drinks as a beverage."

[28]"Social Drinking," *Lutheran Observer* 24 (March 21, 1856): 46; "The Evangelical Lutheran Synod of Virginia," *Lutheran Observer* 20 (November 5, 1852): 816; Report on the State of Religion, Classis of Virginia (1844), in Garrison, *The History of the Reformed Church in Virginia, 1714–1941*, 76–77; *Minutes of the Baltimore Conference* (1852).

[29]Buck Marsh Church Book (December 3, 1803; August 4, 1804). Minutes of the Shepherdstown Session (May 24, 1818; August 16, 1818); Minutes of the Picadilly St. (Winchester) Session, (October 17, 1822).

Hanna's case is in Minutes of the Mossy Creek Session (April 11, 1829; December 23, 1837; May 5 and 6, June 3 and 24, 1855; October 1, 1859).

For examples of discipline for drunkenness see Minutes of the Shepherdstown Session (September 14, 1828; June 14, 1836; October 6, 1852, October 24, 1854; June 10, 1858); Minutes of the Kent St. (Winchester) Session (October 17, 1822); Minutes of the Picadilly St. (Winchester) Session (April 3, 1841); Minutes of the Cooks Creek Session (June 6, 1840); Minutes of the Mossy Creek Session (June 19, 1825; October 12, 1841); id., 1–2; Minutes of the Bethel Session (July 23, 1826; November 14, 1840); Minutes of the Staunton Session (February 20, 1841); Buck

Marsh (Baptist) Church Book (December 3, 1803; September 10, 1825).

30 *The Code of Virginia. Second Edition, Including Legislation of the Year 1860*
(Richmond: Printed by Ritchie, Dunnavant and Co., 1860), 804; Rorabaugh,
Alcoholic Republic.

31 The phrase "basely begotten" appears in Linville Creek Church Book (November 12,
1791). The phrase "not ripe" appears in *Minutes of Lexington Presbytery* (April 26,
1794). See also *Minutes of Annual Conference* (Dunker), 1863, 220; *The Record of
Hawksbill Church, 1788-1850, Page County, Va.*, trans. and annotated by Klaus Wust
(Edinburg, VA: Shenandoah History, 1979), 26; Minutes of the Shepherdstown
Session (April 7, 1822); Linville Creek Church Book (November 25, 1815); Minutes
of the Kent St. (Winchester) Session (July 30, 1842); *Minutes of Lexington Presbytery*
(April 24, 1830). For other examples of discipline for sexual offenses see *Minutes of
Lexington Presbytery* (April 19, 1796), and the case of William Chipley (June 10,
1801; August 14, 1801; April 13, 1802; October 1, 1802; November 11, 1803;
October 10 and 11, 1806); Minutes of the Baltimore Conference (1854); Buck
Marsh Church Book (May 4, 1804); Linville Creek Church Book (April 1766);
Minutes of the Cooks Creek Session (April 2 and May 1, 1838); Minutes of
Shepherdstown Session (April 6, 1827; October 24, 1854); Minutes of Loudoun
Street Session (July 3, 1855), Winchester Presbytery.

32 *Minutes of the Lexington Presbytery* (October 23, 1800); Minutes of the Bethel Session
(April 15, 1820); Woodworth et al., *A History of the Presbyterian Church in
Winchester, Virginia, 1780–1949*, 20.

33 *The Code of Virginia. Second Edition, Including Legislation to the Year 1860*
(Richmond: Printed by Ritchie, Dunnavant and Co., 1860), 804.

34 *Minutes of Lexington Presbytery* (October 15, 1794; August 29, 1793; August 16 and
18, 1799); "Christian Firmness," *Lutheran Observer* 20 (January 23, 1852): 633. It
also warned believers to avoid covetousness to the point that it encouraged accumu-
lation but destroyed benevolent giving. For other criticisms of fashion see Ladies
Department, *Christian Advocate Journal* 1 (December 12, 1826): 64; "Fashionable
Christianity," *Lutheran Standard* 12 (March 9, 1855). See also Fashion," id., 9
(January 1, 1835): 84; "On Dress," id., 18 (February 14, 1844): 108; "The Way to
Spoil Girls," *Lutheran Observer* 28 (December 20, 1860).

35 Wilson, *The Lexington Presbytery Heritage*, 28-29; Isaac, *The Transformation of
Virginia, 1740–1790*, 314–15; Wigger, *Taking Heaven by Storm*, 175–76.

36 Richard K. MacMaster, *Our Strong Heritage, 1778–1988: Asbury United Methodist
Church, Harrisonburg, Virginia* (Harrisonburg, VA: Asbury United Methodist
Church, 1988).

37 Wilson, *The Lexington Presbytery Heritage*, 208, 211–12, 245, 221–22, 334, 337,
340, 375–76; Cassell et al., *History of the Lutheran Church in Virginia and East
Tennessee*, 157, 161–62, 177–78,181–82, 201, 214, 233, 235, 254. Another example of a log structure is St. John's (1793), which lasted until after the Civil War. Other
examples of new brick buildings are Shepherdstown (1795), Stephen's City (1812),
and Bethlehem (1854). Examples of those that used frame are St. Stephens (1841),

a union building with the Reformed, and St. Paul's (Frederick County, 1856). Other new log structures were Salem (Augusta County, 1802) and St. Joseph (Augusta County, 1800).

[38]The phrase "chief architectural ornament" is in Hunter, *Lexington Presbyterian Church*, 49; it is not clear whom Hunter is quoting. See also Peter W. Williams, *Houses of God: Region, Religion, and Architecture in the United States* (Urbana and Chicago: University of Illinois Press, 1997), 119–20; MacMaster, *Our Strong Heritage*, 13, 27, 49; Hunter, *Lexington Presbyterian Church*, 32, 41; *In Commemoration of the One Hundred Seventy Fifth Anniversary of the First Presbyterian Church, Harrisonburg, Va.*; Sanders, *Now Let the Gospel Trumpet Blow*, 50; Garrison, *The History of the Reformed Church in Virginia, 1714–1941*, 428, 439–40; "Church Architecture," *Lutheran Standard* 15 (May 13, 1857); Charles Porterfield Krauth, "A Discourse Suggested by the Burning of the Old Lutheran Church, on the Night of September 27th, 1854, Delivered in the Evangelical Lutheran Church, Winchester, Va." (Winchester: Printed at the Republican Office, 1855), 6–8, 13; Cassell et al., *A History of the Lutheran Church in Virginia and East Tennessee*, 177–78; Phoebe B. Stanton, *The Gothic Revival and American Church Architecture: An Episode in Taste, 1840–56* (Baltimore: The Johns Hopkins Press, 1968), 7, 168, 170.

[39]Don W. Massey, *The Episcopal Churches in the Diocese of Virginia: Alphabetical Listing of Active Churches by Regions and Existing Churches Not Having Regular Services* (Keswick, VA: Diocese Church Histories, 1989), 32, 78, 126; Sorrells et al., Katherine Brown, and Susanne Simmons, *"Conformable to the Doctrine and Discipline*," 18, 42–43.

[40]Asbury, *Journal and Letters of Francis Asbury*; Kercheval, *A History of the Valley of Virginia*, 150; "Church Architecture," *Lutheran Standard* 15 (May 13, 1857).

[41]"Fashionable Christianity," *Lutheran Standard* 12 (March 9, 1855).

[42]"Thoughts on the 'Times,'" *The Virginia Evangelical and Literary Magazine* 2 (October 1819): 466–73; George Baxter Papers, Box 1, file 15. In 1818, prior to the Panic, the *VELM* wrote that extravagance violated republican simplicity; see "Reflections on the Fourth of July, 1818," *The Virginia Evangelical and Literary Magazine* 1 (July 1818): 323.

[43]The description was of John Hersey in Alabama in 1819, but by 1824 Hersey was back in the Baltimore Conference; see Armstrong, *History of the Old Baltimore Conference*, 186–88, 193; Strickland, *The Life of Jacob Gruber*, 85; *History of the Discipline*, 129; *History of the Discipline*, 165; A Sister, "On Dress," *Christian Advocate Journal* 18 (February 14, 1844): 108.

[44]A Sister, "On Dress," *Christian Advocate and Journal* 18 (February 14, 1844): 108; E. W., "On Needless Ornaments," id., 5 (June 17, 1831): 168; "Evils of Dress," id., 6 (February 10, 1832): 96; "Tall Bonnets," id. (June 22, 1832): 172. See also "To the Young Ladies of the M. E. Church," id., 9 (June 26, 1835): 176.

[45]The phrase "I do not lace so tight . . ." is in "On Dress," *Christian Advocate and Journal* 17 (February 14, 1843): 40. The Doctor is quoted in "Dr. Godman on Tight Lacing," id., 5 (September 3, 1830): 4. The phrase "sickly, useless mother" is in

"Extracts of a Letter to a Young Lady," id., 1 (January 11, 1828):76. See also "On Dress," id., 17 (February 14, 1843): 40; "Evils of Tight Lacing and Thin Clothing," id. (December 28, 1827): 68. For secular criticism of fashion see "World of Fashion," *Winchester Virginian* (August 8, 1828).

46Wigger, *Taking Heaven by Storm*, 180–90.

47Strickland, *The Life of Jacob Gruber*, 78, 81, 85, 86. For another lamentation over the decline in nonconformity see Louis Fechtig Sermon Book, 1815 (United Methodist Historical Society—Lovely Lane Museum), 58–60.

48Funk, *Life and Labor of Kline*, 346–47; See also "dress" *Christian Adovcate and Journal* 6 (September 9, 1831): 8. This article was also printed 5 (July 22, 1831): 188.

49Schmidt, *Holy Fairs*, 60, 81–82; William Henry Foote, *Sketches of Virginia, Historical and Biographical* (Richmond, VA: John Knox Press, 1966, originally published 1850), 385.

50John Craig, "Autobiography of John Craig," *Records of the Lexington Presbytery*, Reel 94. It is not clear that Craig's sermon came during communion, but its tone is typical of those preached prior to the Eucharist. See also John Craig, "Sermon" (Records of the Lexington Presbytery, Synod of Virginia).

51Schmidt, *Holy Fairs*, 170–203; Wayland, *Historic Harrisonburg*, 14.

52Not until the 1860s did Quakers began to question their heavily regulated dress; see Hamm, *Transformation of American Quakerism*, 52; "Theoklitus," *Gospel Visiter* 1 (May 1852): 243.

53"Costly Clothing," *Zion's Advocate* 7 (December 1, 1860): 356–57. See also "Circular Letter," Minutes of the Thirtieth Anniversary of the Ebenezer Baptist Association (Front Royal, VA: Printed at the office of *Zion's Advocate*, 1857); Rebecca E. Derr (Philadelphia) to the Editor, *Zion's Advocate* 2 (March 17, 1855): 84–86.

54Ira D. Landis, "The Plain Dutch," *Mennonite Research Journal* 9 (April 1968): 19. This includes the Asbury quote. Mary Jane Hershey, "A Study of the Dress of the (Old) Mennonites of the Franconia Conference," *Pennsylvania Folklife* 9 (Summer 1958): 24–47. The Franconia Conference is in eastern Pennsylvania. *Minutes of the Virginia Mennonite Conference, Including Some Historical Data, A Brief Biographical Sketch of its Founders and Organizers, and Her Official Statement of Christian Fundamentals, Constitution, and Rules and Discipline, 2 vols.*(Scottdale, PA: Virginia Mennonite Conference, 1939, second ed. 1950), I:6. District meeting minutes prior to 1861 are not extant.

55The phrase "spend time" appears in Christian and Ann Coffman to Martin Burkholder (September 29, 1850, I-MS-8, Martin Burkholder Collection, Box 8, Eastern Mennonite University). See also Joseph Funk to John and Mary Keiffer and Jonathan Funk (March 2, 1838, October 9, 1841) Joseph Funk Papers (Eastern Mennonite University). The phrase "a man's life" appears in Joseph Funk to John and Mary Kieffer, August 2, 1840, Funk Papers. See also id., October 9, 1841, and October 2, 1842. The phrase "scrupulously exact" appears in D. A. Heatwole, "A History of the Heatwole Family, from the Landing of the Ancestor of the Race, up to the Present Time," (Dale Enterprise, VA: n.p., 1882), 10. Apparently the author was acquainted with Bishop Heatwole (d. 1842), his ancestor, and also collected information from those who knew him. Asbury quoted in Landis, "The Plain Dutch," 19.

[56] Peter Burkholder, *The Confession of Faith, of the Christians Known by the Name of Mennonites, in Thirty-Three Articles; With a Short Extract from Their Catechism* (Winchester, VA: Robinson and Hollis, 1837), 207, 271, 315; Schlabach, *Peace, Faith, Nation,* 204–10.

[57] The phrase "so-called Christians" appears in "The Simplicity of the Religion of Jesus Christ," *Gospel Visiter* 1 (February 1852): 184; Funk, *Life and Labors of Kline,* 410–12.

[58] The phrase "God made man" appears in *Classified Minutes,* 261; "in conformity to the fashion of the world" in id., 262; "high clothing" in id., 254-6. See also *Classified Minutes of Annual Conference,* 254–56, 261–62; *Minutes of Annual Conference* (1861), 210, 218; (1863), 209; Penelope Byrde, *Nineteenth Century Fashion* (London: B.T. Batsford, Limited, 1992), 90, 92.

[59] Nead, *Theological Writings on Various Subjects,* 400; *Minutes of Annual Conference* (1828, 1840, 1847); Funk, *Life and Labors of Kline,* 378.

[60] "When I Survey the Rugged Cross" appears in John Clark, *The Ebenezer Selection of Hymns and Spiritual Songs, with an Appendix Consisting of Miscellaneous Pieces* (Philadelphia: Henry B. Ashmead, 1858), #74, 59; By a Committee of Mennonites, *A Selection of Psalms, Hymns, and Spiritual Songs, from the Most Approved Authors Suited to the Various Occasions of Public Worship and Private Devotion, of the Church of Christ* (Harrisonburg, VA: J. H. Wartman and Bros., 1847), #80, 69; *Hymns for the Use of the Methodist Episcopal Church* (New York: Lane and Scott, 1849), #145, 93.

[61] F. C. Tebbs, Churchville, Virginia, to the editor, *Staunton Spectator* (August 16, 1859). Tebbs was a Methodist preacher. I found this article at Edward L. Ayers and Anne S. Rubin, "Valley of the Shadow," http://jefferson.village.virginia.edu/shadow2/outlines/secession.

[62] "Report on Class Meetings," Minutes of the Baltimore Conference (1848 and 1851); Andrews, *The Methodists and Revolutionary America, 1760–1800,* 78, 240–41; Mathews, *Religion in the Old South,* 81 97; Wigger, *Taking Heaven by Storm,* 87, 190–95.

[63] Longenecker, "Emotionalism Among Early American Anabaptists," in Longenecker, ed., *The Dilemma of Anabaptist Piety: Strengthening or Straining the Bonds of Community* (Bridgewater, VA.: Bridgewater College, 1997), 61–67.

Notes to The Slavery Debate

[1] "Wrestling with a Slave," Joseph K. Ruebush Collection (Eastern Mennonite University), Box 10. This is a deposition taken from Edward Hatfield, a witness to this event, October 29, 1806.

[2] Charles Ballard, "Dismissing the Peculiar Institution: Assessing Slavery in Page and Rockingham Counties, Virginia," paper presented to the Shenandoah Valley

Regional Studies Seminar, James Madison University (April 17, 1998). I am grateful to Charles Ballard for permission to cite his paper.

[3]Dew, *Bond of Iron*, 107, 148; Ballard, "Dismissing the Peculiar Institution," n. p.

[4] J. Susanne Simmons, "Never a Strong Hold? Deconstructing the Myth of Slavery in Augusta County, Virginia," paper presented to the Shenandoah Valley Regional Studies Seminar, James Madison University (March 1995), 13–15; McFarland Diary, (December 23 and 24, 1856); T. J. Jackson to J.T.L. Preston (December 22, 1862), in Allan, *The Life and Letters of Margaret Junkin Preston*, 152–54; "Wanted," *Winchester Virginian* (April 18, 1828); "For Hire and Rent," *Winchester Republican* (February 2, 1860); "Autobiographical Sketches of the Revd. Dr. William Hill" (William Hill Papers, Synod of Virginia, Winchester Presbytery), 33. For examples of hiring see McFarland (March 7, 1856; December 17, 1856).

[5]The phrase "waves of fireflies" is quoted in "Memoir of Susan Davis Conrad," in Colt, *Defend the Valley*, 35–36. See also Keller, "The Wheat Trade on the Upper Potomac, 1800–1860," 27.

[6]Ballard, "Dismissing the Peculiar Institution"; Dew, *Bond of Iron*, 212–13.

[7]"Carson's" description is in the *Winchester Republican* (October 7, 1859). The phrase"poor deluded victims" is in "Fugitive Slave System," *Staunton Spectator* (October 9, 1850); Joseph Taper, St. Catherines, Canada West, to Joseph Long, New Town, Virginia (November 11, 1840) is reproduced in John Hope Franklin and Loren Schweninger, *Runaway Slaves: Rebels on the Plantation* (New York: Oxford University Press, 1999), 324–25. For other examples of runaways see "Twenty Dollar Reward," *Rockingham Register* (August 11, 1825), "$20 Reward," *Staunton Spectator* (March 23, 1837); "$25 Dollar Reward: Runaway," id. (August 1, 1836); "$50 Reward," id. (September 1, 1836); Dew, *Bond of Iron*, 107–8, 266–67; Franklin and Schweninger, *Runaway Slaves*, 37.

[8]Graybill quoted in Simmons, "Never a Strong Hold?" 9–10. See also "Cash for Negroes!" and "For Sale," *Staunton Spectator* (April 4, 1844); "Negroes Wanted" and "Negro Woman Wanted," *Rockingham Register* (October 13, 1849); "Cash for Negroes," *Winchester Virginian* (July 10, 1839); "For Sale," *Winchester Republican* (February 3, 1831); id. (August 3, 1831); "Servants for Sale, id. (November 18, 1859); Dew, *Bond of Iron*, 107–08, 134–35, 254–56; Claim of Mary Patrick, Southern Claims Commission Records (National Archives).

[9]Claim of Mary Patrick, Southern Claims Commission Records; "30 Dollars Reward," *Winchester Republican* (May 12, 1821); Franklin and Schweninger, *Runaway Slaves*, 61, 73; Ballard, "Dismissing the Peculiar Institution."

[10]Shade, *Democratizing the Old Dominion*, 138–43, 295–96.

[11]Moore quoted in Shade, *Democratizing the Old Dominion*, 197. Faulkner quoted in William W. Freehling, *The Road to Disunion: Volume I, Secessionists at Bay, 1776–1851* (New York: Oxford University Press, 1990), 187. See also Shade, *Democratizing the Old Dominion*, 194–211; Alison Goodyear Freehling, *Drift Toward Dissolution: The Virginia Slavery Debate of 1831–1832* (Baton Rouge: Louisiana State University Press, 1982), 3–5, 122–69, 190–93, 204–8; Freehling, *Road to Disunion*, 162–96.

[12]Henry Ruffner, *Address to the People of West Virginia* (Lexington, VA: R. C. Noel, 1847; reprinted by The Green Bookman, Bridgewater, VA, 1933), 9, 10, 12, 14, 17, 23, 27, 29, 32, 34, 38–39.

[13]Ruffner, *Address to the People of West Virginia*, 7–8; C., "Thoughts on Slavery," *Virginia Evangelical and Literary Magazine* 2 (July 1819): 293–303.

[14]Socrates Henkel (?), untitled, Henkel Family Papers (James Madison University), Box 1, folder 12. The handwriting matches that of sermon notes preached in New Market in the 1850s. To imitate African-American slang the author used the popular practice of misspelling words, such as "were" instead of "where," even if it left pronunciation unchanged. See also *Minutes of the Ketoctin Baptist Association, Holden at New Valley, Loudon County, Virginia* (Baltimore: Warner and Hanna, 1810), 4–5; the query on this matter came from the Buck Marsh, a Valley congregation. See also *Minutes of the Lexington Presbytery* (August 17, 1845), 619–20. For an account of a slave wedding see Allan, *The Life and Letters of Margaret Junkin Preston*, 51–57.

[15]Mintz, *Moralists and Modernizers*, 120–22; Walters, *American Reformers*; Robert H. Abzug, *Cosmos Crumbling*, 133–34.

[16]"A Voice from the South," *Gospel Visiter* 6 (December 1856): 322–24; and C., "Thoughts on Slavery," *Virginia Evangelical and Literary Magazine* 2 (July 1819): 293–303; Minutes of the Baltimore Conference (1851, 1852, 1855). See also "Review of the Reports of the American Colonization Society," 6 (November 1823): 601–11; "Colonization Society," 2 (May 1819): 243–44; "Colonization Society," 2 (December 1819): 581—all in the *Virginia Evangelical and Literary Magazine*.

[17]Douglas C. Stange, "Lutheran Involvement in the American Colonization Society," *Mid-America* 49 (April 1967): 140–42, 146–48; *Minutes of the Lexington Presbytery* (August 22, 1844), 605-6; Ellen Eslinger, "The Brief Career of Rufus W. Bailey, African Colonization Society Agent in Virginia," paper delivered at the Shenandoah Valley Regional Studies Seminar, James Madison University (April 20, 2001), *passim*; *Minutes of the Baltimore Conference* (1854). The Methodist General Conference also approved of colonization; see *History of the Discipline*, 43, 45–46. See also Lacy, "A Sermon on the Death of the Rev. Wm. M. Atkinson, D.D.," 10–11; *Minutes of the Lexington Presbytery* (September 29, 1837), 486; "Autobiographical Sketches of the Revd. Dr. William Hill" (William Hill Papers, Synod of Virginia, Winchester Presbytery), 34.

[18]T. T. Castleman, *Plain Sermons for Servants* (Philadelphia: King and Baird, Publishers, 1851), 40–41; Farwell, *Stonewall*, 134; Baxter Papers, Box 1, folder 15; "The Tract Society Agitation," *The Central Presbyterian* 3 (April 17, 1858): 61; A.H.H. Boyd, "Thanksgiving Sermon, Delivered in Winchester, Va., on Thursday, 29th November, 1860" (Winchester, VA: J. H. Crum, 1860), 12–13; "Circular Letter," Minutes of the Thirtieth Anniversary of the Ebenezer Baptist Association (Front Royal: Printed at the office of *Zion's Advocate*), 1857. See also "The New School Assembly and Slavery," *The Central Presbyterian* 2 (July 4, 1857): 105. Castleman filled an Anglican pulpit in Staunton.

[19]To determine Lutheran slaveholding I used membership lists found in Ambrose

Henkel notebook, Henkel Family Papers, Box 1, folder 6; United States Census, 1840. The notebook includes subscription lists for 1841 and 1842. I also found a list in Rader's Church to Synod, September 21, 1857, Henkel Family Papers, Box 1, folder 11; United States Census, 1850. This petition asks the synod to ordain Soloman Henkel to be their pastor and includes members' signatures.

[20]"The Interest of the Church in the Questions Which Agitate the Country," *Lutheran Standard* 20 (November 28, 1860).

[21]United States Census, 1860; Cassell et al., *A History of the Lutheran Church in Virginia and East Tennessee,* 198, 202, 219; James F. Hutton, Jr., "The Slaveowners of Frederick County and Winchester in 1860" (unpublished ms., March 11, 1963), Rare Book Room, Handley Library; Cassell et al., *A History of the Lutheran Church in Virginia and East Tennessee,* 182.

[22]J. Susanne Schramm Simmons, "Augusta County's Other Pioneers: The African American Presence in Frontier Augusta County," in Puglisi, *Diversity and Accommodation,* 166.

[23]"Subscriptions to Extinguish the Presbyterian Church Debts," 1859, Records of the First Presbyterian Church, Winchester, Virginia, Rare Book Room, Handley Library; James F. Hutton, Jr., "The Slaveowners of Frederick County and Winchester in 1860" (unpublished ms., March 11, 1963), Rare Book Room, Handley Library.

[24]Simmons, "Never a Strong Hold?" 4.

[25]For the year ending June, 1824, McFarland's account book lists twenty-three; of the twelve located, eleven were slaveholders. For the year ending June 15, 1830, the account book lists twenty-two; nine of the ten names located in the census were slaveholders. For the year ending on February 22, 1843, the account book lists eighteen names; I found ten in the census, six of whom were slaveholders. See Francis McFarland Account Book and Census for 1820, 1830, 1840. See also "Our farmers generally occupy plantations of moderate extent, and have only a few domestick servants, and out-door hands, with whom they themselves labor," *Minutes of the Lexington Presbytery* (August 17, 1845).

[26]"The New School Assembly and Slavery," *The Central Presbyterian* 2 (July 4, 1857): 105.

[27]Alley, *A History of Baptists in Virginia,* 125–27; Garnett Ryland, *The Baptists of Virginia, 1699–1926* (Richmond, VA: Virginia Baptist Board of Missions and Education, 1955), 150–54; *Minutes of the Ketoctin Association* (Winchester, VA: Printed by Richard Bowen, 1798).

[28]Buck Marsh Church Book (December 1787; September 3, 1796; April 1, 1797; May 4, 1804; August 22, 1840); Berryville Church Book (November 8, 1857). See also Buck Marsh Church Book (February 28, 1795, June 6, 1795, November 1804, April 3, 1842); Dew, *Bond of Iron,* 178.

[29]Berryville Church Book (November 8, 1857); Linville Creek Church Book (November 12, 1791; January 6, 1805; March 4, 1809 April 16, 1814; August 20, 1814; September 17, 1814; September 12, 1818); Buck Marsh Church Book (January 6, 1805). See also Brock's Gap, Church Book (December 18, 1842; June 17, 1843).

[30]Linville Creek Church Book (May 10, 1794; September 26, 1794; August 9, 1794). See also Betty Wood, "'For Their Satisfaction or Redress': African Americans and Church Discipline in the Early South," in Catherine Clinton and Michele Gillespie, eds., *The Devil's Lane: Sex and Race in the Early South* (New York: Oxford University Press, 1997), 117. Wood believes that Joe accepted the compromise and thereby gave up the woman he loved for his faith, but my reading of the record shows that he was not given a choice. Had he rejected the compromise and left the church, Harrison could still have denied him permission to marry her "wench."

[31]Waterlick Church Book (May 19, 1787; June 16, 1787; September 27, 1789).

[32]Berryville Church Book (July 22, 1855); Linville Creek Church Book (November 7, 1795; March 12, 1796); Waterlick Church Book (April 25, 1789). As early as 1810 the Ketoctin Association decided that blacks would not vote, even if they were in the majority; *Minutes of the Ketockton Baptist Association* (1810), 5. While the church may have denounced Black Joe for being a segregationist—he objected to the seating of a white man in the black section—the general evidence of white control suggests that Black Joe's impertinent challenge of a white man caused his admonition.

[33]The phrase "to wander to other churches" is quoted in *Minutes of the Lexington Presbytery* (August 14, 1857). See also Thomas J. Jackson to J. L. Campbell (June 7, 1858), Thomas J. Jackson Papers (Washington and Lee University), 041a; "Veritas," "The Colored Sunday School," *Lexington Gazette* (October 1860); Hunter, *Lexington Presbyterian Church,* 29; Farwell, *Stonewall,* 125, 133; James I. Robertson, Jr., *Stonewall Jackson: The Man, The Soldier, The Legend* (New York: Macmillan Publishing, 1997), 168–69.

[34]Shepherdstown Church Book (February 5 and 15, 1853); Minutes of the Bethel Session (November 8, 1834; April 9, 1859; February 1, 1863). The session did not know where "Big Ann" had been sold.

[35]See Cassell et al., *History of the Lutheran Church in Virginia and East Tennessee,* 161–62; Charles Porterfield Krauth to his wife (May 11, 1852), in Spaeth, *Charles Porterfield Krauth,* 283–84.

[36]Berryville Church Book (January 1, 1841; September 24, 1841; February 5, 1842; April 3 and 30, 1842); see also Shepherdstown Church Book (November 11, 1855).

[37]Castleman, *Plain Sermons for Servants,* 43, 45, 367–369, 375, 388.

[38]George A. Baxter Papers, Box 1, folder 16; *Minutes of the Lexington Presbytery* (October 17, 1835); Ruffner, *Address to the People of West Virginia,* 8.

[39]Bourne to A. B. Davidson (August 25, 1815), Bourne to Davidson (July 28, 1815), *Minutes of the Lexington Presbytery,* 240–44. The letters are included in the *Minutes.* The affair is described in *Minutes,* 239–44. See also *Minutes of the Lexington Presbytery* (November 21, 1817); Strickland, *The Life of Jacob Gruber,* 60; Wilson, *A History of the Presbyterian Church in Winchester, Virginia, 1780–1949,* 91; *Minutes of the Lexington Presbytery* (December 27, 1815).

[40]*Minutes of the Lexington Presbytery* (November 21, 1817). This evidence is based on Hill's testimony before the Presbytery. See also Letter of July 28, 1815.

[41]Bourne to the moderator of the Lexington Presbytery, Germantown, May 28, 1817,

in *Minutes of the Lexington Presbytery* (September 1, 1817). See also George Bourne, *The Book and Slavery Irreconcilable: With Animadversions upon Dr. Smith's Philosophy* (Philadelphia: Printed by J. M. Sanderson & Co., 1816; reprinted New York: Arno Press and *The New York Times*, 1969).

[42]Bourne to the Presbytery, Germantown (February 21, 1818), *Minutes of the Lexington Presbytery* (April 22, 1818); Bourne to A. B. Davidson (August 25, 1815); Bourne to Davidson, *Minutes of the Lexington Presbytery* (July 28, 1815). See also *Minutes of the Lexington Presbytery* (April 23, 1818); Thompson, *Presbyterians in the South*, I:328–30; Wilson, *A History of the Presbyterian Church in Winchester*, 93.

[43]C. C. Goen, *Broken Churches, Broken Nation: Denominational Schisms and the Coming of the American Civil War* (Macon, GA: Mercer Press, 1985), 68–78; Mathews, *Religion in the Old South*; Thompson, *Presbyterians in the South*, 395–406; Harold M. Parker, Jr., *The United Synod of the South: The Southern New School Presbyterian Church* (New York and Westport, CT: Greenwood Press and the Presbyterian Historical Society, 1988), 40–41.

[44]A. W. Drury, *History of the Church of the United Brethren in Christ* (Dayton, OH: United Brethren Publishing House, 1931), 337–38; "A Reply," *Religious Telescope* (January 24, 1838): 6. The Dunkers' Yearly Meeting considered slavery in 1782, 1797, 1812, 1813, 1837, 1845, 1846, 1853, 1854, 1857, 1862, 1863, and 1865. See *Classified Minutes of Annual Conference of the Brethren: A History of the General Councils of the Church from 1778 to 1885* (Mt. Morris, IL: The Brethren Publishing Company, 1886), 372–78; and "An Essay on Slavery" and "Remarks of the Editor," *Gospel Visiter* 1 (January 1852): 158–59.

[45]Joseph Funk to John and Mary Kieffer (January 9, 1841, and February 22, 1841), Funk Papers (Eastern Mennonite University); *Classified Minutes*, 162-63. The Yearly Meeting's minutes do not give the location of congregations who denied equal seating to blacks or with white members who withheld the kiss from blacks. However, given that most Dunker congregations were in the almost all-white rural North, odds are reasonable that the offending congregations were in the Valley or further south in the Roanoke, Virginia, area. Congregations in southern Ohio are another possibility; see Sammy Weir's story below.

[46]"Bob Spins a Yarn," *Staunton Spectator* (August 23, 1859); Drury, *History of the Church of the United Brethren in Christ*, 337–38; Paul R. Fetters, ed., *Trials and Triumphs: A History of the Church of the United Brethren in Christ* (Huntingdon, IN: Church of the United Brethren in Christ, 1894), 137; J. J. Glossbrenner, "Slavery in the United Brethren Church," *Religious Telescope* 7 (April 5, 1848): 283; Patricia P. Hickin, "Antislavery in Virginia: 1831–1861" (Ph.D. diss.: University of Virginia, 1968), 439–40. I found the *Staunton Spectator* article at Ayers, "Valley of the Shadow," http://jefferson.village.virginia.edu/vshadow2/Browser1/aubrowser/ssaug59.

[47]John Kline to George Shaver (February 1853), in Sappington, *Brethren in Virginia*, 62. Weir resided in Botetourt County, one county south of the Shenandoah Valley; see "The Life of Elder Samuel Weir: A Colored Brother," in Roger E. Sappington, ed., *The Brethren in the New Nation: A Source Book on the Development of the Church*

of the Brethren, 1785–1865 (Elgin, IL: Brethren Press, 1976), 265–72. An elderly Dunker preacher in Ohio gave Weir a home, but the congregation would not allow him to worship with them. Several years later, however, it ordained Weir to preach to African Americans after he gave a trial sermon before the all-white assembly.

[48]The Virginia Yearly Meeting is quoted in Philip J. Schwarz, *Migrants against Slavery: Virginians and the Nation* (Charlottesville: University of Virginia Press, 2001), 84. See also id., 83–84; Hugh Barbour and J. William Frost, *The Quakers* (New York: Greenwood Press, 1988), 155, 159, 162; Weeks, *Southern Quakers and Slavery*, 249–51; Larry Dale Gragg, *Migration in Early America: The Virginia Quaker Experience* (Ann Arbor, MI: UMI Research Press, 1980), 40–41, 50–51, 60–67.

[49]Burkholder, *Confession of Faith*, 419; Funk to John and Mary Kieffer (March 26, 1847), Funk Papers; *Minutes of the Virginia Mennonite Conference*, I:6.

[50]The phrase "an interesting session" appears in Daniel W. Bly, ed., "Extracts from the Diaries of Levi Pitman," (April 18, 1857), 12; the phrase "living up to the Divine rule" appears in Andrew Funkhouser, "Is Slaveholding a Sin?" *Religious Telescope* 7 (December 24, 1847): 174. See also *Religious Telescope* (December 24, 1847): 174; J. J. Glossbrenner, "Slavery in the United Brethren Church," *Religious Telescope* 7 (April 5, 1848): 283; "The Slaveowners of Frederick County and Winchester in 1860."

[51]The Linville Creek statement and the Kline statement appear in Sappington, *Brethren in Virginia*, 63; "Still Hoping," *Rockingham Register* (February 15, 1861). The Linville Creek statement includes signatories and none of these names appear on the slaveholding list; see Slave Schedules, Rockingham County, United States Census (1860).

[52]Forrest G. Wood argues that avoidance of slavery stemmed more from self-interest than altruism, that antislavery Christians were more concerned with their personal salvation and the stain of sin on their souls than with the victims of slavery. Though persuasive, Wood pushes the argument too hard. For example, the effort to emancipate Weir, including his escort to Ohio, and the belief that hired slaves should receive wages demonstrate concern for individual African Americans. It seems a harsh judgment to dismiss society's most progressive on race as preoccupied with self-interest. See Wood, *The Arrogance of Faith: Christianity and Race in America from the Colonial Era to the Twentieth Century* (New York: Alfred A. Knopf, 1990), 287, 315.

[53]Wesley, "Thoughts upon Slavery," *Works*, 11:59-79; Asbury, *Journal*, II:705; Lyerly, *Methodism and the Southern Mind*, 125; Mathews, *Slavery and Methodism*, 5–7, 14–15, 17.

[54]Journal of George Wells (November 9, 1791, April 25, 1792), United Methodist Historical Society—Lovely Lane Museum, Baltimore, Maryland; Emory, *History of the Discipline*, 34–36, 43–45, 80, 274–76; Wigger, *Taking Heaven by Storm*, 140; Lyerly, *Methodism and the Southern Mind*, 126–28; Mathews, *Slavery and Methodism*, 10–12, 19–27.

[55]Minutes of the Baltimore Conference (March 3, 1809); Mathews, *Slavery and Methodism*, 33–37.

[56]Strickland, *The Life of Jacob Gruber*, 52, 60, 130–248; Mathews, *Slavery and*

Methodism, 35–36; Wigger, *Taking Heaven by Storm*, 144. Gruber preached his offending sermon in Washington County, Maryland, which is in western Maryland. Geologically this area is nearly identical to the Shenandoah Valley, occupying the Great Valley that stretches from Roanoke into northeastern Pennsylvania. The social construction of western Maryland also resembled the Valley with its ethnic and religious diversity.

[57] Six of 23 males in class lists owned slaves, and 41 of 940 male taxpayers in Harrisonburg were slaveholders. See 1840 United States Census, Rockingham County; and File 2, Bound Book, Register of Class Members, 1835, Asbury United Methodist Church, Harrisonburg, VA.

[58] The meetinghouse was in nearby Albemarle County; Funk, *Life and Labors of John Kline*, 212–13.

[59] *Minutes of the Baltimore Conference* (1835, 1836, 1841). For another example of slavery through marriage see *Minutes* (1841).

[60] Mathews, *Slavery and Methodism*, 204, 251–55; *History of the Discipline*, 45–46; *Minutes of the Baltimore Conference* (1841, 1842, and 1844).

[61] *Minutes of the Baltimore Conference* (1844, 1855).

[62] In 1841 Shepherdstown had 107 whites and 60 blacks (36% black). In 1860 Shepherdstown had 288 whites and 152 blacks (35% black). See *Minutes of the Baltimore Conference* (1841, 1860).

[63] The phrase "source of ungovernable and angry excitement," appears in *Minutes of the Baltimore Conference*, 1855. See also "Resolution on the Condition of Colored People," *Minutes of the Baltimore Conference* (1844); Official Members and Quarterly Conference Minutes, 1842–1851, (September 23, 1843, June 13, 1846, and March 6, 1847), Market Street Methodist Church Papers (Handley Public Library, Winchester, VA), Box 3. For an example of the Quarterly Conference disciplining white ministers see June 8 and 9, 1843.

[64] MacMaster, *Our Strong Heritage, 1778–1988*, 47–49; *Minutes of the Baltimore Conference* (1848); *Autobiography of the Rev. Joseph Travis*, 180. For a general comment on the Southern sympathies of Valley preachers after the split see George Gilman Smith, *Life and Letters of James Osgood Andrew, Bishop of the Methodist Episcopal Church South* (Nashville, TN: Southern Methodist Publishing House, 1882), 422.

[65] *Minutes of the Baltimore Conference* (1841, 1860).

[66] "The Border Question," 23 (January 12, 1848); Thomas H. Busey (Port Republic) "Border Affairs" (January 12, 1848); "Border Matters," 25 (December 12, 1850): 198—all in the *Christian Advocate and Journal*.

[67] "Report on the Fincastle Resolutions," *Minutes of the Baltimore Conference* (1854).

[68] "Memorials on Slavery," *Minutes of the Baltimore Conference* (1860).

Notes to The Civil War

[1] "The Interest of the Church in the Question Which Agitate the Country," *Lutheran Standard*, 20.

[2]Bly, "Extracts from the Diaries of Levi Pitman," 13; id., (February 4, 1860), 13.

[3]William L. Barney, *Battleground for the Union: The Era of the Civil War and Reconstruction, 1848–1877* (Englewood Cliffs, NJ: Prentice Hall, 1990), 100–5; James M. McPherson, *Battle Cry of Freedom: The Civil War Era* (New York: Oxford University Press, 1988), 213–33; Richard H. Sewell, *A House Divided: Sectionalism and Civil War, 1848–1865* (Baltimore: Johns Hopkins University Press, 1988), 72–76.

[4]"Stephen Arnold Douglass" in "Democratic Candidates Traitors to their Country," *Staunton Spectator* (September 18, 1860), reprinted from the *Spirit of Democracy* in New Market, Virginia. For references to Black Republicans see "Be Warned Ere It Is Too Late," *Rockingham Register* (March 8, 1861); and "Organize! Organize!" *Valley Star* 21 (October 25, 1860); "The Democracy Can Do Nothing in the North," *Lexington Gazette*, new series, 1 (October 18, 1860). The quotations on popular sovereignty are in "How will Old Line Whites Vote!" *Winchester Republican* (October 12, 1860). See also "Douglas Prospects" (July 13, 1860); "The Ledger Candidate" (July 20, 1860); "Our Opinion Exactly" (August 14, 1860)—all in the *Winchester Republican*. "How to Vote," *Staunton Spectator* (September 11, 1860); "Significant Facts," *Staunton Spectator* (September 18, 1861); "The Sofa Party" and "The Signs of the Times" (September 20, 1860) *Valley Star*; "Union or Disunion," *Lexington Gazette*, new series, 1 (September 8, 1860); "Fusion Tickets," Lexington Gazette, new series, 1 (October 11, 1960); Daniel W. Crofts, *Reluctant Confederates: Upper South Unionists in the Secession Crisis* (Chapel Hill: University of North Carolina Press, 1989), 75–85.

[5]"Sen. Douglas in the South," *Valley Star* 21 (September 13, 1860, reprinted from the *New York Herald)*; "Reception of Judge Douglas," *Staunton Spectator* (September 4, 1960); McPherson, *Battle Cry of Freedom*, 223–24.

[6]*Minutes of the Lexington Presbytery* (October 4, 1860); McFarland Diary (November 6, 1860).

[7]Crofts, *Reluctant Confederates*, 81–83.

[8]*Winchester Republican* (November 9, 1860); *Staunton Spectator* (November 13, 1860); *Staunton Vindicator* (November 9, 1860). The Shenandoah County results do not include four precincts that had not reported by press time. The *Vindicator* also reported nine votes for Lincoln in Shenandoah County.

[9]McFarland Diary (November 20, 1860); "Remittance," *Zion's Advocate* 7 (December 15, 1860): 372; Funk, *Life and Labors of Elder John Kline*, January 1, 1861, 438.

[10]"Remember Our Country at the Throne of Grace," *Lutheran Standard* 20 (November 23, 1860); "The Interest of the Church in the Questions Which Agitate the Country," *Luthern Standard* 20 (November 28, 1860); "Our Country," *Lutheran Standard* 20 (December 14, 1860); "Great Excitement," *Lutheran Observer* 28 (November 9, 1860). See also "Day of Humiliation and Prayer," *Lutheran Standard* 20 (November 23, 1860).

[11]A.H.H. Boyd, "Thanksgiving Sermon, Delivered in Winchester, Va., on Thursday,

29th November, 1860" (Winchester, VA: J. H. Crum, 1860). See also Woodworth et al., *A History of the Presbyterian Church in Winchester, Virginia*, 34. For another example of avoidance of the word "slave" see Castleman, *Plain Sermons for Servants*, 7.

12Jackson to Thomas Jackson Arnold (nephew), Lexington, Virginia (January 26, 1861), in Thomas Jackson Arnold, ed., *Early Life and Letters of General Thomas J. Jackson*, (Richmond, VA: The Dietz Press, 1957 originally published 1916), 294.

13McFarland Diary (January 28, 1860); Crofts, *Reluctant Confederates*, 140–42; "Still Hoping," *Rockingham Register* (February 15, 1861); "Be Warned Ere It Is Too Late," id. (March 8, 1861).

14McFarland Diary (January 4, 1861); "Fast Day," *Valley Star* (January 3, 1861); "Fasting and Prayer," *Zion's Advocate* 7 (December 15, 1860): 372.

15Minutes of the Baltimore Conference (1861); Russell E. Richey, *The Methodist Conference in America: A History* (Nashville, TN: Kingswood Books, 1996), 188-219; William Warren Sweet, *Virginia Methodism: A History* (Richmond, VA: Wittet and Shepperson, 1955), 234, 265.

16Pitman Diary (April 20, 1861). See also "War Inevitable!" *Valley Star* 21 (April 11, 1861).

17Crofts, *Reluctant Confederates,* 334–40; "Highly Important Notice," *Zion's Advocate* 8 (April 20, 1861): 114; McFarland Diary (April 18 and 26, 1861); Pitman Diary (November 6, 1860; March 2 and 4, 1861; April 18 and 20, 1861).

18Crofts, *Reluctant Confederates*, 340–41, 346; Durnbaugh, *Fruit of the Vine*, 272; Claims of Daniel Bowman, John J. Garber, Daniel Good, and George W. Hollar, Southern Claims Commission Records (National Archives); Pitman Diary (May 23, 1861; June 1, 1961). I am grateful to Emmert Bittinger for providing me with a photocopy of the Bowman claim.

19McFarland Diary (June 6, 1861).

20Untitled, 8 (January 5, 1861): 1; "Our Brethren in the States Which Have Furnished Troops to the Federal Government," 8 (May 18, 1861): 145–47; "Distress of Nations," 8, (May 4, 1861): 129–30; "Preserving the Union," 8 (June 1, 1861): 161–62—all in *Zion's Advocate*.

21"The Annual Meeting of 1861 A Suggestion," *Gospel Visiter* 11 (February 1861): 62; *Gospel Visiter* (April 1861): 126; untitled, *Staunton Spectator* (April 16, 1861); Durnbaugh, *Fruit of the Vine*, 281–83.

22Thomas, *The Confederate Nation*, 147–48, 290–98.

23See also "Diary of Mary Greenhow Lee," in Colt, *Defend the Valley*, 320; John L. Heatwole, *The Burning: Sheridan's Devastation of the Shenandoah Valley* (Charlottesville, VA: Rockbridge Publishing, 1998), 17–18; Jeffry D. Wert, *From Winchester to Cedar Creek: The Shenandoah Campaign of 1864* (New York: Simon and Schuster, 1987), 147–56; Wert, *Mosby's Rangers* (New York: Simon and Schuster, 1990), 195–96, 213–19.

24The eyewitness account of the devastation is in Samuel Horst, *Mennonites in the Confederacy: A Study in Civil War Pacifism* (Scottdale, PA: Herald Press, 1967), 102–3. The Grant quotation is in Heatwole, *The Burning*, 31. The phrase "hard war" is in Wert, *From Winchester to Cedar Creek*, 153. See also William Blair, *Virginia's Private War: Feeding Body and Soul in the Confederacy, 1861–1865* (New York: Oxford University Press, 1998), 119–20; Gary W. Gallagher, "The Shenandoah Valley in 1864," in Gallagher, ed., *Struggle for the Shenandoah: Essays on the 1864 Valley Campaign* (Kent, OH: Kent State University Press, 1991), 1–18; James M. McPherson, *Ordeal by Fire: The Civil War and Reconstruction* (New York: Alfred A. Knopf, 1982), 188–90, 239–42, 411, 413, 424, 444–46; Schlabach, *Peace, Faith, Nation*, 192.

[25] Allan, *The Life and Letters of Margaret Junkin Preston*, 185; Baer, *Shadows on My Heart*, 36, 140.

[26] Allan, *The Life and Letters of Margaret Junkin Preston*, 163–64, 169.

[27] Ibid., 141–49.

[28] Hildebrand, *A Mennonite Journal*, 57–59.

[29] Jonas Blosser Diary, Blosser Family Papers (Eastern Mennonite University); R. H. Milroy to Mary Milroy, quoted in Peter Svenson, *Battlefield: Farming a Civil War Battleground* (New York: Ballantine Books, 1992), 164; Memoir of Robert T. Barton, in Colt, *Defend the Valley*, 303; Claim of Mary Lamb, Southern Claims Commission Records; Allan, *Life and Letters of Margaret Junkin Preston*, 193. The Blosser Diary is a memoir written in 1874.

[30] Baer, *Shadows on My Heart*, 208–11, 214, 217, 221, 255, 338n4; Frank B. Jones to Susan C. Jones (October 4, 1861), 102; Randolph Barton to Bolling W. Barton (March 3, 1863), 230; Ann C. R. Jones to Lucy R. Parkhill (May 18, 1863)—all in Colt, *Defend the Valley*, 248–50; Claim of Isaac Hardesty, Southern Claims Commission Records; Allen, *Life and Letters of Margaret Junkin Preston*, 193–195; Blair, *Virginia's Private War*, 122–23; Heatwole, *The Burning*, 31, 38, 185.

[31] Blosser Diary.

[32] Blosser Diary; Claim of Daniel Bowman, Southern Claims Commission; Heatwole, *The Burning*, 89–114.

[33] Hildebrand, *A Mennonite Journal*, 23; Pitman (September 21, 1865).

[34] Allan, *The Life and Letters of Margaret Junkin Preston*, 134, 165, 196; Hildebrand, *A Mennonite Journal*, 28, 45, 47.

[35] Baer, *Shadows on My Heart*. Cynthia Lyerly also links Methodist outsiderness with Civil War defeat and suggests that it continued after the war with the Lost Cause mentality; Lyerly, *Methodism and the Southern Mind*, 174.

[36] Funk, *Life and Labors of Kline*, 438.

[37] McFarland Diary (July 28, 1861); *Minutes of the Lexington Presbytery* (September 5, 1861); Sweet, *Virginia Methodism*, 265–66; George Snapp, "Diary," in Sappington, *Brethren in the New Nation*, 375; "Bright Sunny South" (April 10, 1864), Henkel Family Papers, Box 1, folder 12; William E. Baker, "Civil War Sermon" (September 18, 1861; Records of the Lexington Presbytery, Synod of Virginia).

[38] Blair, *Virginia's Private War*, 132–33.

[39] Ray A. Neff, *Valley of the Shadow* (Terra Haute, IN: Rana Publications, 1987), 22–24, 54–68; Hildebrand, *A Mennonite Journal*, 5–6, 11–12, 33.

[40]Neff, *Valley of the Shadow*, 68; June 17, 1861, Records of the Session of Harrisonburg and Cooks Creek Congregation, Rockingham County, Virginia (June 17, 1861; Records of the Synod of Virginia, Lexington Presbytery), 43; J. Nelson Liskey and W. Cullen Sherwood, *Rockingham County Men in the Confederate Service, 1861–1865* (Dayton, VA: Harrisonburg-Rockingham County Historical Society, 1990), 86. I extend appreciation to John Heatwole for information regarding Gabriel Shank's fate.

[41]For an example of a petition seeking exemption from militia duty see "The Petition of the Societies of the People called Mennonists and Dunkards in the County of Rockingham" (December 1, 1784); and for an example of a petition opposing this, see "Petition of the Persons whose Names are hereto Affixed, Frederick County" (October 24, 1793)—both in Petitions to the General Assembly. See also Schlabach, *Peace, Faith, Nation*, 174; Ne Qui Nimis, "To the Mennonites, and Others Opposed to War," *Rockingham Register and Virginia Advertiser* (January 1, 1861; February 15, 1861); Horst, *Mennonites and the Confederacy*, 28.

[42]John Kline to John Letcher (January 30, 1861); Letcher to Kline (February 1, 1861), in Sappington, *Brethren in the New Nation*, 339–40.

[43]Funk, *Life and Labors of John Kline*, 448–53; "The Prisoner's Song," in Horst, *Mennonites in the Confederacy*, 59, 123–24n45.

[44]Henry Kurtz to the Honorable Ephraim Bee, delegate in the Legislature of West Virginia, reprinted in *Gospel Visiter* 13 (September 1863): 278–79; Blosser Diary; Claims of John J. Garber, Daniel Good, and George W. Hollar, Southern Claims Commission Records; Durnbaugh, *Fruit of the Vine*, 273–79.

[45]Blosser Diary; Claims of Mary Blackburn, Henry Early, David G. Garber, John J. Garber, Daniel Good, and George W. Hollar, Southern Claims Commission Records; Durnbaugh, *Fruit of the Vine*, 273–79; Pitman (August 30, 1863); Horst, *Mennonites in the Confederacy*, 39–40. Mary (Patrick) Blackburn's first husband died, and she remarried before filing her claim.

[46]Jackson quoted in Horst, *Mennonites in the Confederacy*, 34–35. See also Blosser Diary; Horst, *Mennonites in the Confederacy*, 28–38; Schlabach, *Peace, Faith, Nation*, 189–93.

[47]Claim of David G. Garber, Southern Claims Commission Records; "Diary of George Snapp," in Sappington, *Brethren in the New Nation*, 376; Pitman Diary (March 16 and 17, 1862; February 3 and March 3, 1864); Funk, *Life and Labors of John Kline*, 474, 477, 479. Joseph H. Sibert is another example of an arrest; see Pitman Diary (May 4, 1864). For another example of draft evasion see id. (March 27, 1864).

[48]*Hopewell Friends History: 1734–1934, Frederick County, Virginia* (Strasburg, VA: Joint Committee of Hopewell Friends), 131–36.

[49]Funk, *Life and Labors of John Kline*, 452, 456–57, 469, 549–60; Hildebrand, *A Mennonite Journal* (August 16 and November 15, 1863).

[50]Conrad was exchanged before the war ended. After the war he became the owner of the Jewelry and Variety Store in Harrisonburg and the town's mayor. He died in 1907. See Sweet, *Virginia Methodists*, 56-7; and Robert J. Driver, Jr., *14th Virginia*

Cavalry (Lynchburg, VA: H. E. Howard, Inc., 1988). See also Horst, *Mennonites in the Confederacy*, 104–6; Funk, *Life and Labors of Kline*, 479–80; Sappington, *Brethren in the New Nation*, 393.

Selected Bibliography

Primary Sources
Manuscripts
   Eastern Mennonite University
      Blosser Family Papers
      Burkholder, Martin, Collection
      Funk, Joseph, Papers
      Ruebush, Joseph K., Collection
   Extracts from the Diaries of Levi Pitman, ed. Daniel Bly
   Handley Public Library, Winchester, Virginia
      Market Street Methodist Church Papers
      Records of the First Presbyterian Church, Winchester, Virginia
   James Madison University
      Henkel Family Papers
   Records of Asbury United Methodist Church, Harrisonburg, Virginia
   Records of St. Francis of Assisi Parish, Staunton, Virginia
   Records of the Lexington Presbytery, Synod of Virginia
      Baker William E., "Civil War Sermon" (September 18, 1861)
      Craig, John, Autobiography of
      McCue, John Marshall, Papers
      Minutes of the Bethel Session
      Minutes of the Cook's Creek Session
      Minutes of the Lexington Presbytery
      Minutes of the Mossy Creek Session
      Minutes of the Staunton Session
      Third Annual Report of the Lexington Missionary Society. Lynchburg,
         Virginia: Published by the Society, October 14, 1820.

Records of the Winchester Presbytery, Synod of Virginia
>   Autobiographical Sketches of the Revd. Dr. William Hill
>   Minutes of the Loudon Street Session
>   Minutes of the Kent Street Session
>   Minutes of the Picadilly Street Session
>   Minutes of the Shepherdstown Session

Religious Petitions to the General Assembly

Virginia Baptist Historical Society, University of Richmond
>   Berryville Church Book
>   Brock's Gap Church Book
>   Buck Marsh Church Book
>   Smith's Creek and Lynville Creek Church Book
>   Waterlick Church Book

United Methodist Historical Society—Lovely Lane Museum, Baltimore,
>   Maryland
>   Fechtig, Louis, Sermon Book
>   Minutes of the Baltimore Conference
>   Wells, George, Journal of

United States Census

Washington and Lee University
>   Baxter, George, Papers
>   Graham, William, Papers
>   Jackson, Thomas J. "Stonewall," Papers
>   McFarland, Francis, Papers

Periodicals

Central Presbyterian
Christian Advocate and Journal
Gospel-Visiter
Lexington Gazette
Lutheran Observer
Lutheran Standard
Religious Telescope
Rockingham Register
Southern Presbyterian
Staunton Spectator
Valley Star

Virginia Evangelical and Literary Magazine
Die Virginische Volksberichter und Neumarketer Wochenschrift
Winchester Republican
Winchester Virginian
Zion's Advocate

Hymnals

The Ebenezer Selection of Hymns and Spiritual Songs, with an Appendix Consisting of Miscellaneous Pieces. John Clark, ed. Philadelphia: Henry B. Ashmead, 1858.

Harmonia Sacra: A Compilation of Genuine Church Music, Comprising a Variety of Metres, All Harmonized for Three Voices; Together with a Copious Elucidation of the Science of Vocal Music. Joseph Funk, ed. Winchester, Virginia: J. W. Hollins, Printer, 1832.

Hymns for the Use of the Methodist Episcopal Church. New York: Lane and Scott, 1849.

Published Diaries, Journals, and Minutes

Alexander, Edward Porter, ed. *The Journal of John Fontaine; An Irish Huguenot Son in Spain and Virginia, 1710–1719.* Williamsburg, VA: Colonial Williamsburg Foundation, 1972.

Allan, Elizabeth Preston. *The Life and Letters of Margaret Junkin Preston.* Boston and New York: Houghton, Mifflin and Company, 1903.

Asbury, Francis. *Journal and Letters of Francis Asbury.* Ed. Elmer Clark, 3 vols. (Nashville: Abingdon Press.

Baer, Elizabeth R., ed. *Shadows on My Heart: The Civil War Diary of Lucy Rebecca Buck of Virginia.* Athens: University of Georgia Press, 1997.

Burkholder, Christian. "Third Address." *Useful and Edifying Address to the Young on True Repentance, Saving Faith in Christ Jesus, Pure Love, etc.* Lancaster, PA: John Baer and Sons, 1857.

Burkholder, Peter. *The Confession of Faith, of the Christians Known by the Name of Mennonites, in Thirty-Three Articles; With a Short Extract from their Catechism.* Winchester, VA: Robinson and Hollis, 1837.

_____. *A Treatise on Outward Water-Baptism*, trans. Abraham Blosser. Dale Enterprise, VA: 1881; originally published Harrisonburg, VA: Lawrence Wartman, 1816.

Bourne, George. *The Book and Slavery Irreconcilable: With Animadversions upon Dr. Smith's Philosophy.* Philadelphia: Printed by J. M. Sanderson & Co., 1816; reprinted New York: Arno Press and *The New York Times,* 1969.

Boyd, A.H.H. "Thanksgiving Sermon, Delivered in Winchester, Va., on Thursday, 29th November, 1860." Winchester, VA: J. H. Crum, 1860.

Caldwell, John Edwards. *A Tour Through Part of Virginia in the Summer of 1808,* ed. William M. E. Rachal. Richmond, VA: The Dietz Press, 1951.

Castleman, T. T. *Plain Sermons for Servants.* Philadelphia: King and Baird, Publishers, 1851.

"Circular Letter." Minutes of the Ketocton Baptist Association. Winchester, VA: Hervey Brown's Cheap Book and Job Office, 1851.

"Circular Letter." Minutes of the Thirtieth Anniversary of the Ebenezer Baptist Association. Front Royal: Printed at the office of *Zion's Advocate,* 1857.

Classified Minutes of Annual Conference of the Brethren: A History of the General Councils of the Church from 1778 to 1885. Mt. Morris, IL: The Brethren Publishing Company, 1886.

Doctrine and Discipline of the United Brethren in Christ. Hagerstown, MD: Gruber and May, 1819.

Edwards, Morgan. *Materials Towards a History of the Baptists in Pennsylvania both British and German.* Philadelphia: Crukshank and Collins, 1770.

Eichelberger, Lewis. "A Sermon on the Death of the Rev. Ebenezer G. Proctor, Late Pastor of the Lutheran Churches Constituting the Smithfield Charge." Winchester, VA: Hervey Brown's Book and Job Office, 1851.

Hildebrand, John R., ed. *A Mennonite Journal, 1862–1865: A Father's Account of the Civil War in the Shenandoah Valle.* Shippensburg, PA: Burd Street Press, 1996.

Hill, William. "A Sermon Upon the Subject of Confirmation." Winchester, VA: Samuel H. Davis, 1830.

Hughes, Thomas. *A Journal by Thos. Hughes: For His Amusement, and Designed Only for His Perusal by the Time He Attains the Age of 50 if He Lives So Long (1778–1789).* Port Washington, NY: Kennikat Press, 1947; reissued 1970).

Ireland, James. *The Life of the Rev. James Ireland, who was, for many years, Pastor of the Baptist Church at Buck Marsh, Waterlick and Happy Church in Frederick and Shenandoah Counties, Virginia.* Winchester, VA: Printed by J. Foster, 1819.

Krauth, Charles Porterfield. "A Discourse Suggested by the Burning of the Old

Lutheran Church, on the Night of September 27th, 1854, Delivered in the Evangelical Lutheran Church, Winchester, Va." Winchester, VA: Printed at the Republican Office, 1855.

_____. "Popular Amusements: A Discourse Delivered in the Evangelical Lutheran Church, Winchester, Va., on the Afternoon of Whitsunday, June 8th, 1851." Winchester, VA: The Republican Office, 1851.

MacVeagh, Lincoln, ed. *The Journal of Nicholas Cresswell, 1774–1777*. New York: Dial Press, 1924.

Minutes of the Annual Meetings of the Church of the Brethren. Elgin, IL: Brethren Publishing House, 1909.

Minutes of the Ketoctin Association. Winchester, VA: Printed by Richard Bowen, 1798.

Minutes of the Ketoctin Baptist Association, Holden at New Valley, Loudon County, Virginia. Baltimore: Warner and Hanna, 1810.

Minutes of the Virginia Mennonite Conference, Including Some Historical Data, A Brief Biographical Sketch of its Founders and Organizers, and Her Official Statement of Christian Fundamentals, Constitution, and Rules and Discipline, 2 vols. Scottdale, PA: Virginia Mennonite Conference, 1939, second ed. 1950.

Nead, Peter. *Theological Writings on Various Subjects; or a Vindication of Primitive Christianity, As Recorded in the Word of God.* intro. William Kostlevy. Dayton, OH: 1866; reprinted Youngstown, OH: Dunker Springhaus Ministries, 1997.

Newcomer, Christian. *The Life and Journal of Christian Newcomer, Late Bishop of the Church of the United Brethren in Christ.* Ed. John Hildt. Hagerstown, MD: F.G.W. Kapp, 1834.

Ruffner, Henry. *Address to the People of West Virginia*. Lexington, VA: R. C. Noel, 1847; reprinted by The Green Bookman, Bridgewater, VA, 1933.

Schmucker, Samuel Simon. *The American Lutheran Church*. Religion in America Series. New York: Arno Press and The New York Times, 1969; originally published 1851.

Simons, Menno. *The Complete Writings of Menno Simons, c. 1496–1561*. Ed. John Christian Wenger. Trans. Leonard Verduin. Scottdale, PA: Herald Press, 1956.

Travis, Joseph. *Autobiography of the Rev. Joseph Travis; A.M., A Member of the Memphis Annual Conference.* ed. Thomas O. Summers. Nashville, TN: Southern Methodist Publishing House, 1856.

Wesley, John. "Friendship with the World." *The Works of the Rev. John Wesley, A.M.* London: 1872.

Secondary Sources
Books

Abzug, Robert H. *Cosmos Crumbling: Americans Reforms and the Religious Imagination.* New York: Oxford University Press; 1994.

Alley, Reuben Edward. *A History of Baptists in Virginia.* Richmond, VA: Virginia Baptist General Board, n. d.

Anderson, Fred. *Crucible of War: The Seven Years' War and the Fate of Empire in British North America.* New York: Alfred A. Knopf, 2000.

Andrews, Dee E. *The Methodists and Revolutionary America, 1760–1800: The Shaping of an Evangelical Culture.* Princeton, NJ: Princeton University Press, 2000.

Armstrong, James E. *History of the Old Baltimore Conference from the Planting of Methodism in 1773 to the Division of the Conference in 1851.* Baltimore: King Brothers, 1907.

Arnold, Thomas Jackson. *Early Life and Letters of General Thomas J. Jackson, "Stonewall" Jackson, by his Nephew, Thomas Jackson Arnold.* Richmond, VA: The Dietz Press, 1957; originally published 1916.

Barbour, Hugh and J. William Frost. *The Quakers.* New York: Greenwood Press, 1988.

Behney, J. Bruce and Paul H. Eller. *The History of the Evangelical United Brethren Church.* Nashville, TN: Abingdon Press, 1979.

Bilhartz, Terry D. *Urban Religion and the Second Great Awakening: Church and Society in Early National Baltimore.* Rutherford, NJ: Fairleigh Dickinson University, 1986.

Bittinger, Emmert, ed. *Brethren in Transition: 20th Century Directions and Dilemmas.* Camden, ME: Penobscot Press, 1992.

Blair, William. *Virginia's Private War: Feeding Body and Soul in the Confederacy, 1861–1865.* New York: Oxford University Press, 1998.

Bowman, Carl F. *Brethren Society.* Baltimore, MD: Johns Hopkins University Press, 1995.

Brackney, William H. *The Baptists.* Westport, CT: Praeger, 1994.

Breen, T. H. *Tobacco Culture: The Mentality of the Great Tidewater Planters on the Eve of the Revolution.* Princeton, NJ: Princeton University Press, 1985.

Brunk, Harry Anthony. *History of Mennonites in Virginia,* 2 vols. Harrisonburg,

VA: Published by the author, 1959.

Buckley, Thomas E. *Church and State in Revolutionary Virginia, 1776–1787.* Charlottesville: University of Virginia Press, 1977.

Cassell, C. W., W. J. Finck, and Elon O. Henkel, eds. *History of the Lutheran Church in Virginia and East Tennessee.* Strasburg, VA: Published by the Lutheran Synod of Virginia, 1930.

Colt, Margaretta Barton. *Defend the Valley: A Shenandoah Family in the Civil War.* New York: Crown Publishing, 1994.

Crofts, Daniel W. *Reluctant Confederates: Upper South Unionists in the Secession Crisis.* Chapel Hill: University of North Carolina Press, 1989.

Dew, Charles B. *Bond of Iron: Master and Slave at Buffalo Forge.* New York: W. W. Norton, 1994.

Durnbaugh, Donald F. *European Origins of the Brethren: A Source Book on the Beginnings of the Church of the Brethren in the Early Eighteenth Century.* Elgin, IL: The Brethren Press, 1958.

_____. *The Brethren in Colonial America: A Source Book on the Transportation and Development of the Church of the Brethren in the Eighteenth Century.* Elgin, IL: The Brethren Press, 1967.

_____. *Fruit of the Vine: A History of the Brethren, 1708-1995.* Elgin, IL: Brethren Press, 1997.

Eisenberg, William Edward. *The Lutheran Church in Virginia, 1717-1962.* Roanoke, VA: Trustees of the Virginia Synod, Lutheran Church in America, 1967.

Emory, Robert. *History of the Discipline of the Methodist Episcopal Church.* New York: G. Lane and C. B. Tippett, 1845.

Fischer, David Hackett. *Albion's Seed: Four British Folkways in America.* New York: Oxford University Press, 1989.

Fitzkee, Donald R. *Moving Toward the Mainstream: 20th Century Change Among the Brethren of Eastern Pennsylvania.* Intercourse, PA: Good Books, 1995.

Franklin, John Hope and Loren Schweninger. *Runaway Slaves: Rebels on the Plantation.* New York: Oxford University Press, 1999.

Freehling, Alison Goodyear. *Drift Toward Dissolution: The Virginia Slavery Debate of 1831–1832.* Baton Rouge: Louisiana State University Press, 1982.

Freehling, William W. *The Road to Disunion: Volume I, Secessionists at Bay, 1776–1851.* New York: Oxford University Press, 1990.

Funk, Benjamin, ed. *The Life and Laors of Elder John Kline, the Martyr Missionary.* Elgin, IL: The Brethren Press, 1900.

Funkhauser, Abram Paul. *History of the Church of the United Brethren in Christ, Virginia Conference.* Ed. Oren F. Morton. Dayton, VA: Virginia Conference of the United Brethren in Christ, 1931.

Garrison, J. Silor. *The History of the Reformed Church in Virginia, 1714–1941.* Winston-Salem, NC: Clay Printing Company, 1948.

Hamm, Thomas. *The Transformation of American Quakerism: Orthodox Friends, 1800–1907.* Bloomington: Indiana University Press, 1988.

Hart, Freeman H. *The Valley of Virginia in the American Revolution, 1763–1789.* New York: Russell and Russell, 1971; originally published by the University of North Carolina Press, 1942.

Hatch, Nathan. *The Democratization of American Christianity.* New Haven, CT: Yale University Press, 1989.

Heatwell, John L. *The Burning: Sheridan's Devastation of the Shenandoah Valley.* Charlottesville, VA: Rockbridge Publishing, 1998.

Heyrman, Christine Leigh. *Southern Cross: The Beginnings of the Bible Belt.* Chapel Hill: University of North Carolina Press, 1997.

Higginbotham, Don. *Daniel Morgan: Revolutionary Rifleman.* Chapel Hill: University of North Carolina Press, 1961.

Hofstra, Warren R. *A Separate Place: The Formation of Clarke County, Virginia.* Madison, WI: Madison House Publishers, 1999.

Holton, Woody. *Forced Founders: Indians, Debtors, Slaves, and the Making of the American Revolution in Virginia.* Chapel Hill: University of North Carolina Press, 1999.

Hopewell Friends History: 1734–1934, Frederick County, Virginia. Strasburg, VA: Joint Committee of Hopewell Friends.

Horst, Samuel. *Mennonites and the Confederacy: A Study in Civil War Pacifism.* Scottdale, PA: Herald Press, 1967.

Hunter, Robert F. *Lexington Presbyterian Church, 1789–1989.* Lexington, VA: Lexington Presbyterian Church, 1991.

Isaac, Rhys. *The Transformation of Virginia, 1740–1790.* Chapel Hill: University of North Carolina Press, 1982.

Jennings, Francis. *Empire of Fortune: Crowns, Colonies, and Tribes in the Seven Years War in America.* New York: W. W. Norton and Company, 1988.

Johnson, Paul E. *A Shopkeeper's Millennium: Society and Revivals in Rochester, New York, 1815–1837.* New York: Hill and Wang, 1978.

Kanter, Rosabeth Moss. *Commitment and Community: Communes and Utopias in Sociological Perspective.* Cambridge, MA: Harvard University Press, 1972.

Kercheval, Samuel. *A History of the Valley of Virginia.* Harrisonburg, VA: C. J. Carrier Company, 1981, fourth ed.; originally published in 1833.

Koons, Kenneth E. and Warren R. Hofstra, eds. *After the Backcountry: Rural Life in the Great Valley of Virginia, 1800–1900.* Knoxville, TN: University of Tennessee Press, 2000.

Kraybill, Donald B. *The Riddle of Amish Culture.* Baltimore: Johns Hopkins University Press, 1989.

Levy, Barry. *Quakers and the American Family: British Settlement in the Delaware Valley.* New York: Oxford University Press, 1988.

Little, Lewis Payton. *Imprisoned Preachers and Religious Liberty in Virginia: A Narrative Drawn Largely from Official Records of Virginia Counties, Unpublished Manuscripts, Letters, and Other Original Sources.* Lynchburg, VA: J. P. Bell Co., 1938.

Laurie, Bruce. *Artisans into Workers: Labor in Nineteenth-Century America.* New York: Noonday Press, 1989.

Longenecker, Stephen L. *Piety and Tolerance: Pennsylvania German Religion, 1700–1850.* Metuchen, NJ: Scarecrow Press, 1994.

Loveland, Anne C. *Southern Evangelicals and the Social Order, 1800-1860.* Baton Rouge: Louisiana State University Press, 1980.

Lyerly, Cynthia Lynn. *Methodism and the Southern Mind, 1770–1810.* New York: Oxford University Press, 1998.

MacMaster, Richard K. *Land, Piety, Peoplehood: The Establishment of Mennonite Communities in America, 1683–1790.* Scottdale, PA: Herald Press, 1985.

Marietta, Jack D. *The Reformation of American Quakerism, 1748–1783.* Philadelphia: University of Pennsylvania Press, 1984.

Massey, Don W. *The Episcopal Churches in the Diocese of Virginia: Alphabetical Listing of Active Churches by Regions and Existing Churches Not Having Regular Services.* Keswick, VA: Diocese Church Histories, 1989.

Mathews, Donald G. *Religion in the Old South.* Chicago: University of Chicago Press, 1977.

_____. *Slavery and Methodism: A Chapter in American Morality, 1780–1845.* Princeton, NJ: Princeton University Press, 1965.

McPherson, James M. *Battle Cry of Freedom: The Civil War Era.* New York: Oxford University Press, 1988.

_____. *Ordeal by Fire: The Civil War and Reconstruction.* New York: Alfred A. Knopf, 1982.

Mintz, Steven. *Moralists and Modernizers: America's Pre-Civil War Reformers.* Baltimore: Johns Hopkins University Press, 1995.

Moore, R. Laurence. *Religious Outsiders and the Making of Americans.* New York: Oxford University Press, 1986.

Price, P. B. *The Life of the Reverend John Holt Rice, D. D.* Richmond: The Library of Union Theological Seminary in Virginia, 1963.

Puglisi, Michael J., ed. *Diversity and Accommodation: Essays on the Cultural Composition of the Virginia Frontier.* Knoxville, TN: University of Tennessee Press, 1997.

Ragsdale, Bruce A. *A Planters' Republic: The Search for Economic Independence in Revolutionary Virginia.* Madison, WI: Madison House, 1996.

Rhoden, Nancy L. *Revolutionary Anglicanism: The Colonial Church of England Clergy during the American Revolution.* New York: New York University Press, 1999.

Richey, Russell E. *Early American Methodism.* Bloomington: Indiana University Press, 1991.

_____. *The Methodist Conference in America: A History.* Nashville, TN: Kingswood Books, 1996.

Sanchez-Saavedra, E. M. *A Guide to Virginia Military Organizations in the American Revolution, 1774–1787.* Richmond: Virginia State Library, 1978.

Sanders, I. Taylor II. *Now Let the Gospel Trumpet Blow: A History of New Monmouth Presbyterian Church, 1746–1980.* Lexington, VA: New Monmouth Presbyterian Church, 1986.

Sappington, Roger E., ed. *The Brethren in the New Nation: A Source Book on the Development of the Church of the Brethren, 1785–1865.* Elgin, IL: Brethren Press, 1976.

_____. *The Brethren in Virginia: The History of the Church of the Brethren in Virginia.* Harrisonburg, VA: Committee for the Brethren History in Virginia, 1973.

Sarna, Jonathan D., ed. *Minority Faiths and the American Protestant Mainstream.* Urbana, IL: University of Illinois Press, 1998.

Semple, Robert B. *A History of the Rise and Progress of the Baptists in Virginia.* Richmond, VA: Pitt and Dickinson, Publishers, 1894.

Schmidt, Leigh Eric. *Holy Fairs: Scottish Communions and American Revivals in the Early Modern Period.* Princeton, NJ: Princeton University Press.

Schlabach, Theron F. *Peace, Faith, Nation: Mennonites and Amish in Nineteenth-Century America.* Scottdale, PA: Herald Press, 1988.

Sellers, Charles. *The Market Revolution: Jacksonian America, 1815–1846.* New York: Oxford University Press, 1991.

Shade, William G. *Democratizing the Old Dominion: Virginia and the Second Party System, 1824–1861.* Charlottesville: University Press of Virginia, 1996.

Sheriff, Carol. *The Artificial River: The Erie Canal and the Paradox of Progress, 1817–1862.* New York: Hill and Wang, 1996.

Smith, Merritt Roe. *Harpers Ferry Armory and the New Technology: The Challenge of Change.* Ithaca, NY: Cornell University Press, 1977.

Smith, Timothy L. *Whitefield and Wesley on the New Birth.* Grand Rapids, MI: Francis Asbury Press, 1986.

Sorrells, Nancy, Katherine Brown, and Susanne Simmons. *"Conformable to the Doctrine and Discipline": The History of Trinity Church, Augusta Parish, Staunton, Virginia, 1746–1996.* Staunton, VA: Lot's Wife Publishing, 1996.

Spaeth, Adolph. *Charles Porterfield Krauth.* Religion in America Series, 2 vols. New York: Arno Press, 1969.

Stanton, Phoebe B. *The Gothic Revival and American Church Architecture: An Episode in Taste, 1840–56.* Baltimore: Johns Hopkins University Press, 1968.

Stokes, Melvyn, and Stephen Conway, eds. *The Market Revolution in American Social, Political, and Religious Expressions, 1800–1880.* Charlottesville: University Press of Virginia, 1996.

Stowe, Steven. *Intimacy and Power in the Old South: Ritual in the Lives of Planters.* Baltimore: Johns Hopkins University Press, 1987.

Strickland, W. P. *The Life of Jacob Gruber.* New York: Carlton and Porter, 1860.

Taylor, Alan. *William Cooper's Town: Power and Persuasion on the Frontier of the Early American Republic.* New York: Random House, 1995.

Thomas, Emory M. *The Confederate Nation: 1861–1865.* New York: Harper and Row, 1979.

Thompson, Ernest Trice. *Presbyterians in the South, Volume One: 1607–1861.* Richmond, VA: John Knox Press, 1963.

Tillson, Albert H., Jr. *Gentry and Common Folk: Political Culture on the Virginia Frontier, 1740–1789.* Lexington: University Press of Kentucky, 1991.

Titus, James. *The Old Dominion at War: Society, Politics, and Warfare in Late Colonial Virginia*. Columbia: University of South Carolina Press, 1991.

Walters, Ronald G. *American Reformers, 1815–1860*. New York: Hill and Wang, 1976.

Ward, Harry M. *Major General Adam Stephen and the Cause of American Liberty*. Charlottesville: University Press of Virginia, 1989.

Wayland, John W. *Historic Harrisonburg*. Staunton, VA: Published by the author, 1949.

_____. *Twenty-Five Chapters on the Shenandoah Valley, to Which is Appended a Concise History of the Civil War in the Valley*. Harrisonburg, VA: C. J. Carrier Company, 1976; first ed., 1957.

Weeks, Stephen B. *Southern Quakers and Slavery: A Study in Institutional History*. New York: Bergman Publishers, 1968.

Westerkamp, Marilyn J. *Triumph of the Laity: Scots-Irish Piety and the Great Awakening, 1625–1760*. New York: Oxford University Press, 1988.

Wigger, John H. *Taking Heaven By Storm: Methodism and the Rise of Popular Christianity in America*. New York: Oxford University Press, 1998.

Williams, Peter W. *Houses of God: Region, Religion, and Architecture in the United States*. Urbana and Chicago: University of Illinois Press, 1997.

Williams, William Henry. *The Garden of American Methodism: The Delmarva Peninsula, 1769–1820*. Wilmington, DE: Scholarly Resources, Inc., 1984.

Wills, Gregory A. *Democratic Religion: Freedom, Authority, and Church Discipline in the Baptist South, 1785–1900*. New York: Oxford University Press, 1997.

Wilson, Howard McKnight. *The Lexington Presbytery Heritage: The Presbytery of Lexington and its Churches in the Synod of Virginia, Presbyterian Church in the United States* (McClure Press).

Wood, Gordon S. *The Radicalism of the American Revolution*. New York: Alfred A. Knopf, 1992.

Woodworth, Robert Bell, Clifford Duval Grim, and Ronald S. Wilson. *A History of the Presbyterian Church in Winchester, Virginia, 1780–1949*. Winchester, VA: Pifer Printing Company, 1950.

Worrall, Jay, Jr. *The Friendly Virginians: America's First Quakers*. Athens, GA: Iberian Publishing Company, 1994.

Wust, Klaus. *The Virginia Germans*. Charlottesville: University Press of Virginia, 1969.

Articles, Dissertations, Papers, and Theses

Ballard, Charles. "Dismissing the Peculiar Institution: Assessing Slavery in Page and Rockingham Counties, Virginia." Paper presented to the Shenandoah Valley Regional Studies Seminar, James Madison University, April 17, 1998.

Buckley, Thomas J. "After Disestablishment: Thomas Jefferson's Wall of Separation in Antebellum Virginia." *Journal of Southern History* 61 (August, 1995): 446–80.

Calhoon, Robert M. "'Inescapable Circularity': History and the Human Condition in Revolutionary Virginia." *Reviews in American History* (March, 1983): 38–41.

Davidson, Katherine Hoge. "Anglicanism in the Valley of Virginia." Master's thesis, University of Virginia, 1941.

Durnbaugh, Donald F. "Religion and Revolution: Options in 1776." *Pennsylvania Magazine of History and Biography* 1 (July 1978): 8.

Eslinger, Ellen. "The Brief Career of Rufus W. Bailey, African Colonization Society Agent in Virginia." Paper delivered at the Shenandoah Valley Regional Studies Seminar, James Madison University, April 20, 2001.

Foner, Eric. "Why Is There No Socialism in the United States?" *History Workshop: A Journal of Social Historians* 17 (1984): 57–80.

Gorrell, Donald K. "'Ride a Circuit of Let It Along': Early Practices That Kept the United Brethren, Albright People and Methodists Apart." *Methodist History* 25 (October, 1986), 9–11.

Hofstra, Warren R. "'The Extension of His Majesties Dominions': The Virginia Backcountry and the Reconfiguration of Imperial Frontiers." *Journal of American History* 84 (March, 1998): 1281–1312.

Hutton, James F., Jr. "The Slaveowners of Frederick County and Winchester in 1860." Unpublished ms. (March 11, 1963), Rare Book Room, Handley Library.

John, Richard. "Taking Sabbatarianism Seriously." *Journal of the Early Republic* 10 (Winter 1990): 517–67.

Landis, Ira D. "The Plain Dutch." *Mennonite Research Journal* 9 (April 1968): 19.

Lindman, Janet Moore. "A World of Baptists: Gender, Race, and Religious Community in Pennsylvania and Virginia, 1689–1825." Ph.D. diss.,University of Minnesota.

McCleskey, Turk. "Rich Land, Poor Prospects: Real Estate and the Formation of a Social Elite in Augusta County, Virginia, 1738–1770." *Virginia Magazine of History and Biography* 98 (July, 1990): 449-86.

Noll, Mark A. "Methodism Unbound." *Reviews in American History* 29 (June, 2001): 192–97.

Simmons, J. Susanne. "Never a Strong Hold? Deconstructing the Myth of Slavery in Augusta County, Virginia." Paper presented to the Shenandoah Valley Regional Studies Seminar, James Madison University, March 1995.

Spangler, Jewel L. "Becoming Baptists: Conversion in Colonial and Early National Virginia." *Journal of Southern History* 68 (May 2001): 243–86.

Stange, Douglas C. "Lutheran Involvement in the American Colonization Society." *Mid-America* 49 (April 1967): 140–48.

Zirkle, John F. "Buckskin Imperialists: Some Activities of the First Virginia Regiment, 1754-1758." M. A. Thesis: James Madison University, 1981.

Websites

Edward L. Ayers and Anne S. Rubin, "Valley of the Shadow," http://jefferson.village.virginia.edu/shadow2

Index